The Letters of Aunt Mary
1868-1970

October 2013

To Martin,

with thanks,

from John.

Published in Ireland by the Author.

ISBN : 978-0-904081-07-7

Layout and typeset by Grace McCullen.

Cover Design by Sirocco Design.

Printed by Anglo Printers, Drogheda.

Previously Published by the Author

More Outstanding in the Field – 2010

Outstanding in the Field – 2008

Shoulders to the Wheel – 2006

Bill Crimmin's Drogheda - 2004

My Dearest Annie - 2003

From the Nanny to the Boyne (with Margaret Downey) - 1999

Jingles of the Harness – 1999

The Brass Thimble - 1996

The Call of St.Mary's - 1984

Dedication

To the Gathering of McCullens at Kilsharvan 2013.

'More than kisses,

Letters mingle souls.'

John Donne (1571-1631)

Acknowledgements

This has been a project in preparation for several years and I wish to heartily acknowledge the constant support and enthusiasm of Dr.Oliver, Fr.Dick and Mary, the family of Jim who provided the initial spark to collect, collate and publish the letters of Aunt Mary.

Similarly the response of cousins, nephews and nieces, far and near, has been unfailing. By the nature of things, my wife Ann and my own family have been invaluable assistants in enabling me to cover tables with obscure documents and escape with a pen, from other occupations.

Particular thanks is due to Peter for his cover design and artistic ideas since the first page was written, and to Grace who provided the enormous work in layout, typing and the final production. Her contribution is the key to the unlocking of Aunt Mary's treasure trove.

In order to afford background information on many of the unexpected references in the letters, I am grateful to my consultant friends in County Meath, Drogheda, Clonmellon, Laytown and Bettystown, Tullyallen and Termonfechin, who filled in gaps and joined dots. Photographs by Bill Crimmins, Vin Duffner, Kieran Campbell, Austin Cooper, James Clarke, Terry Collins and Newsfile are acknowledged.

For particular images and writings included, I thank my several cousins, Nora for the beautiful photographs of the 1966 event, Barry Cassin for use of his material on pages 151-152, Dermot for his artistic depiction of a grand aunt he only knew by reputation, Gavin and Orlaith Duffy for a launching pad, and Peter Kierans and Anglo-Printers in Drogheda for a splendid printing creation.

John McCullen

October 2013

Contents

Introduction

When my cousin Jim died in 2008, he left his various financial affairs in my hands, and after all kinds of disbursements were made, there was some small surplus, of money, and also a large surplus of documents in the basement of his former residence at 33, Laurence Street, Drogheda. These varied from the remnants of the gun of Collier the Robber to the Certificate of First Holy Communion of Richard Moore of Duleek Street, given in 1866. Painstakingly my godfather, Dr.Oliver would arrive weekly and hand over several shoeboxes of old letters, with the command; *'You look after these now.'*

Many of the letters were written by Mary F. McCullen, or to her, or stored and passed on by her to Jim's Mother, Eva, thus stretching from 1868 to 1970. Gradually, I realised that the mixing together of the small surplus of money and the large surplus of dusty letters could be a fitting memorial to Jim and Aunt Mary, both of whom loved nothing better than an audience who appreciated history.

With the full support of Jim's family this endeavour has been simmering for five years and now is cooked and ready to be consumed. There is a reflection of Aunt Mary's style in that the selection of material is very wide and does not, in my father's words, 'stick to the point'. She was not one to be categorised, and so history, gossip, genealogy, fashion, property, politics, sport and human behaviour all mix in a hotch-potch, and then she would say;

> *'The phrase 'hotch-potch' of my little book dates back to the Roman writer, Juvenal, and he lived from 60-130 AD. There could have been some descendants on Lambay Island, but they may have moved to grow vegetables around Rush or Lusk.'*

I hope that you enjoy the world of Aunt Mary Frances McCullen.

CHAPTER 1

THE BACKGROUND

Over a thirty year period, from 1941, Mary Frances McCullen was a summer fixture, strolling on the beach at Laytown and Bettystown, with her stick and usually a companion listener. If you managed to break into the conversation and were to ask her;

'Who are you, Mary and where did you come from?'

She would hesitate, because of being more at ease speaking of others and then sensing an escape route in ancestry, begin a lecture on McCullens, Moores, Hammills and Hoeys. By the time you had reached the Nanny River both you and she would be immersed in some one individual, in any of the four families, perhaps two centuries before and you might think;

'How did I get myself into this Pandora's Box and where will it end?'

In Mary's thoughts, events in Ireland were marked by The Reformation (1530), Cromwell (1649), Catholic Emancipation and Dan O'Connell (1829) and the Famine of 1845-51. On this scale of things, The McCullens and Taaffes, her grandmother's family, were 'Old Residenters', meaning living in the Beabeg / Beamore / Platin locality of East Meath, for several hundred years. This meant Catholic, as well as Irish. The Moores had come from The Queen's County (Laois) via a slaughter at Mullamast and the Battle of the Boyne (1690) and settled at Kellystown, Donore and then moved into Drogheda to operate shop businesses. Annie Moore came from one of these general stores at Duleek Street and Mary was her only daughter. Annie's mother was Mary Hoey who originated in the townland of Whiteriver in the parish of Mosstown and Barony of Ardee. As would have been 'normal' in the Ireland of the nineteenth century, there was no shortage of traumatic events in Mary McCullen's immediate origins.

- ❖ Bridget McCullen (nee Hammill), Mary F's great grandmother died suddenly in 1836, leaving her husband Patrick, a widower with a family of six, aged from toddlers to 19.
- ❖ Ann McCullen (nee Taaffe), Mary's granny died suddenly in 1853, ten days after her only son, Patrick, was born leaving her husband James with an infant.
- ❖ The Taaffe family were evicted twice (1850's) from farms in Beamore and Platin by landlords, before finally settling at Newtown, Donore.
- ❖ In Annie McCullen's (nee Moore) family, five of her siblings died, two of whom were drowned at sea, before she married Patrick McCullen, and her father also died two years before her wedding.

The diagram in figure 1 may help to make all these relationships a bit clearer.

These family details give some genetic background to Mary, and the environmental atmosphere into which she arrived as the second child of Patrick McCullen and Annie Moore, on Friday 28th September 1883 and was no less hectic.

Her brother, James, had been born 21 months beforehand, on December 12th 1881. When Patrick and Annie married, their 'honeymoon' was a pilgrimage to Knock Shrine in Co.Mayo, in February 1881, where apparitions of Our Lady were seen in 1880. The first organised pilgrimage was on 15th May 1880 led by Rev. Fr James Anderson O.S.A and numbered thirty people from Drogheda. A woman was allegedly cured of an ulcer on that occasion.

The political milieu around the time of the arrival of Mary Frances into the world was just as unstable as the sociological situation. Another famine in 1879, a spell of severe weather, Evictions, the founding of the Land League by Michael Davitt, and the second imprisonment of Charles S.Parnell in October 1881, with the Home Rule Bill for Ireland a very live issue, all added to the turmoil.

Quadrilles involving Miss Macken, race meetings in Bellewstown and card-games of the previous decade would have become more animated events in the early 1880's, and Land Reform was also on the horizon, with a first Land Act in 1881, introduced by Mr Gladstone.

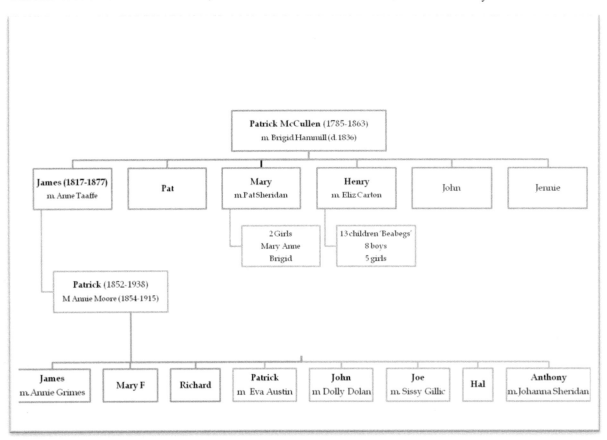

Fig 1 - Ancestry of Mary Frances McCullen

John Moore (b 1700's) great grandfather of Mary McCullen was married three times and Mary's mother came from the second of these unions. John Moore had at least nine children with his three wives, and two of these were called 'John' which easily led to confusion, as well as to various step and in-law relationships. One of these established the connection to the Macken family of The Naul in County Dublin, and since the publication of 'My Dearest Annie' (2003) three letters from Ellen to Annie Moore (born 1854) have come to light.

My Dear Annie,

I received your kind and welcome letter and I would have answered it before now only I have been to Ardcath every day since and as the Mission closed on Tuesday last I was away the whole day. I have been made a child of Marie and a child of the Sacred Heart on Friday by Father Sebastian the Conductor of the Missions.

Dear Annie, I have seen Mary a few days before your letter arrived. She is very busy preparing for the examinations which will take place on Monday week, and as visitors cannot stay any time, on that account, it would be better for you to wait and have a long day with her when she comes home. I daresay you are going to the races. We will not go this year. Joined by Mamma and Dada in fondest love to your Mamma and Dada, Brothers and Sisters and hoping to see you all soon. I remain as ever affectionately yours,

Ellen Mackin, Enfant de Marie, C.S.H

Ps. I hope your Dada is quite recovered. I suppose Richie does not know Drogheda – he is so long away. Give my love to him. PPS. Please write soon.

My Dear Annie,

Naul,
May 19th 1872

I would have replied sooner to your kind and very welcome letter but as I was stopping in Clonswords I thought it better to wait until my visit terminated. I enjoyed myself greatly. We spent Sunday week with Mrs Brennan of Balgeen and had a pleasant evening. Mr & Mrs McGrath and the Brennan's of Saddlestown were there. We danced a few quadrilles but were obliged to leave early as John Macken was going to the fair next morning. I came home on Wednesday last.

We drove to Clonswords yesterday. Mrs Gaffney and family were there – we had a little game but as usual I did not win, I daresay you are delighted at the news that there is some hope of a races in Bellewstown. I believe that gentlemen of that district are collecting funds and doing all in their power to keep it up.I think I forgot to mention in my last letter that Annie Macken sent us a carte of herself and husband from America, he is a very fine looking man. Annie does not look as well as when she went away. I do not think she likes Nebraska as much as the other. She writes that her husband intends to settle in some other state after a short time. Dear Annie you must be weary reading this epistle so I will conclude joined by all in best love to each,

Believe me, Your attached friend, Ellen Macken

Naul February 29th (no year)

My dear Annie,

It is now a long time since I had the pleasure of hearing from you, and I hope you are quite well. Did you get many Valentines? I got four including yours and Richies for which I am very thankful . I seen Mary last Tuesday. She is quite well and said she did not hear from you this long time.

Dear Annie I will now conclude with fond love to all and hoping to hear from you soon, I remain as ever affectionately, Ellen.

PS I hope the fasting is agreeing with you and also that your Dada is quite well. Mamma wishes to be remembered to your dear Mamma and joins me in love to all. PS Write a long letter soon.

These family details give some genetic background to Mary and the environmental atmosphere into which she arrived as the second child of Patrick McCullen and Annie Moore, on Friday 28th September 1883 was no less hectic. Her brother, James, had been born 21 months beforehand on December 12th 1881. When Patrick and Annie married, their 'honeymoon' was a pilgrimage to Knock shrine in Co.Mayo, in February 1881, where Apparitions of Our Lady were seen in 1880. The first organised Pilgrimage was on 15th May 1880 led by Rev Fr. James Anderson OSA and numbered thirty people from Drogheda. A woman was allegedly cured of an ulcer on that occasion..

Mary Frances was blessed in her parents, both of whom were thrust into responsibility early in life and both believed in Education. Her father, Pat, became breadwinner at 24 when his father died suddenly and left him a full household, and several farms. He was largely self educated and a voracious reader, while his wife Annie had been very well eductated at the Mercy Nuns and later in the Siena Convent with Dominican Nuns. As the eldest daughter, Annie had also played a central role in the shop and public house business in Duleek Street. At marriage, she was 27 years old and her husband was 28. Both were very capable, optimistic and ambitious. While a quadrille with Miss Mackin would appeal to Annie, the focus for Pat was business, money and achievement. A close friend of his, a McQuillan from Duleek Street in Drogheda once remarked;

' You will never be happy Pat, till you are chained in a gold-mine!'

Pat & Annie McCullen

James Mc Cullen (1817-1877)

CHAPTER 2: 1893 - 1901

SCHOOLDAYS

It would be true to say that none of this book could be written if it were not for the unusual respect given to the written word by Annie's daughter, Mary Frances. The vast bulk of the letters were sewn together in packs, according to author, and carefully stored in some desk, drawer or press, often along with the most unusual bedfellows like the plait of Sister Anthony of Padua, the palm from the pilgrimage to the Holy Land in the 1920s, the coral pieces which came home in the trunk of Captain Richard Moore, or the wedding shoes and bouquet of February 1881.

Not alone did Mary file and store, she also read voraciously, and my father would sometimes upbraid us for being like Auntie Mary – "with your head stuck in a book" , especially at a time of crisis, with suckling calves or kale crying out to be wed. Mary kept up a correspondence with many people and received postal deliveries, from at home and abroad, at several different addresses. Not alone did she write letters, she also did sections of genealogy on old Christmas cards, paper wrappers, old envelopes and pages torn from school copy-books. Several hundred of these items survive, covering history, geography, genealogy, archaeology, gossip and social affairs, horse-racing and farming, but at this juncture, we concentrate on the first batch, written to her mother. Like Aunt Sissy, she commences with the "school letter".

Sacred Heart School, Drogheda.
My dear Mother,   *December 20th, 1894*

You shall be glad, I am sure, to receive this little letter from me, as it is my first. Our examinations are now over and I think that I got on very well, and got good marks. We shall get vacation tomorrow and hope the weather will be fine for us to enjoy ourselves. Today the Xmas hamper with some nice prizes will be raffled, in aid of the Holy Childhood. I hope I shall be lucky and win something. As this is my first, you cannot expect a long letter. I will now conclude, wishing you all a very happy Xmas.

I remain, your fond child,
Mary.
                                                                            December 12th, 1895

I am delighted the time for writing our letters has arrived as it gives me an opportunity of letting you know how I am getting on at my studies…successful…raffle in aid of the Holy Childhood…twopenny lottery…I hope I may get something nice

While Sister Anthony of Padua was agitating for Mary to be sent to schools as far as Hertfordshire and Galway, to get used to the colour of the Benedictine habit, and perhaps create a tourist trail to Bartestree, Mary was eventually sent to the Loreto Convent School in Navan, which at the time had a direct rail link to Drogheda, passing through McCullen's farm. Most of Mary's letters to Mother are undated by year, an omission she could not be accused of in later life. It seems likely that she went to Navan in 1897 and graduated to home in June of 1901.

The great news is that I was put into Second Year junior grade class by Mother Rosalie and I commenced German also...we were all presented to the Bishop on Monday...a long walk on Wednesday, James' special hatred, I thought very nice...commenced music with a Miss Bennett...very nice...Christina Morrin, stayed with Mrs. Monks, her aunt in Lusk...commenced a tea cloth in Mountmellick work. Please send me a half-crown P.O. before Tuesday and flannel bodices with 63 and my name on them. You had better come down to see me, or I might get too fond of this school, and might not come back at all...

October 13th

Enclose my monthly marks...the Bishop is now much better, and the Nuns are coming back today...

The Farmhouse and yards at Beamore from where Mary wrote the following letters.

October 24th

...Mr. &Mrs. Corry were here on Friday...Cattie Dodd will be coming here in a short time...Is it true that Aunt Cissie only writes to Nuns, now?...I hope the Drogheda Musical Society is a success. Did Father get the English Grammar for me yet?...Sister Ignatius told me to tell you to come before Advent, as you cannot see any of the Nuns otherwise. Do any of the Beabegs ever come down on Sundays? How is Uncle Harry?

October 2nd, 1897

As James came in this week, you need not expect a very long letter from me. I received the music, shoes and marking ink all right, the ink was a very good kind and just what I wanted, but the shoes are not the right sort, if you could get a pair of black canvas, I would be obliged, if not, you need not send any...Fr. Crean was to call the next day to see me, but he did not... I was very glad you all remembered my Birthday, John was very good to send me such a pretty picture, and as for Paddie!

James (standing far right), with his classmates at St Finians

...very much disappointed that Father did not come...send me four yards of pink ribbon about an inch and a half wide, a pair of white silk gloves and a pair of <u>nice</u> dancing shoes...Do you hear how Mrs. Reilly or Ida Symington are now?...I am taking a bath every morning now, so you may expect to find me very strong when I go home...

Undated

...Last Sunday we celebrated Mother Rosalie's feast day and got out to Delanys. The Bishop brought us over to Athlumney Castle and into the Mercy Orphanage...the Nuns looked very odd, without cuffs...

November 28th, 1898

...Please send me the "White Heather Waltzes" by J. Westwood Oliver. I think they are 1/6 in Kearneys...I am glad that the Corporation have a more docile Town Clerk as it would have been inconvenient for them if they could not bring all their grandeur to Fr. Curry's ceremony...Is Anthony talking yet? I am sure he can walk this long time. How is Margaret getting on? Is she in the hospital at present? Please remember me to Catherine...

PS. Please send me some chilblain ointment.

November 6th, 1898

Many thanks for the parcel and letters…Father was telling me about all the trouble you went to get one of the books…I saw Ricardo on Tuesday…the operetta is "Red Riding Hood", which they had some time ago in the Sacred Heart School…

December 12th

Many thanks for Postal Order…all about the concert in Drogheda papers…please keep me one of them…did the pictures you sent me last week come from Hereford or Mayo? Tell Joe that I am preparing a good number of new stories for him…

March 5th

…The boots were too large, so I sent them over to Richard with a pattern of the right size to send home in his bags…My chilblains are not as bad as before vacation, although the weather is very cold, we have snow every second day. Which of the helps were invalided? I hope Dominic was not. Is the Cemetery to be on the site Father proposed?

Mary, pictured with younger brother Richard.

May 1st

…The music examinations are on Wednesday next – say a good prayer for me at 12 o'clock. If Father is not going to Diamor next week, please send me an order for 2/6. Did you notice any improvement in my writing yet? I suppose you saw in the papers that one of the girls here, M. Ryan, won a Christening cake at the St. Vincent de Paul Bazaar in Dublin…

May 23rd

Please send me 6/ - I want 2/6 for Rev. Mother's Feast day and a small silver locket for a child's birthday – when sending it, do not say what I want it for, or that it is a new one… Did Aunt Cissie condescend to attend St. Mary's during the Mission? Hoping <u>somebody</u> will keep their promise to come and see me

November 4th, 1900

I got the portmanteau on Thursday evening when Dick was over – he was in great form and expected to be able to see me next Sunday again…everything here is just the same as usual…no news…unless I take to penning descriptions of the girls, which you would not find very interesting…

November 19th

…I suppose you heard that the Bishop is coming to, or has arrived in, Mullingar…I am very glad to hear that Hal is improving. I suppose the other youth is as extraordinary as ever in the eyes of his Aunt…I would be very glad to get letters from any of the scholars, though I won't promise to answer them…

I suppose you consider that Father's visit last week will free you from the obligation of writing to me for the next month but I do not have the same opinion… If Paddie is not too much taken up with his classical studies, I would be glad to get a letter from him. Are the ladies of the Bazaar Committee having any more entertainments? I remain, Your fond child,

Mary.

The pressure from Sr. Anthony was consistent and forceful;

April 1896

Tell Mary the Sisters wear white. I am sure she would like it.

May 11th 1896

I am so glad Mary was successful with her music. That was a good number of marks and will encourage her. Get Cis to enquire from Nelly Macken of Clonswwods about Bellingham School. Her sister is a nun there and Dr. Adrian's children are there, it is not far from Hereford. Mary might like it and then I would see some of you.

May 23rd 1896

I am sure 'Sweet Marie' as I need to call her did not approve of Bellingham, nor would I, so I hope to see you by some other means. The Prayer for Ireland, for Marie (M.F), 'May it again become a seat of learning and religion. May the rising generation see it's rights restored.' What would you say to the Dominican Convent Galway, for Mary ? She would get accustomed to the white habit...

Dec 21st 1896

Will Marie ever forgive me for not writing to her but that shows how quick the time goes in a convent – is that one of her objections to them ? I believe she is not very partial. I am afraid she will agree with her Aunt Cissie...

A surviving letter to Mary herself.

My Dear Mary,   *April 19th 1899*

....We are preparing for Holy Profession, secure all the prayers you can get for us....you will have to make an attempt at singing when at home with all these brothers, as I expect you will be a model sister.

To Annie,   *July 3rd 1901*

...As for Mary.....I am glad you are keeping her from school, for your own sake.....so much anxiety over that.....

December 19th 1903

......As for Mary, I am sure she forgets she ever had an Aunt May !...

Mary always loved reading, was interested in people of all ages, and had a very absorbent brain, so we can easily deduce that school life was an enjoyable experience for her. The discipline and reflection associated with religious exercises would have come easily to her.

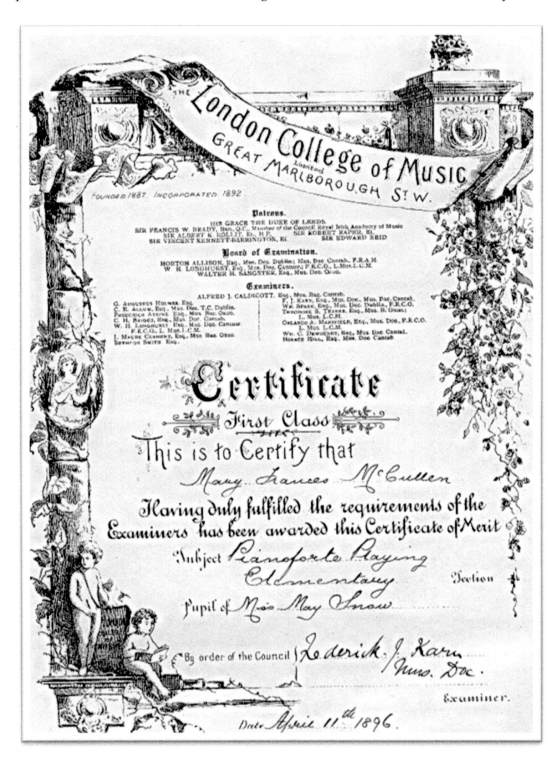

First Class Certificate Awarded to Mary Frances in 1896 by London College of Music.

CHAPTER 3: 1901-1915

AT HOME WITH MOTHER

To arrive home in the summer of 1901, from the ordered academic life of the Loreto Convent in Navan, to the hectic life of a farm with a family of ten and ten workmen, plus a 'help' in the house, must have been a dramatic change for Mary. The care of Hal , now aged seven, and Anthony, aged three, would have challenged an eighteen year old girl with hobbies of reading, music and conversation.

As I can testify from personal experience, cooking food for humans was not her favourite occupation, but it seems that her mother had a great way of managing people into their strengths. Almost immediately, Mary took over the book-keeping and wage-book, and gradually also picked up the job of family scribe to the 'scholars' away at Colleges. Richard had announced his attention to his father in 1897 to be a priest, and pursued that aim from the age of twelve years through the Seminary in Navan, to Maynooth, and ordination in 1909.

While he laboured in the Colleges the letters from his sister give a clear insight into the daily debates, farm work, gossip and local news in Beamore and also show the rapid maturing of Mary under Annie's tutelage. There are nine of these which survive, covering the period 1903-1910.

Dear Dick,   *Beamore, January 27th*

I have looked everywhere for the quotation you mention, but I cannot find who on earth wrote it…Paddy wants to know if you have a Bury's History of Rome…Long got it for South Dublin by 1500 votes. "Boss" Croker late of Tammany who is at present living in Stillorgan lent five motor cars to Hazelton to bring up voters…the gentleman who declared he was not a relieving officer was "thrun" out by his high-souled constituents…"The Freeman" has been making very merry over the failure of the "thirty bobbers" to impress their views on the British workmen…

It was a pity the donors of the stained glass windows did not encourage Irish manufacture. "The Tower of Glass" in Pembroke road turns out beautiful work, some destined for Loughrea Cathedral, was exhibited at Ballsbridge Horse Show, was really splendid. John wants his tea now, so I must stop. He has had toothache on and off for the last week, so Pa thinks it is a case for intervention of "Web-foot", alias Connelly.

Mary.

My dear Dick,   *March 4th, 1903*

…Hal took the measles last week from Anthony and is still in bed with them. All the children of St. Mary's and adjoining parishes seem to have resolved to settle the attendance problem by going on the sick list, some favour measles but the majority favour whooping cough.

"St. Stephen's" is unusually good this month. Cruise O'Brien is the president editor. He is also Secretary of the Young Ireland Branch of U.I.L. – the time he can spare to his studies can't be much.

A Dublin barrister named Byrne took the prize at the Theatre Royal Pantomime for a lyric –

> *"If I were Mr. Balfour, I would, I would*
> *When sick of Parliamentary life,*
> *I'd stick to golf, and seek a wife I would, I would."*
> *and so on....*

The Protestants are putting up a little wooden hut for S. Cooper. We had a visit from Mr. Parr, Sen., who is superintending the job and Peter Farrell who is attending the putter up, of said edifice.

The Saw Mills is about to be closed up…it is said that F. Smith is going out to his brother in law in America. I was in Navan, and saw a youth giving the gates of the Seminary a kick, clearing the chasm on his way to McGillicks…

The first car in Drogheda belonged to Dr. Parr. Reg. No. IY45. A Panhard Levasso model. (Photo courtesy of Mr. P. Fullam)

Dr.Parr's Car – the first in Drogheda !

My dear Dick,   *May 8th, 1904*

…Poor Jas. Reilly died at Stillorgan and was buried in Athlone. Thos. McCourt was buried the same day in the new Cemetery St. Mary's…died of congestion of the lungs. You have doubtless heard of Mr. & Mrs. Macken's marriage. They are at present stopping at Laytown, and intend residing at Bryanstown when that dwelling is done up…Father and James were in Mullingar Fair last week but did not go to the dedication ceremony…then the Pater patronized the M.G.W.R. for Ballinasloe… Last week, I read J. Eliot's "Mill on the Floss" – it's a wonderfully able book. Almost all the minor characters belong to the one class of people, rather stupid, very honest, and intensely middle class and narrow-minded, in their ideas, but still each one has an individuality of its' own. The King and Queen did not call on you this time, as far as I can see, their visit has been something of a fizzle. E. Delany's mare, St. Corrine won some great race at Punchestown. The King was greatly struck with her and offered Edward £2500 but the latter wanted £3000. Of course, all this must be taken "cum grano salis". We are all very busy boiling all kinds of things for a calf afflicted with an interesting disease known as "Timber Tongue"…nothing further to relate.

Your affectionate sister, Mary.

My Dear Dick,   *1-11-04*

As the house is very quiet at present (Ang is in Duleek St. J at mass time) I am taking the opportunity of sending the long promised letter. The Pater was in Trim last week on the Grand Jury. One case was of a militia man up for escaping from Mosney on someone else's bicycle. He was acquitted and beguiled the railway journey between Trim and Navan by relating how the deed was done to an admiring audience of Jurors.

As you don't read the newspapers, you probably have seen nothing of the row in the R.U.I. The Senate did not give admission tickets for degree day to the grads/undergrads who applied for them. The excuse given was 'that there was an exceptionally large number of candidates receiving degrees this year and their friends would have first claim.' Some few of the others managed to get in and made up for their scarcity by the vigour of their voices. Then a band of radicals drove up and tried to rush the doors. The Senate sent for the Police and the Chancellor left the chair in disgust, without delivering his address. The Mob broke in, breaking any glass they met en route, and left the Hall again, after one of them had delivered a Chancellors address, touching on that vexed question of Irish University Education.

I suppose you are having a concert tonight – you might send a programme, and some account of it. James hasn't been in Scotland for a fortnight. Up to that he was across almost every week. Willie Corry has gone to A.J Keogh the Auctioneer, as a Clerk. The services of P.Maguire, Junior, were dispensed with last week, and it is expected that the old man will also walk the plank before long. Fr.O'Farrell was saying the other day at the station that almost £40 had been collected for the Cathedral. Mother wants to know the raison d'etre of the band of red flannel encircling your neck when Paddie saw you. She also hopes you have got rid of your cough.

The Leader has been rather dull of late, especially since M.O'R. stopped writing. I will enclose one page of A.M.W. If I can find it, the best piece he wrote in a long time. I saw by the paper, the Bishops were thinking of conforming the curriculum to suit the R.U.I. programme. One of the Clonliffe Professors, Rev. M.Cronin, got a Junior Fellowship in Mental and Moral Science the other day. John Redmond is to be presented with the Freedom of Drogheda by the Corporation. The Corporation won't sell its agricultural property, so the tenants (on the Pater's motion) are going to present an opposition address drawing attention to the defects of the Land Act, the cruel oppression of Professing Patriotic bodies and so on, ad infinitum. They are beginning to draft it already so I can't keep on writing.

Yours, etc, Mary

My dear Dick,   December 5th, 1904

…Beginning at the wedding – I did not see it, as I was in bed with a bad cold…the attendance rivaled that of a last night of a mission…"Boiler" had a tall silk hat and was best man…Lizzie and Katie went with Mattie and Mrs. (McC.) to Miss Carroll's marriage with Davy Sheridan…it was a very swell turn-out, one of the clergy present was from Castleknock!

I was at a performance of Hamlet in Theatre Royal – house packed. Hamlet & Polonius and gravediggers were very good, the Queen only middling and Ophelia good only when she went "dotty", as P. Guilfoyle put it. James was in Ayr & Glasgow last week…the only topic of conversation in railway carriages was the "free kirk" and the "wee kirk" questions…

I read Johnson's Life of Grey…his criticisms of G.'s poetry are too ridiculous for anything and he seems as cockshure as Macaulay about everything. John wishes me to tell you he hasn't time to write to you anymore…Mr. McDonnell of Kilsharvan died a fortnight ago, and the attendance at the funeral was very large, including Fr. Curry and Fr. Clavin…Paddie is imploring me to remove the <u>two obstacles</u> to his peace, to bed, so I conclude,

Mary.

P.S. P. says there is a son of the "Leader of the Irish Race at home and abroad" in his class at Univ. College.

My dear Dick,   *December 8th, 1906*

Will you please send me a complete set of the Dungannon Club Postcards (not written of course). Emily O'Reilly is going to Irish classes in Rathgar – she says Dr. O'Daly is an ideal teacher…Now that the purchase of Reays has left us municipal rate payers, I'm thinking of joining the free Library…The Cardinal revoked his panegyric of last Easter, and now seems to regard the Libraries as "a compound of the seven deadly sins with a dash of bubonic plague thrown in".

Mr. Egan, Miss Durnin's husband, seems to be determined to make things hum in Beamore. He intends to stall feed and is building a shed for the purpose. As we are at present using the cultivator in the Road field, you may guess that every brick that goes on is carefully watched. The Irish Unionist alliance had a meeting in the Rotunda…the "Great Irish" poet Edward Dowder presided. Balfour had intended to come but then he funked. Mother says you may expect a letter and remittance in a few days, so that you won't have to work your passage home. At present, there is a strenuous campaign being opened on Reays – fencing, gates hung, posts sunk, etc. James and my Father are going to a fair in Limerick on Monday.

Yours, Mary.

Dungannon Club Postcard

My dear Dick,   *February 18th, 1908*

The only books I have had out of the Library are Scott's Peveril of the Peak, and Old Mortality and two books on St. Patrick. Old Mortality is really a good book. When driving up to Salmon recently, Father, J.A. and J.K. stopped to inspect the ploughing match at Gormanstown. Everyone expected that Tommy, alias Mouse, Markey would take first prize, but he only got second, a ploughman of McKeevers of Elm Grove taking first. Mother and Anthony were in Dublin last week and visited the new Art Gallery…

Harry Mallon and Kirwan intended leaving this year but have since reconsidered. T. McCann, J. Moore's boy, has had a very bad attack of pneumonia and is in the Cottage Hospital…the lambs are only making their appearance just now, Turlough was tied up early in the week…Mother and Father saw Paddie last week…Mr. Ginnell is still in jail…the despot of Prince's Street will retire from chairmanship of the Freeman as soon as he can. As you may guess, Father's feelings on the subject are simply indescribable, I think he'd like to choke the three head participators, Redmond, Healy and O'Brien…

Has your book appeared on the world yet?

Cover from Titian's 'The Tribute'

Joe is warning me, so I must desist –

Yours, as ever, Mary.

In recent times, due to the diligence of Dr.Oliver, I have discovered two more letters from Mary to Dick during 1909, and one during 1904.

My Dear Dick,   *18th July 1909*

As I am going out to Drogheda just now, I'll send you any correspondence that came for you this week. Just now, we are very busy. John is in Salmon. Joe is at home and James is at present staying in Carolans though he expects to get finished with Diamore this week. Paddy and I were at Navan Show on the 10th. It was a boiling hot day. Fr.Swan was there bringing around some female relations. There was any amount of other young clergy there. Fr Murphy (formerly in the Sen?) was finishing up his vac; the earlier part of it, he told Minnie Reilly, had been spent in Norway. The Show itself was no great shakes – a great decrease in entries of every sort except horses, and a very bad attendance except towards evening. We paid a visit to Loreto, where all the Nuns were expecting you to get the blessing.

Just imagine, I have been down every evening at the sea to bathe since Thurs. last (except Sat of course). That being the case, I have time for nothing else and actually not been in the library for nearly a fortnight. We got a postcard from the G.N.R yesterday, saying that your luggage had come at last. They will probably send for it today.

A great number of people went on the trip to the Isle of Man on Sunday last. Amongst others were Maggie and William Taaffe and Mrs Carroll (their sister). Teresa got a ticket but slept it (not the ticket) out. However she consoled herself when the returning travellers said the trip was 'no great thing'. There was a heavy fog outside Douglas Harbour which delayed landing by two hours on shore ('Time to run up the town, get your tea and run back'..... one of Jas Collins shop boys told John) while to crown all, some of the 'Duleek Gates', Terry McConnon (Do you remember Galbraith's fat red face breadman?) a cart man of Tighes and others too numerous to mention missed the boat, have not returned to the bosom of their families.

I want to try and get 10 o'clock mass so I'll stop now with best love as ever,

Your sister, Mary.

P.S. Paddie is just now knocking his fingers against the window, I asked him to cover the last page for me but the mean thing won't. Henry and he are exchanging remarks about the relative mortality of lambs, cows and horses.

Note : For a more cheerful account of the trip to Douglas, see the Old Drogheda Journal No.19 (2012) in an article by Frank Gallagher.

My Dear Dick,   *27 October 1909*

Enclosed is a list of all the greek books I came across. I do not think there are many more about. Katie told me that Rose Lynch is to be married before Advent to Mr.Ryder of Beauparc. You may remember he owned the first inside car we bought.

For the past six weeks Drogheda has been simply revelling in the Bell and Hammill cases before the Magistrates. The first case was that of an overseer in Ushers Mill charged with embezzling some of the Worker's Wages. When the police went on with the case they arrested two or three of his brothers for taking and carrying away from the Mill a varied collection of articles ranging from towels to ropes, shuttles and machinery. Since then the police have been searching the houses of brothers-in-law and cousins, so that it is almost as interesting as a game of 'consequences'.

Nobody knows whose place will be searched next. The Hammill case was even more dramatic, if the Drogheda papers reach your benighted district, you should study the reports.

John and Joe say that there is always a pound on at Hallow Eve and that perhaps you could come home. I need not say that if so we will all be delighted. Paddie was down last Sunday. He seemed absorbed in the University appointments, which had not then been made public. The Commissioners seem to have made a good selection. My friend, Mr Sheridan, the dentist, secures one of the dental lectureships. Paddie said that the competition for the Chair of National Economics was tremendous. Some men with messages to the Nation, even offered to take the chair for nothing. However, the final choice lay between Kettle and Donovan (also from the Freeman) Poor Skeffy did not get anything!

Everyone is busy looking for a threshing mill. Last week, we thought we had secured one. It came down into the haggard and then turned around and went away. The driver sternly steamed past Flanagans, McEntaggarts and half a dozen other places, the owners of which had their eyes out their eyes out on sticks for a mill. It is supposed he reined in somewhere in the Co.Louth from which he had received a retainer.

Hoeys gave a great party last week to Mr & Mrs Byrnes, some of the visitors came from Scotland. Two of the Miss Paddie Lenehan's have been sent to Loreto, Navan. I hear that two of Johnnie Lenehans daughters have been sent away to school, I suppose to Navan, too. Mr Murphy Sn of Coola Bridge (alias Weasel) was enquiring lately from both Father and James about you and your future movements. He is very anxious to have you in St.Mary's as he admires your style of delivery and thinks you are thrown away in the uncivilised district known as 'down the country'.

By the way, did you hear anything about Fr. Crean? James was talking to his brother about a fortnight ago, but since then we have heard nothing. The next time you are writing you might tell us when we may expect to see you and oblige,

Yours affectionately, Mary

PS. List of fourteen Greek Books (titles and publishers) follows.

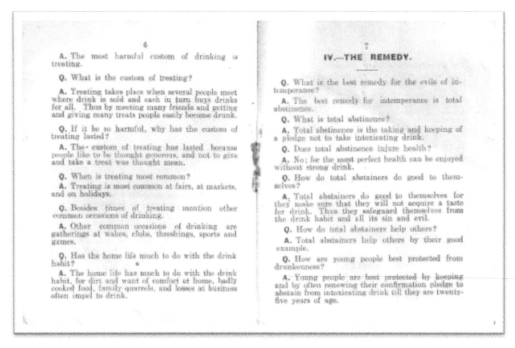

Mary's 'Temperance Questions' booklet.

In case the reader might imagine that Sister Anthony of Padua had given up her recruiting role for Convent Life, there is a letter from her to her nephew, Dick.

My Dear R.   *7 September 13th 1906*

Your dear letter gave me quite a surprise last evening. I need not say how pleased I was to receive it, as I am rarely treated to one by any of my affectionate nephews. Many thanks for the dictionary which I shall treasure all the more as it was used by yourself. I tried to recognise the small photo in the front but find it very changed from my recollection of Richard. I often wondered you and James have never sent your photos as I am sure you have one. I have a nice one of Joe. What is he going to do with himself? I had hoped he would follow your example. I hope Paddy is getting stronger as Teresa did not think him very well in the summer. Perhaps the study is so difficult when preparing for examinations.

What a dear little boy Antoine is – I am sure you will all spoil him when you are at home. I was delighted when your mother took him over here. I wonder Mary never writes to me – Do you think she will ever become a nun? I hope she will as there is not much to live for in the world and then she has so many gifts which would be so useful if she gave herself to the Religious Life. However I hope she will be happy whatever life she choses. I was in hopes of seeing her as I thought she would be over with Teresa. I suppose you study a great deal who gives the Retreat – Is it one of your own Fathers? I had a postcard with a view of the College, it is very fine. I will expect a letter sometime from you now that you have broken the ice and it will not compensate for my disappointment at not seeing you.....

Yours affectionately,

Sister M St.Antoine Moore

M.Anthony (first nun on left).

CHAPTER 4

THE DEAR TROUBLESOME BROTHERS

Leaving Richard for the moment, the others whom Mary had to deal with were James, Paddy, John, Hal and Anthony, all younger than her, except James who was the eldest. The bulk of his surviving correspondence is to his mother and father, but Mary is often referred to and even merits a letter or two herself. He writes

> *Dear Mary,*   *St.Finians, 19th October 1895*
>
> *I wish you success in your music. I am sure you will do something in it. It will not be long until xmas vacation. It is nine weeks today. I hope you will not have your party until then. I am, as ever,*
>
> *Your fond brother, James.*

In letters to his mother in 1895 and 1896.

> *....If Mary and Richard are going to write, let then, enclose it in yours...*
>
> *....I suppose the nuns are busy selling tickets for the raffle and that Mary is having her revenge on Richard by selling as much as possible and gaining as much importance...*
>
> *....I hope all are well....especially Mary.*
>
> *...Others never saw the sea before and several mistook Aunt Cissie for my sister. This, you may tell her is a very high compliment to pay her – you might also send me a pair of studs for in the bag.*

Referring to an excursion to Gormanston

> *....I hope Mary is getting better.*
>
> *....By the way, a boy from Mullingar asked me to get a hat for him, so I ask Mary to get one from Brady's.*

For the rest of their lives, Mary was more than happy to search for whatever James might require, whether it was food, clothing, hats, tickets or even coats buried under the ground. The latter refers to an old smelly coat he wore handling sheep, which his wife buried in order to get rid of it, but M.F acted as a whistleblower much to James' delight and his wife's disgust.

Paddy was always busy as a student or as a Doctor and even his mother remarked in 1903, that he surpassed himself, by sending her a letter with five lines in it. However, five new letters were unearthed by Dr.Oliver, all written to Richard, which give us an insight into his life, three from a lodgings at 38, Cabra Park in Phibsboro. No dates are given, but they would be 1905-1908.

Dear Richard,   *Colaiste Droichead Nuadh*

You must excuse my not answering your letter before this, as stamps were very scarce, I had to wait until I got some from home. They have put up a laundry here.... A young lad named Guirrini from Dublin got his walking papers the other day for stealing a watch and trying to sell it in the town. They are going to allow papers in the Library...

I hear that the Japs are hammering the Russians...five or six warships being sunk on the latter. If St.Thomas's day is fine, I might struggle over to see you but don't count on this as several things might happen between that and this to prevent my going. John tells me that Collinge (?) has changed his mind about the play and has them learning the 'Pirates of Penzance'. I don't think there is any more news about here, so I will end this.

Dear Richard,

I received your epistle yesterday and was much disappointed in not getting the brushes. You might send them on as soon as you get them. Although there has been fine weather here during the week, the Liffey has been flooded since Sunday which shows there must have been very heavy rain somewhere about. Had you any? We got 4 new students during the week, 3 from Kerry and 1 from Whitehaven. I think what Weynes failed in at the Intermediate was Greek because I saw that he only got 55 in Greek. Will you ask Walsh for his and McGuirke's numbers and I'll send you on their numbers from the book. I hadn't a letter from John yet.

Hoping you will write soon – I remain,

Your fond brother, Paddy .

Paddy at his Graduation

Dear Richard   *St.Thomas' College, Newbridge*

You must excuse me for not answering your last letter sooner but to tell you the truth I had not time. On Ascension Thursday, I was at a hurling match in Fermoy, between our team and theirs. On account of the early win they got last year, the Fermoy lads were expecting as they said themselves, that they would have a game of ping-pong, but on account of some new arrivals here last Christmas, among them two lads who go to Dublin nearly every Sunday to play (and who were on the Leinster team in the match Leinster vs Munster a few weeks ago) the Fermoy lads got a great drop. At half time when the score was even, and all their men were nearly dead, they brought on a ball which was afterwards found to be 31/2 oz , half the right weight; Our lads wouldn't play with this until one of the priests made them. So at full time, they were two points ahead. But as there was a dispute about a goal we were one point ahead.

The College below is a very nice one. It is all in one building stretching along a very high hill but there is hardly any grounds, and not a tree near it. It is very bleak looking. The journey down was about 5 hours, so that we arrived there near three; as we left shortly after nine, we did not arrive here till four the next morning. We had to get up at 10am on Friday, and go to class, the second part of the day. Yesterday, their team came up to play the return;

They came up about one, so the match was about half past two. You may bet that they were beaten here because they wouldn't be let play with the ping-pong ball. At full time they were beaten by nine points, the score being 1-14 Newbridge and 0-8 Fermoy.

Our goal was put in from the fullbacks – they got a fifty, which was caught about one yard from our goal by the fullback, who has the Long Puck Championship for Leinster. They stopped here last night, and have just gone. Please excuse the writing and grammar of this, and I want to finish it before the Prior comes back from seeing the Fermoy lads at the station. Fr. Reginald Walsh is stopping here for the past few days, as there is no centre for matric and had to sign for Dublin, so we will be in the same place.

When are you going home? I don't think there is anything more about here, only that the Fermoy lads, because they were beaten by our lads, would not speak to any of the fellows here. Hoping you are very well, I remain, P.D.McC

Dear Richard,   *38, Cabra Park, Phibsboro*

I received your letter all right the other evening, and I tried Webb's for the Catechism. He had not got it and I did not try Clerys for it yet, but if I get it before I go home, I will let you know. I expect to go home on Friday evening.

I suppose you heard that Mrs L.Lenehan was operated on by the Farnans in the private hospital – Eccles St., about a fortnight ago. As there is nothing else to record from here, except bad weather, I will draw this to a close, with a word of congratulations to you on your finding out that it was your turn to write, Your amicable brother, Paddy

Dear Richard,   *38 Cabra Park, Phibsboro (undated)*

I returned here on Tuesday and since that day I have been engaged in looking for the two books and pictures. The only place I heard anything about the pictures was in Gills where they said they would

be getting some of the Perry Series early next week so if you still want it you might drop me a note before Tuesday. As you will see by the enclosed cutting, I got a second class honour in the exam , the great surprise here being that Stewart did not get an honour.

I could not get the Staenkiste (spelling?) up to this although Clerys expect to have it second hand shortly. Fr. O'Farrell left Drogheda last week for Ballymore and we got in his place Fr J. Connor. I had intended to send you an account of the conferring but mislaid the paper here. I don't think that there is anything else except that the medical board of the mater are giving a smoking concert (free of course) in the Gresham to the students of the hospital next Saturday night....

P.D.   Selection of pictures from the Perry Series..

Dr.Paddy was appointed Medical Officer for Stamullen after obtaining an Honours Degree from N.U.I in 1910. There was only one applicant and all members of the Local Board spoke highly of him. The Chairman described Dr.McCullen as 'the right man in the right place

Somebody must have messed up Mary's filing system at some stage in the last century, because I came on the longest letter written by Paddy to anyone, in an envelope containing a letter of Annie's to Fr.Richard. It has moved on from student life.

Dear Richard,   *Stamullen, Balbriggan, 10.5.11*

As I am not extremely busy this evening I thought I might write to know if you were in the land of the living. Practically every man, woman and child in the Julianstown end of the district had just put the measles over them and you can guess that I had a busy time. Just now there is a lull although I have been out every night since last Tuesday. They are expecting the Bishop here on June 3ʳᵈ though what will happen if the youngsters get the measles I don't know. I suppose you heard that James and myself broke out on Easter Monday and drove to Fairyhouse where I met practically all my class, both qualified and not, along with many others. There is a retreat on at present in St.Mary's and it is wonderful to see how anxious each of them is at home about how the others attend, anyway a new bicycle, was got to enable Mary to do so !

I was speaking to Fr.Leonard some days ago – anxious to hear about you etc., when will you be free for the summer ? My mother tells me that you don't intend to go anywhere this year, if so, you might arrange to spend most of your time here, as this place is ideal just now, and will be more so when one can get an odd feed of fruit. Anyway 'I do feel lonely' (see popular lyric) and any break in the monotony, even a letter at present would be welcome.

John is about to get up a hayshed in Salmon this summer so that there is strict scope for the family genius in the line of building. Would you mind sending me anything you want to get rid of, in the way of reading material, even old newspapers or a few volumes of the Encyclop.... Britannica (not sure of exact spelling but you know what I mean). I really think that I read more since I came here than since I went to school. I am going to Dublin on Saturday morning, by invitation, to assist at an operation. I just mention this to show you that us Dispensary Doctors are cultivated by the 'Square' now?, some of whom were very pressing in the invitations to accompany them in their motors to Punchestown and Leopardstown a few weeks ago. Anyway, whatever the cause, I never thought that they were worth so much 'crawling on your knees after', to make use of Joe's favourite expression.

Yours etc,

P.D. McC

John, my father was two years younger than Paddy and spent his term of imprisonment in St.Finians from 1903 to 1905. In addition to the 19 missives sent to his mother and featured in 'My Dearest Annie', six more have surfaced in 'Laurence Street Cellars'.

Dear Richard,   *7ᵗʰ November 1903*

You may excuse me for not writing sooner.The Bishop was in today and gave us a free day on Monday. Mary was down to the Convent on Wednesday. Two of her companions were being received, one being a sister of E.Gibbons, who is going to teach the second year course of drawing here. I hear Father T.Gogarty is curate in Tullyallen along with Fr.Breagy who was curate in Drogheda, before he got to be P.P. of that place.I heard Paul Kelly saying that one of the McQuillans went to Australia. I suppose that my mother told you that Mrs Fay of Peter St., and Mrs McGoldrick of Duleek St., were dead.

I can't think of anything else except that Paddy says he is the only one from Drogheda, in Newbridge. There was a very exciting football match played here on Sunday week between the Independents and the Isles of the Sea. The Isles won, therefore are Champions of Leinster for another year. There are 80 students here this year. I must conclude now.

Hoping you are well, I remain, your fond brother, John.

P.S. I suppose you heard that Dr.D. Sheehy is M.P. for South Meath.

Dear Dick,   *8ᵗʰ October 1904*

We received your nice long letter during the week. I forget what day it was, but it was not on a wet day. There was a very strong wind here during the week, and it is awfully cold since then, so cold that I have seen a lad with chilblains already. Joe does not mind being here now as he is used to all the tips and the hot tea (which he thought to be shocking , instead of the half and half) and other things. I hear that Bermingham is gone to America and Fennon to Liverpool. There is a rumour that hurling is going to be introduced here....... it would be well liked.... Fr Gibbons teaches the drawing class.... I sent home the bag this day week and I did not get an answer or anything yet, you would think they were all dead. If visiting soon, I want you to send (as you told me you could) some money. I can't think of any more 'rubbish' to say so I remain,

Your loving brother, John.

'Now he would be one of the McQuillans of West Street – Vincent who joined the Vincentians. His brother Fr.Joe was a Dominican in the South Seas Islands... Oh! Dolly's mother, Mary Jane Dolan, was the only sister.Pardon me, there was a younger girl but she died at the age of nine'. This would be a sudden interjection by Mary!

Dear Dick,   *St.Finians, 5ᵗʰ November 1904*

I was surprised to get a letter from you lately. I suppose 'Macbeth' came off with great success on Tuesday. You must write me a good account of it when you next write, which I hope will be soon. The great love which everybody bore to Fr.Gibbons soon died away. Everyone has a great dislike to him. He is too particular about small matters. He would near eat you if you went up to to the dormitory without asking. For instance on Tuesday night (the night of the Big Feast) he went around, all the dormitories when the fellows went up their swops and put them down. He is always preaching......

I had a letter from my mother on yesterday and she said that Paddy went down to see you on Tuesday. I suppose he is pounding horrible hard now. I hear that Bermingham lost his vocation and that is why he went to America.

We done the Jubilee here on last Thurs, Friday and Saturday. We made 3 visits in the town Chapel on Thursday, on Friday there was a general confession and we also fasted on Friday eating only two slices of bread with our tea in the morning, at dinner time we ate as much as we could, and for supper we get only half a slice of dry bread with our tea and on Saturday we went to Communion.

We do have Purcell (The Drill Master) in now. I would not take any pleasure in walking round the field as fast as you could and your legs are dropping under you, Hoping you are well,

I remain, John.

P.S. If you have any spare moments you might write to Biddy.

Dear Dick,   *11th February 1905*

As you delayed a long time before you wrote to Joe, I thought that I might have the same liberty by delaying to write to you .... How did you like Ash Wednesday ? I got over it alright. Mary came down on Tuesday..... Fr.O'Farrell and Fr. Clavin were in here on Thursday week (there was a conference) but I was not talking to them. Joe and P.Kelly were. The Bishop is in Navan nearly a fortnight but he did not come near us until yesterday. But his visit did not do much good for he was in the Refectory when we were at our dinners and managed to disappear before we left. We are to have a catechism exam on Tuesday.

I can't think of any more nonsense to say, but hope you are well and free from chilblains and that you will reply soon,

I remain, John.

'That would be Biddy Cunningham who lived in Beamore beside us. They would be locals since before the Reformation...'Old Residenters'. John bought the land afterwards from Tommy Clarke in the 1950's'. Another interjection!

Dear Dick,   *1st April 1905*

.....You should have written a decent letter and not your few lines on a postcard. The fellows are beginning to practice for the sports now since we got to be out in the field at six..... you never gave me a description of the plays which were on 17th. I don't get very many visits from James or another anyone else now. If it is not to you inconvenience you might send me some money for the entrance to the sports. I am in a hurry to post this before the bell. I can't think of anything else to say, but I will write to you very soon.

Hoping you are well, I remain, John.

Dear Dick,   *St.Finian's (undated)*

I am sorry I did not get a letter from home or the books. Did you get them when you were going back ? We had a free day on Tuesday. M. Weymes got an exhibition and W.Moran got 2 book prizes and as you can tell about them. P.McDonnell is prefect and a very kind, easy fellow he is too. He was asking for you. P.Leonard is senior. The fellows who have charge of the vestry are E.Murtagh, W.Cooney and M.McKeever. The fellows who have the dormitories are P.McDonnell, P.Leonard, T.Keeffe, E.Murtagh and J.Merlehan, I got my marks today.

They are Arithmetic 315, Algebra 300, English 195, French 313, History & Geography 240, Latin 230 and Euclid 270.

Joe Larrigan got into All Hallows and D.Mulvany. At present there are 86 fellows in the House. I can't think of any more rubbish to say only that if you are writing home during the week, you can send my marks. I saw P.Connell going back on Tuesday. Fennon went to Liverpool. I think it is time for me to wind up, so

I remain,

John.

In Autumn of 1904, Joe was dispatched to the seminary, in the company of his older (by two years) brother, John. Three previously unknown pieces of correspondence have surfaced. These are from Joe and John to Dick .

Dear Dick,   *4th Feb 1905*

I hope you are quite well and I hope your teeth are all right. I arrived back here on Monday 16th, all wet and cold. We had one feast since then and we got 3 new lads, the two Lenehans and a small lad the name of Foley, aged 15, and he is about the size of Ang (then aged 7). How many teeth did you get pulled and are you going back ? Were you under gas?

There are about 20 lads in bed at present some with colds, others with toothaches. Thank Goodness there is nothing on me or John. I am at the same table and in the dormitory. John Keegan was asking for you. He does have to get his dinner with himself as he has to get a bottle of stout with it, because his arm burst and it is like a map with spots. I think I am getting on all right. We had a free day on Tuesday and we passed it all right as it was not wet and there was no walk. I found a watch in the field but it was P.Mac Donnells. Write soon as I have no more news. Your loving brother,

Joe McCullen

Dear Dick,   *18-9-05*

I arrived here safely last Friday night. I am in the Junior Grade and they are not teaching Irish in it and I am not learning Greek. There is a brother of John Conner's if you know him. There are over 20 new lads here. Young Fergus Casey is here. Father was down at the Fair here and was in seeing me, yesterday. There is a new Priest here in place. I had a letter from John this morning. He said N.Conner is going to be ordained in a short time.

I am sleeping in the Big Dormitory, and T Keeffe is over it. J Merlehan is senior. How is it that J.Keegan has such a liking for you – he is always asking for you.

I remain, Your Loving Brother, John McC

The final piece of correspondence is a postcard scene of Market Square, Navan.

Dick,

You must excuse me for not writing to you sooner. A brother of   ?   came back on Friday and went away on Sat morning. We expect a free day tomorrow. There are a few new lads back. I was never as lonesome coming back as this year. I hope you got back safe. There is nothing startling about here these times. Big Dick is not back this year, as he has to stop at home to mind the lambs.

Write soon, Joe.

Amongst Fr.Dick's collection of letters is a copy of College Rules for St.Finians, when it transferred to Mullingar in 1908. This gives a flavour of the approach of staff to the hard-pressed students...

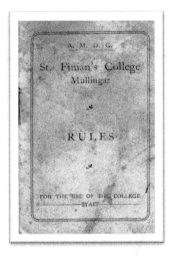

St.Finian College Rules

(2)

Programme will be in keeping with the requirements of the Holy Father for the faithful generally. The Instructions will be given by all the priests of the College in turn, and will not occupy more than a quarter of an hour. The servants of the College will attend at these Instructions, special days being reserved, as occasion may require, for addresses special to the Students themselves.

IV. As the proper conduct of the Students is mainly in the hands of the Deans, they will take week about on duty as at present arranged.

V. The Dean on duty will be at all times accessible to the Students. He will preside at night prayer, and will secure the punctual attendance of Students at morning prayer and meditation.

VI. He will superintend the morning and evening recreations, preside at

(3)

the commencement of studies, and, in general, make his presence felt wherever the Students may be engaged at their exercises.

VII. He will pay frequent and un-expected visits to the study hall during the hours of study—a duty which may be shared in simultaneously by all the priests of the College. He will also visit the rooms and dormitories occupied by Students, and satisfy himself that neither there nor in any place to which they may have access is anything introduced which may be forbidden to the Students of the College.

VIII. Whilst maintaining discipline in the refectory, and preventing un-necessary waste, he will consider it part of his duty to see that the Students are properly catered for, and thus pre-vent a recurrence of any possible complaints that may be made in regard to the dietary of the College.

Two letters from Anthony to Dick are included in the bundle of the dear, troublesome brothers.

Dear Fr. Richard   *Beamore, 19th Feb 1910*

As I have a very sore toe and being at home from school but having the use of my hands, I thought I might scribble these few lines to you. I have been getting special grinding from Mr. McQuillan since you left, the fee being ten shillings per month. We have two lambs at Beamore and Joseph has great trouble herding, nobody started to stop up with the sheep yet.

We have had the mill since Tuesday, but it left yesterday. The reason why it stopped so long was that they were unable to thresh very much on Thursday because of great wind and rain. There is a retreat being given by the Redemptorist Fathers in St.Peter's and Fr. Sutton is one of them. Hoping you are well,

I remain, Anthony.

Dear Richard   *Beamore, Monday.*

I managed to get time to write to you this line. I suppose you are anxious to know about my studies. I am in division of weights and measures. I am beginning to like gaelic very much, I think it is easy enough. I went over 26 of the props of Euclid. I suppose you heard about my illness of a fortnight. I think Mr McQuillan is easy enough. I know I would sooner be there than in the Nuns, I will now close,

Yours truly, Anthony.

Letters from Anthony are extremely rare ! The other dear, troublesome brother for Mary was Hal, who was handicapped, suffering from epilepsy and was very prone to lung infections. Annie refers to him as 'My Treasure', but from 1901 to 1911, Mary seems to have devoted a lot of her time to his care. Hal left home in 1911, to become a residential pupil with the Brothers of Charity in Belmont in Waterford and then onwards to the Strop, a residential home in Ghent, Belgium. It is likely that the enormous patience and tolerance shown by Mary in her later life was borne out of her dealings with Hal during that ten year period after she returned from the Loreto in Navan.

'Pardon me ! Alex McQuillan lived on the Old Hill and was a great teacher. He used to give grinds. Some of the Doctor's family went to him to do Irish Lessons. Mary would have been with him'. Interjection by Mary F.

Original Homesteads in Beabeg

Beabeg House (home of 13 cousins) and Dermot & Lucy McC on mudwalls after collapse in the 70's

CHAPTER 5

THE PRIEST'S ROLE

Apart from Dick's provision of a listening ear to his younger brothers, and a literary peer for his sister Mary, he played a huge role as a confidant for his mother, Annie, and also for many of his fellow students. However, there is also the previously unknown involvement by him in preparing and publishing a book. This was a popular version of the Abbe Constant Fouard's 'The Life of Christ – The Son of God', which was to be sold for six pence.

Looking at the project from the vantage point of a century later, it seems very unusual for a 22 year old clerical student , two years from Ordination, to carry off such a project. In his own papers which made their way to 33, Laurence Street, Drogheda, via Aunt Mary, and then to Beamore, via Oliver, 20 letters survive, mostly responses from the Publishing House of Longman's Green & Co, 33 Paternoster Row, London E.C. They commence thus;

(Note in Dick's writing – 'answered 16th May).

There follows a long series of letters from Longman's Green & Co, and the Archbishops House in Westminster. The Archbishop would not provide an 'Imprimatur' for the book until he checked the final proofs.

Longmans Green & Co would publish 30,000 copies on cheap quality paper, with 268 pages, and obtain permission from Abbe Fouard's Executors who were living in America. Dick was to provide an 'Old Master' painting selection for the cover and proof read the book – all for a fee of five guineas.

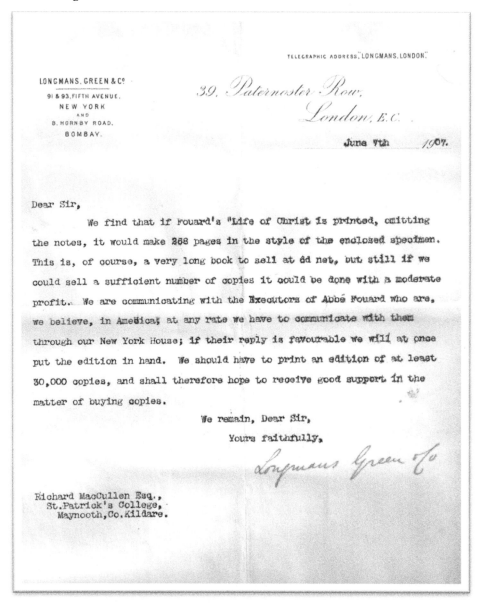

Their letter of November 8th 1907 states –

> 'We have decided to use the Titian 'The Tribute Money' on the cover and so will not trouble you to send in the 'Da Vinci'! We have pleasure in enclosing our cheque for your work, as agreed'.

The Printer had trouble however and it was not until March 10th 1908, that six copies were dispatched to Mr. R Mac Cullen, by parcel post.

Dick, who inherited a large genetic ability for thriftiness from his Mother and Father, obviously started marketing immediately. A letter dated March 19th 1908 is included in the archive.

My dear Mr McCullen   *All Hallow's College,*

I am very glad to renew an old acquaintance. I can assure you it was through no ill feeling that I gave you that 'atque', for having to end my list somewhere, it must have so happened that I ended it with your name – the merest chance.

I am very thankful for the copy of Fouard's life of Christ which you sent me. It is the first, and I believe the best Catholic Life of Christ that combines deep scholarship with solid piety. I happen to have all the Senior House in my Scripture Class and half the Junior House in the Humanities Class and am therefore in a position to recommend it' and I shall strongly urge them to get it, for I believe it is a book that should be in the hands of every student as it may now be had for 6d.

With renewed thanks and all best wishes, I am, your very sincerely,

M.O'Brien

Whether or not it was due to Rev Professor O'Brien, a letter from the Publishers arrived on April 29th 1908;

TELEGRAPHIC ADDRESS "LONGMANS, LONDON".

LONGMANS, GREEN & Cº
91 & 93, FIFTH AVENUE,
NEW YORK

8, HORNBY ROAD,
BOMBAY.

303, BOWBAZAR STREET,
CALCUTTA.

*39, Paternoster Row,
London, E.C.*

April 29th 1908.

Dear Sir,

   We are obliged by your letter of April 27th., and we are happy to say that the publication of the cheap edition of Fouard's "Life of Christ" has started very well:up to the present date we have sold about 10,000 copies, which we may regard as very promising. It is, of course, necessary to sell a very large number of copies of the book to make it commercially successful considering the extremely low price.

       We remain, Dear Sir,

       Yours faithfully,

       Longmans Green & Co

Richard MacCullen Esq.,
 St.Patrick's College,
 Maynooth,Ireland.

When Fr.Dick was ordained, he spent a short while as a 'supply priest' in the parishes of Dunboyne and Mount Nugent during the summer of 1909, and was then appointed on September 13th to succeed Fr.Lynam, as Professor of Greek at St.Finians Seminary which was now based in Mullingar. This must have given him a degree of satisfaction when linked with a letter of seven years earlier from Fr.Duffy (who had crossed swords with my father).

My Dear Dick,   *St.Finians 2nd Sept 1902*

I am afraid your score in Greek will prevent you in getting an Exhibition – you might be too proud if you got one. I enclose your marks and those of a few others. Note that all subjects have the same value 400 marks. In pass subjects the gross marks are given. In Honours Greek, the excess over 100 is given. In other honours subjects the excess over 200. Thus in the pass papers you got 395 in Algebra and 275 Geometry. In the honours papers your gross marks are Greek 180, Latin 225, English 270 and French 275. Send me a telegram when you know the result of your exam in Maynooth,

With best wishes to all of you, J.E. Duffy

Editor's Note: There is a strange irony in the Duffy-McCullen saga, in that my father left the seminary with an abiding dislike for the reign of Fr.Duffy, Fr.Dick who did not get the 'Exhibition' is then appointed Professor of Greek and one of my own unpleasant memories of education was when I could not spell 'handkerchief' in the class of an old Nun with a woollen shawl at St.Joseph's in the 1940's. Her name was Mother M.Philomena Duffy – a niece of Fr.Duffy!

An interesting letter from a fellow student arrived to Fr.Richard, within a few days of his appointment to St.Finians.

St.Mary's Maynooth,

Dear Rich,   *25 Sept 1909*

Would you have a commentary on St.Matthew that you would lend me till Xmas? Joe recommends McCarthy and Maas. I hope you like the Seminary. A Professor ! A grand title. I believe the Seminary got on fairly well at the intermediate level this year. I heard Hugh Conlon made a good howl ?. I wonder what kind of year we are going to have here. It would seem that there is punishment ahead, from two resolutions of the Bishops – one withdrawing permission for all the newspapers and magazine's previously allowed, and the other ordering the inaugural meetings of all societies to be postponed until after their (bishops) October meeting. We had a letter from Paul Walsh this morning. He is not coming up till about the time of the distribution. He likes his parish immensely. I think he was in for the matriculation a few days ago.

I was just thinking over the B.D ? lately and I don't know what to make of it. I suppose I am nearly certain not to be let back next year even if I should get the B.D. Assuming that, I would like to get out of the B.D class altogether. The appearance of last year's candidates (or some of them at least) about the 1st of June was a sufficient lesson to an average type. However, I have some misgivings as to how the Bishop would take it, if I should ask to be dispersed. Could you throw any light on the problem ?

We had a great gallery affair yesterday. Connell, the Bank Manager from Donegal, whom you saw here with Joe Tinny, was in at a spread the other night and stopped here the next day when he placed his motor-car at the convenience (Mercy, I should say) of the students. After breakfast , the Dunboyne men drove it until something went wrong and during lunch it went round and round the park N?

Times bringing a new batch of fellows every time. You would think it was the hobby horses. He had a great chat with certain members of our diocese, with whom he left his card and invited them to meet him.

If Patsy Connell wants his book on the psalms, I will send it to him. If not, I will keep it till he comes up sometime, Nothing strange at present,

Yours faithfully,

William Moran

The Gym and St.Finians, Mullingar, after improvements by Fr.Dick.

About 34 other letters to Fr.Dick survive – from fellow priests and students who give advice, seek advice or spar intellectually in a style of debate which must have been their usual kind of repartee during years together in College. I have taken a sample of each of six of these, in addition to William Moran.

Rev. Paul Kelly writes from Ushaw, Durham on 24.10.08 to thank Dick for sending him books. Paul was from James St. Drogheda and the two would have grown up together. He was ordained in 1911 – it seems a bit delayed, because of ill-health. He writes

> *'Since I wrote to you last, I have received tonsure and full orders minor. Ted Smith is the same. P.Macken got the diaconate, so you see the Meath men are advancing, slowly and steadily....'*

Ursa Major Alias the Polar Bear writes from Eglish, Dungannon in August '09.

> *'Might I insult you by asking you to take some 2/6 int, to be said in ordinary time. I know well the arrogance of newly ordained priests puffed up with 5&10 / int each morning. Design to reply by next post, saying how many, if any , you can oblige by taking'. Re your suggestion about my military training etc. I would advise you to send on that tip to + Michael Cardinal etc. But I fear that much against my will, I am destined to be made a 'kid-walloper' in an intermediate school'.*

Note: Int = Intentions, to be included at masses said by the priest. Cardinal Logue was in situ.

Fr. Con writes from St.Jarlaths, Tuam, on 9-9-09 listing several Greek text books and bits of advice for a budding Professor at a Diocesan Seminary, and suggesting that named Publishing Houses would supply copies of books ' gratis' if you write to them.

> *'Make sure that you send me a postcard when next calling to Ballinrobe ! At all times, I will be at your back to do whatever little thing it is in my power to do for you'*

He concludes – *'Make sure that the boys like you!'*

Fr Muiris O'Connaill writes from Dunboyne House on 10-5-10, to explain that he is standing by his appointment to Enniscorthy and not going Meathwards. After some philosophising he says-

> *'Excuse my paper not having the seasonable verge. He was a great king and bore himself well on his lofty perch. I remember well when he was crowned, a certain Irish paper was suppressed for calling him a 'bald-headed gnome' and rising such naughty words as 'lecher' in the same column'. (reference to King Edward VII).*

Rev. E. Connolly, based in a city in Missouri, reminisces about the past, long disappeared (!) in January 1911 – in response to some news pieces sent on by Fr.Dick.... *'So the old place is falling into decay – peace to it's ashes – I will always retain kind memories of it. I am glad to hear that the faces of Mornington and Drogheda still retain their contented peace, and smiling countenances. All my relations are living in Dublin now, but if I ever go back to Erin's isle, I will visit the old haunts'.*

Rev. Donal A. Reidy, a Kerryman, carried on a correspondence with Fr.Dick from 1909 to 1912 some of it from home, some on the boat to Australia, and more from his Mission Station on the other side of the world. Commencing with a 12 page missive from Beaufort, Co.Kerry on 20/7/09 he discusses the various appointments after the Ordinations and remarks; *'I was surprised and somewhat disgruntled at another example of Irish Episcopal Management, Lord save us ! Are young priests like mere pawns in a chess board that no allowance is ever to be made for aptitudes, tastes and inclinations. It is a very defective and unstatesmanlike system of administration.'*

His short-term future was as a 'quasi C.C' No.6 in his own parish - *'I keep always from the PP, who is a 'type'. Innovation would be dangerous and I hang on to the text 'Nemo propheta in terra sua'! The , mountains must be moved by faith and come to Mahomet'.*

Donal mentions the Bishop of Ballarat in this letter, and wonders how did his own Bishop know of his contacts..... Three weeks later he writes again, after a long cycle into the Kerry Mountains, with several punctures. His CC ship expires the next day and reflecting on his work – one funeral service, no sick call, five confessions and his only ; *'One day of mortal terror that a deaf old-woman might throw her arms around me and whisper her tale in my ear (no confessional!).'*

'He mentions the case of O'Hickey who is in a dispute with the Bishops and going to try Rome for a resolution of it. *'At any rate , the Church or Irish won't be the better of the whole affair' and 'I know the Bishops put their feet in it in the beginning and have tramped on through the mire since. I havn't a scrap of sympathy for insubordination (agitation is different) but I detest high-horsey dignity.'* Referring to restriction on newspapers for the 'Dunboyne men' he writes *'I suppose An Claidheamh too, will be considered too sharp for children to play with.*

Whatever took place in the Diocese of Kerry, Donal writes a letter of congratulations to Dick on his lectureship in Greek at Mullingar, and is already packed for Australia on 10.09.09, to arrive on 27th October in Melbourne. c/0 Rev L.O'Neill, St.Patrick's Cathedral, Ballarat. He promises that the next letter would be written 'out upon the ocean wave'.

However, there is a postcard of a High Cross, posted at North Wall Station, Dublin, 7.15pm on 15.9.09, written in Irish. Was this for privacy, as a last kick at the Shoneen Bishops ? or because he felt more Irish to be leaving home ?

 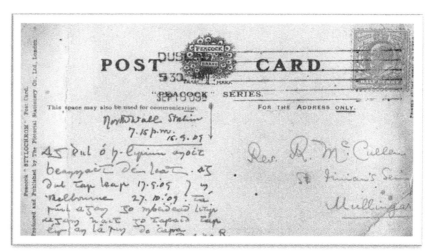

Sure enough, the next letter comes on 18.10.09, written on board the R.M.S 'Orontes',

Suez to Colombo in Ceylon was dreadfully wearisome, the heat was oppressive and very exhausting.... lowlying coral islands now in our final ten days to Freemantle, covered with cocoa palms and little shoals of flying fish....busy with letters, and sermon for Sunday week....Port Said has the name of being the dirtiest and wickedest town to be met with..... I smelled them from a good distance.... drank delicious Egyptian coffee....a suggestion for your classical stories, get a guide book and pictures of Greek and Roman life and buildings, or go for a trip there yourself.

This will give an additional interest and life to your lectures... I have a good many things to do in 5 years....wonder what percentage of them will get done ?

What kind of restrictive measures were being discussed by the House of Lords in Maynooth ? Did they sink deeply in the mire or float themselves on rafts of platitudes? Is Maynooth a boarded out child of the University ? Of course we are going to get Home Rule at the next General Election. Tis going to come but will Ireland be half English by the time it comes ? Are we going to see it ?

One month later, Donal was in a different place;

St.Patrick's Cathedral
9.2.10-25.2.10

My Dear Dick,

How busy, How worried, How unsettled I've been for the past three months... if he ever intended having me as Secretary I think he has put that notion out of his head..... My new Parish of Watchen (100 miles south of Ballaral) has three churches and I must drive a pair of horses (I never drove a horse by myself before last xmas!)... I haven't read a book price since taking up Missionary Duty here .... have received a letter from Maynooth that will leave me unsettled for some time longer. McCaffrey writes to urge me to apply for Deanship at Maynooth, saying that he had spoken to all the members of the Council about it who would look favourably on my application! Result will be cabled in June..... I would have liked more experience first....

The sermons are killing to me, the children's sermon spoiled my preparation for my Sunday ones... Your letters have been as welcome as the breeze on the brow of the Ancient Mariner....couldn't tell you how dissatisfied I have been, a mixture of homesickness, dissatisfaction at unsettlement, and solitude in a crowd. I didn't, on purpose make any lay friends... In confessions, it is heart sickening sometimes to find the acquaintance young people have with evil ... Australians want their Bishops to be involved in social activity. The Priests at home don't know what they could do with their people if they took the trouble to make them good, the priests must have a lot to do to keep them Catholics.....

I have just heard from Ireland that the 'Blocks' is coming with a crozier to Melbourne. He wouldn't be the best man, he would be far more suitable for an Irish Diocese. Mannix or O.Dea would be very suitable.... If I am to return I shall be in Ireland by the end of August.

It was not to be. The next letter is dated 20-26th March 1911, a year later, and Donal mentions that his health has never been better, since before he had a breakdown in early Maynooth life, the winter in Watchem is pleasant and warm, and he believes that he is getting into Missionary work because there is so much to be done, and this gets him over the lack of comradeship and the loneliness, for home. Having received photographs of St.Finians from Fr.Dick, he comments:

'The dormitory is an exception to the other fine buildings. These two double-rows remind me of an orphanage I visited not long ago in Ballarat. God help any non-hippopotamus-hided 'Mamma's Darling' that fate should bring to that dormitory. If there be one work of charity more necessary than another in boys schools, it is that those in authority should seek every means to put down bullying and petty persecutions with a strong hand!'

He concludes: 'I can be perfectly happy here !'

My Dear Dick,

9th September 1912

In explanation of my contribution to the 'Austral Light' re. Mannix, it was done in answer to a pressing request from the Editor, and on the following days... Health very good lately. Hope you are doing well and making progress in that difficult study. Boy-psychology, more difficult than Plato, I imagine.

With Kind Regards, Your Sincere Friend,

Donal A. Reidy

Apart altogether from the matter of improving the Gaeilge, Rev Padraic _____ was no slouch when it came to selling the charms of 'the best of Connaught' which he could organise with visits to Galway, Clifden, Wetsport, Killary, Kylemore, Cong and Annaghdown, where Johnny Heneghan was. Fr.Dick made a visit to Ballinrobe, to visit his fathers' two first cousins, nuns in the Mercy Convent, Sisters Elizabeth and Magdalen who wanted his special blessing and to show him the Convent Gardens, 'laden with tempting fruit'. Fr.Padraic was to get a train from Ballinasloe to Ballinrobe but the communications broke down and Dick was back in the East before Padraic got the letter. This was what happened to envelopes addressed in Irish...they were sent to Dublin for translation!

Resulting from this disappointment, Padraic suggests that they could go to the college in Tourmakeady and spend a while in a large tent in mid-September during holiday time. The final letter explains how he could come to Mullingar and deal with the Irish-speaking group of 4 1/3 Priests (Dick's Description). The censorship mentioned in the other correspondence of the time, surfaces here too. Padraic writes (in Irish)

'The work with you is hard enough, but not as hard as here. There are only 5 priests in the Dunboyne and their life is not nice at all. No society can start on any work, without the Bishops coming with rules. No papers of any kind are allowed. This means 'An Claidheamh', 'The Irish Rosary', everything! I have not started to teach Irish yet and I am worried and lonely.... Say a little prayer for Irish in Maynooth.'

Bernard J. McGuirk

There is a mountain of surviving correspondence from BJMcG – in very small writing and in great detail , including reports on football matches, exams, smoking up the chimney, superior English students, and his feelings on all kinds of topics. These are funny, irreverent, sad and often very scattered and he writes of how often he has a 'writer's block' or even tears up half composed letters. Most of the letters are not 'year dated' until after his ordination but certainly last from 1903 to 1914. A selection of sentences from his letters may give a flavour of the man and his education at Oscott College in Birmingham.

· 'The cost of postage is frightful'. Letter 1 penny, Postcards ½ penny.
· 'I haven't yet come to the age when I'll look back on St.Finians as a paradise. That young brother of yours is a disgrace or else you didn't train him as you trained Paddy.'
· ' I was cutting up a frog and at a delicate part of the operation when Professor O'Hanlon' (a convert – 65 y.o), came around and began to hug me . He is as mad as a March Hare.'
· 'You Irish Schoolboys feel exhultation at the approach of Vacation, coming from those great Prisons they call Colleges, but We English won't stand that kind of treatment.'

- 'We have a fellow from Dingle who reads Irish as fast as he likes, but isn't much at understanding it except for a middling stock of phrases, he doesn't know much!'
- 'I got a great letter from the Daw lately. His ironical references to St.Finians are the best bits ever I saw, I am thinking of getting it framed....'
- 'I am writing this during Church History Lecture and I haven't opened a book since I came back.'
- Since then, I have like Mark Twain, regularly 'got up, washed and went to bed' every day. Such a performance is quite unnecessary when a fellow jumps out of the bed at 6.29am and has to be in the Chapel at 6.30.
- 'I have become a regular smoker here as we generally smoke cigars after Dinner every day, and it is a 'contra regulos'. I didn't eat much for Dinner....but I drank like a fish, and felt mad getting up at 6 yesterday morning.
- 'Tim O'Farrell was late for his entrance exam, and had to get a special exam. Jimmy came to his room to give him his mathematics, and went to hug him. Tim not knowing him thought he was a student and gave him a gentle reminder by getting a chair and whacking him out of the room. This is the kind of Professors we have and most of them are Irish.'
- 'Last Saturday, immediately after Dinner, 3 of us rushed off to see the villa play Fulham in the 3rd round of the English Cup at Aston. They won 5-0, with an attendance of 53,000 gate of £1646.'
- 'This is a crocky bit of a letter for a 'Scholastic Philosopher' as I ought to be. We have Retreat starting for a whole week, and I've got the blues, badly at such a thought. Pity me !'
- 'We are entirely free here (the Pension is £60 for the few who pay) £1- £2 per term is allowed for the Dentist. Altogether, I think this is a very good place.'
- Oscott, Nov 24th 1906 – St.Cecily's Day is a real red letter day in music mad Oscott, and I have never had such a time as the last 48 hours. I have been elected Master of Games or Captain this year, am President of a Debating Society and a Literary Society so have little time for letter writing. PS. I saw in an Irish paper that struggled this far, that you got a prize for an Essay on Edmund Burke.

St.Gregory's, Longton, 17-5-11, now ordained and in a curacy , Bernard writes again to excuse his delay in sending a long letter due to all his duties in the parish. Having made a resolution to do the deed on a Sunday, his day was stolen by unexpected duties, so at 8pm, he suffered 'collapse of resolution, followed by bad language, weakening of the will, darkening of the intellect, etc'

1-6-11

'Delighted to hear that you are coming to visit and inhale our smoke from the Potteries. Let me know when you will arrive at Crewe. Now I have to hear confessions. These are first Fridays even in pagan England'.

Longton   31st March 1913

'I acknowledge your last three letters. I have been laid up and am going to Belgium to squat, for a rest. I have had a rotten time, coughing day and night and absolutely off my oats. My return to this place is problematical, but my chest does not get on well with the smoke. I hope to see the Grand National on Friday, and a decent winner would provide funds for a complete cure....

Caversham, Reading.   31 March 1914

At last, I have got my release from Longton which did not agree with me. My Rector here is quite a young man, and altogether I am in clover. The Chaplaincy is along with a small Mission (about 350), so you see, I am resting. This is an ideal place to do London from, so it would be great to have you as a visitor, since we are on the Main Line. The last time you came to Longton you went to Hereford from London if you remember.

In the last line is concrete proof that Dick visited his Aunt in the Convent at Bartestree, in 1913, and just before the War of 1914-1918. Amongst the latest cache of correspondence is one from Mother Mary of St.Anthony of Padua.

My Dear Richard,   *Dec 16th 1918*

It seems some time since I received your interesting letter, but even the eyes of a drone bee could never see the photo which never came. I do not care for these Country gobs at all events I should expect a respectable photo. How are you ? Escaped the 'flu', I hope. Our holy and revered Chaplain is just recovering from a bad attack. We had 150 girls and a dozen of the sisters in bed at the same time. They must have been very bad as several were anointed and we had six deaths during the time. We escaped T.G., but all the Sisters of the Novitiate got it at the same time, it is well we were left to take care of them. They are all well now.

I hope you have made use of the Biretta. I cannot imagine you going on the Altar without it. As for the Pyx bags, I am astonished as they are in great request here. Are you very glad the War is over, I think it dreadful to hear of the Ladies getting seats in Parliament. It is bad enough their having votes. How do you spend Christmas? Very busy I imagine. Just give us a special remembrance in your good prayers. Paddy has taken your bad example with regard to letter writing , it is impossible to get a line from him. God bless him, he is always busy doing good like yourself. I never got the address for new Residence. Like a dear, write me a nice letter, as I am rather in a state of depression, with all this illness.

With Best Wishes to Beamore and Salmon, Yours devotedly in Our Lord,

M. Anthony of Padua Moore

Fr. Dick with his biretta .

CHAPTER 6: 1903 - 1915

ANNIE'S LETTERS TO DICK

Sixty letters survive from this period, and sometimes contain additional inserts, like reports from Anthony, or John or Joe, on their activities and more intellectual pieces from Mary or Paddy. Since these letter tumble from the Mother's envelope, I include them in that order, and print the main portions of the letters.

13th April 1903

You may pay the £1 fee to the R.U.I for registration by P.O. without delay. James went to Glasgow this week and Paddy got 1st place in English at the exams, one of three equal firsts in French and second in Maths. Don't make any allusion to these in your next letter, lest the cry be 'my mother tells everything!'. The Leader of the Tenants Committee waited at the August Body of the Corporation and demanded to be heard. Each body then resolved to arm themselves with a Solicitor and in the presence of Messrs McCann and Tallon, a letter was dispatched to the L.G.B to secure their approval for sale of lands. No reply has appeared. Mary tells me that she has three clumps of daffodils, four jonquils, and tulips coming into bloom. Paddie was told today he will hardly require a protractor, which is a thing for measuring angles with.

23rd April 1903

I had a letter from P. During the week in which he said that had been at the Curragh Races and gloriously remarked they were not near as good as Bellewstown. Also that they walked six miles to the Hill of Allen. Now I want you to pray very earnestly for the next nine days for my intention. There has been a larger rift than usual between James and the Pater and we want all the light and Grace to do what is the will of God. Don't for a moment think that James had done anything very wrong, as it all arose over a trifling incident. Don't make any allusion to this in your letter but pray earnestly. Mary and your father will arrive on the 14th. After considerable prodding, got Paddie to write enclosed directions to Myles Keogh, 4 Lower Mount Street, Dentist and enclose 15/- , you should get both extracted for 5/-. Mention who you are !

11th Oct 1903

I enclose Gill's invoice. Father saw John on Friday for a few minutes. He is still very lonely. There are 78 boys there now. He sleeps in Finegans. He thinks they teach drawing and science better in the Christians. We are minus any male help in the House as Albert has departed. It is still very wet and rain. Sheehy was returned for Meath by a large majority but J.H. Parnell secured over one thousand votes.

19th Nov 1903

I felt considerably relieved in getting your letter this morning. I enclose letter received from Paddie and the pound required. Mary was sitting opposite your friend Rev Joe Kelly at the dinner after the ceremony in the convent, I hope you will get on well at the Matric. When I read Dr. O.Dea's recommendation I just expected Maynooth would enter ' en masse'. James saw John yesterday. He is not much enamoured of the sem. Yet and is as small as ever.

PS. I threw all the Leaders in, except one that goes to Clonlusk. So you will have what survives Hal's tidying up. Save up your 'Rosarys'' to bring home at Christmas.

PPS. Father went to attend sale of farm named ' Salmon' two miles from Balbriggan today which belonged to Kelly of Weston. To my surprise I received telegram announcing that he bought it. Price will be up to 1900 pounds. There is no residence.

Dear Richard,   *November 21st 1903*

Please find enclosed cheque for value £6-0-0 together with £1 note. You shall endorse cheque before handing it to college authorities. I am pleased to see that you have taken up the matriculation course as I know you will do your best (which should be very fair) as I believe legible writing is not a subject. Yours as ever, Father.

DearDick,   *January 25th 1904*

I enclose letters for you from John and Paddie. Master R.Moore from Athboy arrived here this morning. Father Clavin arrived on Monday last selling tickets to a concert and variety entertainment in the 'Parochial Hall' ie. The Boys School at the top of the Old Hill. It is to come off tonight. We were all flabbergasted at the letter from the Archbishop. Mary's correspondent in Dublin told her that the coughing in the Church during the reading, prevented them knowing of it till 'the paper next day'. Mr M.J McCarthy's speech (enclosed) is the most fitting proof of the necessity for an organisation if Catholics are to live in the Country for the future. Fr.O'Farrell interviewed John when done at the conference.

They are having a lively time in St.Peter's at present. You may remember to have heard Paddie and John speak of young Pearson's in Palace St. Well, the Paternal was carrying on a 'soup' house under the auspices of the 'Irish Church Missions'. Frs. Clarke and Finnegan went and demanded admission (which was refused) to see some of their flock, who were attending the 'classes'. The delinquents, were hurried away out the back door. Things were denounced from the altar on Sunday night and on Monday night, crowds assembled and playfully broke the windows accompanied by the music of melodeons. Police were protecting the premises, when Joe was passing to school and ballads have been circulated with the refrain; 'To down your souls, for penny rolls, some soup, and hairy bacon', which is chanted on all occasions, by the small boys. Joe says it is also the correct thing to mutter 'soup' in a stage whisper when passing a Protestant. Greenhills was sold on Saturday to Mr Leland for Hill, it is supposed. We had the Mill last week, 'Osbornes'. The car arrived home from Macallisters and looks very nice. The Chariot was sent to be raised and painted.

 The kid has not yet penetrated to the front as Ang herds him continuously. Mary is contemplating a frame only she had no sawyer at hand. Your friend Master Hoey has been dispatched to school and the other young gentleman went into a ditch at the hunt and had to be pulled out with ropes last week. I am not sure if you remember a man named Pat Gregory who lived on Platten Road, and worked on the railway. He went into your Aunt's to do some shopping after coming from his work on Saturday night and died off before half past seven…. Enclosure from John –

Dear Dick   *28.1.1904*

The Bishop is in Navan since Wednesday week and was in here on Sunday, but it was not for all the good it has done us. Ford nor Harte would not go up for a free day. We were out in the town chapel listening to him preaching on Sunday. Joe Fagan nor Roger Moore did not come back. Roger is gone to Newbridge. Buddy McDonnell was asking for you. They had a great concert in St.Mary's. There is to be a great play here called 'The Grand Duke'. I hope you will excuse me for writing on such paper but I forgot to bring up some. Hoping you won't get vexed at the 'rubbish'.

I remain, John.

12ᵗʰ February 1904

Mary was in Navan yesterday at profession of two nuns. She saw Dr.Gaffney, Fr.Murray and Dr.Dooley there. Poor John is suffering from chilblains, but seems otherwise resigned to his fate. Paddie says they now have permission to read the papers in the Library for half an hour on week days. As the Japs and the Russians are at war now, I am sure they are delighted. All the Christian (Bros) boys are in favour of the Japs and Joe takes it as a personal insult if anyone says Russians will win. The first two lambs arrived in Salmon. James has got a new black, frieze, overcoat, something the shape of yours.

Mrs Cepta May was married during the week to Mr.Farrell, Solicitor. Some say the bridesmaids were in pink and bride in blue, but I suppose you don't mind if it were vice-versa. Ang is very busy at his lessons and the first chapter of his Catechism. What will become of the young lambs of the weather won't get dry ?

20ᵗʰ Feb 1904

I am on invalid's list , so cannot use my tongue due to hoarseness….more time for replying! The death of Mr. J McCann M.P caused a great shock and much regret. Fr.Farrell and a deputation called on Mrs McCann requesting her to have him a public funeral in Navan. She declined and a special train started from Navan at 7.00 for the funeral – he was buried in the O'Connell Circle.

The Yankee woman who lived in Whearty's was found sitting dead at the fire by Tighe's breadman on Wednesday. When the funeral was about to start next day, the police stopped it to have an inquest held. Mr.Corry arrived yesterday and James was seized as a Juryman as your father was in Salmon. Andrew hid in the hayshed, Dominic ran over the fields. Of course, the verdict was 'Death from Natural Causes'.

Ang was very disturbed by the appearance of policeman taking James, and wanted a full explanation. In Paddie's last letter he said he expected to do honours in three subjects and is jubilant over his expected half hour to read the Chronicle. The Prior considered that the Leaders of the 'Freeman' and 'Independent' were unfit ! They are adding hot water pipes to the other comforts of the students. Do you expect all your correspondents to have a microscope to decipher your epistles ? as ordinary glasses would not be expected to meet the requirement. We are having alternatives of frost and rain and just had a respectable fall of snow.

Write soon – with best love – Mother

9ᵗʰ March 1904

I enclose the Birth Cert as requested. Mary J expects you will be glad to know she has been successful in her efforts to get the lace fan and collars exhibited in the St.Louis Exhibition. She sold them at her own price to Mr.Reardon who was making arrangements with the Technical people. She is very jubilant because he engaged to have them exhibited under her name and marked 'sold'. James was speaking to the Crillys who have returned unexpectedly. A cow has had 2 nice calves that are alive, and the 'grippers' visited Mrs Conner yesterday as the final scene of the Turkey Case. Apart from such events, there is nothing very exciting to tell.

Love from all, as ever,

Your loving Mother.

My dear Richard,   *18ᵗʰ March 1904*

I am very sorry to inform you that Mrs.Taaffe of Newtown died quite unexpectedly this morning. All the males had gone out on their usual avocations, when one of the girls found her lying in on the bed quite dead. R.I.P. Father went on Tuesday to a series of Fairs in Connaught and we did not expect him till Monday next, but if this never reaches him (I am sending telegram to Balla) I daresay he will be home tomorrow night.

I suppose you had great festivities last night. Of course, we had to drown the shamrock in lemonade with due ceremony. I enclose a little bunch of leaves. In Paddy's last letter, hope was dawning that he might come home Easter week..... we are still having rain here. Joe cannot often bring his cycle. When your father returns, he will send the cheque. I suppose you received Mary's letter.

The Hon Mac Carthy has retired from the fray (I suppose they had to pay him well). We are all down on Horace Plunkett now on account of his book (a la McCarthy), Your friend McKeon is at home in the sulks as the Board wanted to get rid of him, and Cavan Co.Co would not elect their candidate, and wanted to pare away his pay then, so he won't go out! Frank Moran has a motor bicycle.

As ever, Mother.

                                                                                            3-5-04

......Thank God that prayer prevailed in the matter I spoke of last time. Poor James Reilly died in Stillorgan on Saturday. Mr.McCourt of the Bull Ring died and was buried in 'Calvary' today – Fr.Curry's new cemetery. There was a fire in St.Finians last week which was extinguished by the aid of the police before the students awakened from their slumbers.

Your Aunt Cissie arose one morning last week, went to six o'clock mass, breakfasted in McDermott's, dressed and drove in a carriage to Mornington Chapel accompanied by the third Miss McDermott and was married to Mr.Macken there. They then drove to Laytown Station on a hack and went to Bray. On Wednesday, they returned to Laytown to a cottage there. Joe and Mrs Crilly are staying with Teresa still. I had a letter from Paddie this week...20 hurlers going to Fermoy. He wrote for bathing drawers, so I suppose the Liffey will suffer.

                                                                                            31-5-04

I hope you will accept enclosed tie although late for your Birthday. I hear that Bessie Flynn and daughter sailed for The States last night..... The pet lambs were dispatched to Ballestrand yesterday but committed awful depradations in the garden before they left. They even extended operations on some drills of peas James had coming up beautifully. Let me know if you require any money sent for coming home... Father called to Newbridge and found Paddie looking well, face thin, colour returned, but big and athletic looking. He was bathing in the Liffey yesterday and took a cramp – it evidently does not agree with him. The Prior says ' he is one of the few very good boys we have'.

                                                                                            11-6-04

I received your blue epistle....John favoured us with a copy of the group of himself in the fairground, we thought it extremely good. I hope you are satisfied with the exam results...... John is very anxious to know will he be home for the Regatta, on 22-23 June. Father is away in Longford and I think Balla Fair is today. I expect him home tonight...Dr.Mannix must have some consideration for the mere laity when he made such sensible arrangements for their convenience. I hope you have saved up for the 'Rosary', because I am already thinking of a cup of tea and a rest on the sands.

Joe is trying to get all the dirt off the bike before the two owners return and has already had several bathes. He renewed his acquaintance with the fisherman, who was asking for you.

25-6-04

Many thanks for your programme of Union received this morning. It was a rare treat to be present. We had a good account of it each day in the Freeman.

You were fortunate in getting such good prizes. I think Father will be much disappointed if he cannot see Dr.Healy's book. Look through your sheets, shirts etc., to see if any renewals are required before returning. John reached home as fresh as paint and is quite satisfied except for the Latin. They attended the Regatta both days and Father actually brought Ang yesterday.

PS. James saw J.Tallon at the Regatta. Don't leave the prize list behind, please.

27-9-04

I am sure it caused universal gloom to have expended 9 shillings on the books to have a look at them., but I suppose it is one of the usual disappointments. Mary desires me to tell you that she will be well satisfied to receive the series singly with your valued autograph and a few words of wisdom on each but don't let that prevent you sending letters.

I think John done very well. They will put him on for an exhibition next year. I had an appeal from Joe to throw out the Greek but I told him not. It will not be worse for him than other beginners. Mr.Connell, the Bank Manager who was in Navan called on Teresa with the motor and gave her a drive to Clogher in the machine. He called again on his way back to Donegal....

I am sure your roomy attic is a change from your small compartment at home, will you have a companion? Ang is not reconciled to school yet but goes off every day...Mary, James and I spent Sunday evening at Duleek Gate. Johnny and Mrs and Corrys were also there .

The Pub in Duleek Gate (formerly Moore's)

Father sends cheque for three pounds. Please invest some of the balance in stamps, as we have an objection to paying double postage, same as last time. Father met Fr. Flynn in Dublin (He is disappointed in Joe but enthusiastic about John). Everything is very busy here but weather continues fine.... Mary is much obliged for the card and intends to write a long letter when she has time. I think you are right not to try for the Gilmartin as you will have quite enough to study.

The morning you were leaving I sent over to Brogans for steak and we received a communication a few mornings after from McCourts that the pony backed against the brass guard, breaking it and they were having it repaired, followed by a bill from Cooney for thirty shillings.

N.Conner went with two ploughs to Salmon today and 'Kiddie' was sent. He intends to plough a field there immediately. Your father has had a cold for the past three weeks; I think you should write to him next week. We had a miller here between the two hands. McCabe was struck on the arm with a shovel by the other gladiator and he broke his arm, so had to go to hospital. Dominic has been re-instated, and is to mind the sheep and lambs. Gorman is the new mayor, there were three other candidates. Mrs Hughes of the 'Argus' is dead and also the P.P. of Tullyallen. Paddie tells me they got a good many new boys, he mentioned Brogan from Trim and Moore from Athboy and a youth born, in and through, the siege of Kimberley.

My dear Richard,   *20-11-05*

There was a large attendance at the meeting on Sunday. The Agricultural Tennants of the Corporation aroused the ire of that body by resolving to present an address of complaint....at the Banquet, Fr.Curry made the speech of the evening and surprised the town generally. The abundance of champagne floored many imbibers. Your father left early (9 o'c) but before that saw a Corporator slide gently from his chair to the floor when one of the stewards called two attendants to carry him into seclusion. But he was only one of many. Paddie was waiting outside with the pony and trap tickled at the exits, which afforded unqualified fun for the masses. The proceedings continued until half-past four on Monday morning.

It is said the Hoey-Sheridan wedding is to come off next week with great e'clat ? . On the same day Miss Carroll of Dunleer is to be married to Mr.Sheridan of the Tredagh Hotel. Mary went down on Friday to see John & Joe. I was uneasy about the the latter, as your father thought he looked thin and pale. He said he was not sleeping well but was getting enough to eat. Mary reported he now looks as well as ever, and says he is alright. Ang commenced learning Elocution on Friday but that night I discovered a spot of ringworm on his head, so will have to get his hair cut and remain at home, till it is well.

As ever, Mother.

29-1-05

I was beginning to wonder why you were not writing ..... Mrs Cassidy (Fr.Cassidy's Mother) is dead and to be buried in Glasnevin tomorrow R.I.P. Tall hats are always worn at funerals as well as weddings....John and Joe got to the Pantomime on last Saturday, as well as Paddie. I paid a visit to Mt.Granville on Sunday. M.J was downstairs but did not go out as far as the road. I think they are very lonely and unsettled. Paddie had a very sore finger, a beeling or Whitlow, I fear he will lose the nail .

The Ballinrobe Nuns sent a box of nice things for Hal for his birthday. Wasn't it kind to remember it ? Paddie remained on this evening for a lecture on 'Recent Excavations in Crete' by Rev.H.Browne S.J.

John sent home his Intermediate Certificate. Joe wants to give up Greek but won't be let. Maguire is leaving Salmon in May. The other men are remaining. The big grey is wholly invalided with his leg. A cow died supposed to have a piece of turnip in her windpipe. Ang has not enough hair on his head to go to school but it is growing. Your father met R.Sheridan in the Land Commission Office – he got there through Landlord influence from the stamp office. He does not seem satisfied as he told your father 'There is nothing else like a farm' and said he would prefer Trinity to the Royal since there is no social life in the latter. My breath was almost taken away! All this is strictly entre nous, of course!

29-1-05

Father said 'Is he alive at all?'. Mary's crocuses are not in bloom yet – she had so many in blocks and encloses some. As the Queen remarked ' That is nothing to what I could do if I liked.' Mr.Gogarty's death caused universal shock and Mr.McCullough was again defeated at the election by Gerald Daly. J.Monahan and Waters were conducting agents for Mr.Daly, on Yankee lines, with the incorruptible voters imbibing all the liquid refreshment offered by the candidates. Old Simcox collected voters and drove them in a wagonette to the polls.

There is a lull in sale of Corporation Land – I hear that the vulnerable official is ill again. Douglas Hyde lectured under Mons. Segrave's wing in Drogheda last week. Mary was anxious to go but Fr.Clavin arrived with tickets for Parochial Hall Concert. Duffy's gramophone and Mr.Kearney were the principal features. There does not seem much prospect of the Railways Scheme being carried out.

Dear Richard,

I may as well plunge into gossip at once by telling you that Mrs. Conner's case was dismissed , with each side to pay costs. Then your Father received sub-poena as witness in lawsuit, over Tom Carpenter's will. There were 15 other witnesses, brought up to the Four Courts on Tuesday last including Jemmie Smith. When all legal expenses been incurred and two or three witnesses examined the case was settled . So your Father was not called. He had to go again in a land case the next day, including P.Lenehan.

Fr.Curry's concert was very crowded – he says he cleared between thirty and forty pounds. The noise of the 6d people was something awful. I felt as if there was an avalanche behind my back which might come down any moment. It was impossible to hear any of the instrumental pieces, as they did not seem to approve of <u>that.</u>

Then, an unfortunate medical gave them 'God Save Ireland' in response to an encore (they seemed to encore everything) and they immediately commenced to help until he seemed actually afraid of them. He was a Mr.Murphy from Brittains and probably was unaccustomed to their playful ways. Fr.Clavin said he heard or saw nothing as he was relegated to the back, to subdue the tumult, I suppose. James and I resolved that as we had performed our duty, Mary and your Father will do theirs next time. Joe was in ecstatics as there was a running fire of audible criticism kept up.

27-2-05

Poor Tommy Taaffe died during the week under very sad circumstances. He had got into financial difficulties, held a meeting of his creditors which resulted in the shop being closed last week. He was buried in Kilsharvan on Saturday.

19-3-05

About your postcard of the 'O'Growney Tomb design, I'd prefer one I saw in the 'Evening Telegraph' some time ago. There was unexpected destruction here last night on the lambs by a dog worrying them. He destroyed six and I have a poor fellow here at the fire, whose neck was bitten. I needn't tell you that elaborate preparations have been made for his reception tonight. Father went off with the enviable frame of mind to some Western Fairs this morning. Paddie was sent to Mrs Lynn's funeral from Tullyallen to Ballymakenny at 2.00. She was a sister of J.MacQuillan late of the North Road. Joe has settled down to conquer the Greek.....

3-4-05

....Mary's flowers are going on lovely. Last week, we invested in wire netting from the lane gate to your gate and it affords calm satisfaction, to view the enemy from the window, marching along the centre length looking for a weak spot.... The lambs came off safely since, a cat and dog fell victims.... Hal put his 'imprimatur' on Paddy's enclosure...

17-4-05

Paddy got first place in Latin and second in Physics in the exams – you can ask him all the questions next week. Fr Cassidy of Ardcath is coming to preach on Friday evening and Fr.Barr O.P. in the Dominicans, he is from Tallaght and said to be a great Preacher. John & Joe will be home on Saturday, I expect. P.Flanagans son in law at Bettystown met with a very sudden death. He was found dead outside the door in his shirt one morning. It is supposed he walked out the window in his sleep and was killed. On the same day, Bernard Ryan fell off a load of coals beyond at Kate Kelly's and was killed also.

3-4-05

To show you that I can rise above the inevitable tie for your Birthday, I enclose a penwiper!.... I would not accomplish the knitted tie in time..... I did not attend the Retreat as often as I would have liked. Didn't I envy Mary sailing off on her bike and we could not go together. I enclose John and Joe's impressions of the Excursion which are diametrically opposite....

.... I suppose you heard that Miss Kelly of Bull Ring is to be married to Fullam (Bicycle man)... Paddie came home, today, much elated, with a Brookes saddle (never ridden on) which he bought at a cycle house in the green for one shilling, because there was a fire. So the seat of torture is dispensed with and he enamelled 'singer' and got a new tyre and cover, it is expected to take the lead this summer.

Out of this envelope came the two letters of John & Joe, to home, reporting on the famous Excursion. The Letters are dated 13th May 1905. Joe's Letter (aged 12) reads;

'We had an Excursion on Wednesday to Mullingar which was very nice, as we had not much rain. Went as far as Clonsilla on the 9.00am train - got a special train to Mullingar about 11.15, went out to the New Seminary with the Bishop and looked around it - a splendid building, very large, met the two Gogarty's there.

Walked out to Lough Owel and had our dinner there. Walked back and left about 5. We saw Maynooth and the Bog of Allen. Paul Kelly brought his camera and he took a lot of photos. Please send some money. It is not my turn to write. Was there any accidents at the Big Fair of Drogheda ?

Write soon, Your loving son, Joe.

John's Letter (Aged 14) ;

'I was disappointed at not getting a letter from you during the week as I have no money. Send also some laces. We had the excursion to Mullingar on Wednesday, it was a very ugly excursion, hardly anyone enjoyed it. I suppose the fair was very large yesterday. I can't think of anything to say as I only wrote this note asking you for the money for which I am in great need.

Joe in 1902   John, aged 10 (at his First Communion)   Anthony in 1908

24-9-05

I hear that butter is now given in the evening but you did not say who were to be ordained. Joe is back in the Seminary in Junior Grade (not studying Irish) and has thrown Greek overboard. He says there are 30 new boys, including Bellew, and a brother of Paul Walsh; Andrew and Dominic are absent here, so Paddie is commandeered and John is just going on as usual. Aug is in school presided over by M.M Raphael. I think Arnotts offer splendid value.

Do you require toilet covers? I don't think the blankets can equal the home-mades. How did the curtains work? Hal seems to know this time that he is not to expect you home as he never enquires from Paddie about you, but often talks about you. James was down in Diamor last week.

Mary went up to Saddlestown to see M.Reilly (who got a spill from her bike) and found her after returning home from Jack Moran's wedding....

30-9-05

Paddie paid five shillings each for the two enclosed books; if you enclose order for Clery's for five shillings they will order Vol II for you and send it direct to Maynooth. The other book is out of print. Paddie received the microscope this morning.

Paddie has been every day to Cecilia St., since the Registrar has been giving lectures there every day. Merriman was first for the vacant fellowships and Skeffington second. Fr.O'Driscoll was among the rest of the eight candidates. We had the Mill this week and threshed all. It left yesterday, and we held our Station this morning. Father started here for Longford on Saturday night, reached here on last train last night and went to Land Court today to give evidence for value on four different parties. John is in such trouble about the Acrostic that he won't let me defer it any longer. I enclose the beastly thing which has got on my nerves since Friday. The united brains of the Family have failed to solve one line, even so if you can manage it, send it on direct. He has succeeded in all the rest, except two words. Fr.O'Driscoll was beaten by the modern female in the person of Miss Boland who was also an unsuccessful candidate for the Fellowship.

12-11-05

... We had a station on Friday last. Fr.Glynn called for the first time. They had a marriage in St.Mary's last week which was rather unusual ... P.Walsh was telling us about it first that the bride had gone to a place during the summer (ticket cost her a pound). 'Where you'd walk on sharp cinders for your sins in your barefeet.' She there met a wealthy widower with one daughter with the result that they were married after two meetings. Her parents are in a situation with Cairnes of the Glen, so the story goes. I nearly forgot to tell you that Miss Durnin got married to the man who had her grass, last year. His name is Egan and he appears to be on the shady side of forty if not more.

The Shed is nearly finished in Salmon and I am not sorry. The Mill is working here and weather very fine. They entered into possession of Reay's on the 1st and have opened a gate to cart manure below Faulkners. Best love from all.

22-11-05

I enclose 'St.Stephen's.' Mary wishes you to know that Teresa has been seized with the postcard collecting disease, so please send any old Maynooth pictures before Christmas, at intervals, to her. Fr.Clavin has been appointed P.P of Kilbeg and shook the dust, or mud of St.Mary's off his feet on Saturday last. James was to Kells on the same train.

For some reason, only a small number of letters from 1906 survive....

22-2-06

I have quite given up the idea of getting John to study here . He is not getting stronger apparently and could not stand any more study **at present**. *Meantime he seems quite happy and content.*

We are minus Dominic and Flaker now and Paddy Walsh is installed instead. Of course they are extra busy with the lambs. Anthony has been ill since Wednesday last, is in bed, and measles also appeared. The Doctor was dosing him to put out the measles but he is all right now. I hope you are keeping free from colds – above all. Wear your newest shirts and drawers now till the warm weather sets in. Nothing will give you cold at this time more than thin underclothing. Mrs Reilly of Saddlestown died last Thursday from some heart affliction. Many went to a Profession in Navan and reception for 150 people, performed by Mons. Gaughran. She visited Joe as well –some boys very ill with measles. Write to the Pater, next time you are describing the play....

1-10-06

I have been so busy preparing Paddie's clothes and had no time to write. He is staying at 38 Cabra Park, and hopes to see you next Sunday. Could you have the old striped jersey parcelled up for him. Mrs John Hand died yesterday – she had been recovering in Lucan. There has been an arrival at the corner – they called the Young Lady Elizabeth Patricia and Mr & Mrs Macken were sponsors. Fr.Doran was telling me about the brilliant Tuam boy who eneterd Maynooth, Hubert Treston. Fr. Healy O.S.A is his uncle.

15-10-06

Paddie never got to see you; his trains did not suit, and I was disappointed to have no news. He seems quite happy with his companions and the work. Yesterday he had to get his fees, and Landlady's charges for the ensuing month. They were stiff enough. Poor Mrs Lenehan died last week, there are nine children, the eldest about Paddie's age. Christy Burke was buried in Tullyallen yesterday. When Joe returned, he was put into Junior Pass class, Your father was not satisfied and called to remonstrate with the two Fr.Flynns. Rev. J declared Joe unfit for honours at all, at all! Rev. D. Not so immovable. Would have to wait on his marks. Now Joe tells me he is put in honours class. Exhort him to study when you write. We are threshing in Salmon today and after the potatoes are in, expect the mill here.

15-3-07

John

I hope you will get rid of the troublesome teeth as soon as possible. Father encloses the cheque for £6-0-0.... John seems to be taking kindly to the 'camping out' in Salmon, in spite of the severe weather. He was down for the Fair as well as the usual Saturday to Monday visit. As the cough your Father was complaining of was very troublesome, he paid a visit to Dr.Dempsey and is much better since he finished one of the 'bottles of physic'. We expect Paddie down for St.Patrick's Day. I hear he has indulged in a brown frieze double breasted overcoat, with huge collar. Poor Mattie Geraghty was buried on Friday last. R.I.P.

16-5-07

As I have not been on a shopping expedition since I got the sore feet I had no chance of getting anything new for your birthday. In spite of pressure of business, you might have spared a quarter of an hour to write a line in the last six years. Mary has been hinting at a possible famine in pens and paper in Maynooth.

29-5-07

We are glad to receive the piece of foolscap this morning; it was a slight improvement on the ruled leaf of an exercise which Paddie sends.... I suppose you will be so busy with exams now, that I may not hope for a line at all. You know I get fidgety lest anything be the matter when two or three weeks pass over without having a letter from you. Joe inquired 'were you dead or alive' and Anthony frequently regrets the nice postcard he bought with his own money and wasted on you !   *29-5-07*

I enclose laces – found yet again – and supposed hidden by Hal.... The perfidious McCullough sent the suit, with two pairs of pants home for Paddie, but nothing for you. Hal made up his mind evidently that you were not to come back as he did not inspect your bed that night or next morning. Before going to bed he heard the dogs barking, came to me and whispered 'Dick', then opened the back door. Mary had to be making all kinds of excuses for you, even Anthony had to be explaining.

Teresa had a visit from Mr O'Reilly from London, who was doing Clonmacnoise. They brought 80 horney. In Drogheda, on Saturday which is supposed to be enough. Edward measured the porch but proceeds no further yet.

An unenclosed single page from Annie to Richard, describes an 'invitation to Julianstown to meet Mr & Mrs Jack Moran, on their arrival home. The Julianstown Band went to meet them and played around the house at intervals all night. The bride is very pretty, golden haired, blue eyes, perfect complexions and has reached the mature age of sixteen on her last birthday. As the mamma seems to be the predominant partner, the pa is a quiet man, not much to speak of. The Bride has four elder sisters, and the Dublin contingent were very musical . The house guests included Minnie Reilly and Miss Eva Heeney R.I.A.M. We had a delightful musical event and we were the first to leave'.

14-9-07

We have searched every imaginable place for the book... I have the boots and will send them ....Mary thinks the book is still in your trunk........John & James are sojourning in Balbriggan as intervals.... Mary is glad you found the conclusion of W.Ewart which proved conclusively that 'Mary is always right'. Your father said. She has indulged in Aubrey de Vere's poetry in the library this week.

1-11-07

I expected you would give your opinion on the clothes in your last letter. Mrs McCullough declares 'they were the best Tommie ever were turned out' and wanted a verdict from the family. Fr. J.O'Connor has come among us – Anthony's verdict 'Long and Slender'. After considerable difficulty we succeeded in catching a slater and carpenter and only want a plasterer to finish the porch. We derive considerable benefit from the comfort of the outer door, since it was put up. Gustavav Adolphus and his comrade were out to the fair on Tuesday but H.Mallon could not get the reserved price. We were then given quotations from Navan Bacon Factory and they were sentenced to be sent there on Monday.

James, Mary and your Father were at the High Mass on Sunday in Shop Street - at the collection in the Church afterwards, nearly one hundred pounds were raised. The skinning of Lord A. is a much more protracted operation or rather series of operations. My interview with the great may have ended when he suggested I consult my friends and call in the following week, which I did, accompanied by your Father. We agreed the 23 years purchase, he agreed to forgive the forthcoming half year's rent,

then wanted 3 ¾ cent till sale be completed . We wanted it at 3½ . Finally, he told me to take form he had drawn up and return it by post. Father returned it by hand on Wednesday and talked him into 3½ , for submission to Lord A. There it stands.

Between ourselves, I think Paddie was downhearted at the result of the R.U.I exams. He was third. Don't make any allusion to it in your letters.

Shop Street, Drogheda (1908)

5-2-08

Get rid of that cough even if you have to visit the hard hearted Doctor every day...I was in Dublin, visiting Guinness and Mahon re. Salmon. Eventually, I signed the purchase document on the terms offered in November. I am to have game rights. Did you hear from Longmans or the Archbishop since and when will the book be out ? Mind yourself, for goodness sake, even if you have to double the number of garments. James, Mary and Joe were off spending the evening in Miss Moores to meet Fr.Houlihan O.P.

18-10-08

Paddie was advised to go for a studentship as a resident , and he met Dr.Coffey in Dame Street, who visited him for tea, and was very helpful. Since he will have to wait on each member of the Staff, and attend at the Hospital, he decided to move back to Dublin next week. We had our Station yesterday and Fr.Kelly was asking of you.

I had a letter from Mrs J.Moore, sent back in a steamer, when passing Newfoundland. She said they had 6 young priests on board who played fifteens with Johnnie. He was sick, but she 'never missed a meal'. A postcard came from Washington saying that they had spent 2 days in New York, unearthed 3 of the Reilly's, were having a good time, and intended to stay a few days at Chicago before they reached the Rockies. M Woods is in Salmon, building the offices to the Labourer's Cottages (of concrete). There is quite a flutter here among all the old folks trying to find their correct ages for the pension....

1909 dawned and with it the ordination of Father Dick. His own letter to his mother, as published in 'My Dearest Annie' bears another airing.

Maynooth,
The Morrow of the Ordination

My dear Mother

Business first, Dawson says he sent on the bicycle on the 15th June; queer: let him see to it. Today, I said my first Mass here, all right for all in Beamore. I am not rightly recovered from the drunkenness of yesterday's joy; all I realize is that there are others in the same position as me. I am told that it is the joy of a lifetime, so let me enjoy it while it lasts.

They are having the D.D. Concursus today in the Aula. The younger members of the family will be pleased to know that the objectors (8 of them) representative of religious orders and theological faculties are xxxx & Revd. "Dinny Flynn". The results of the B.D. are out. I have held my place pretty consistently. Out of 16 candidates, 11 are through, 5 stuck;

> *Walsh (Meath) leads*
> *Keogh* (Kildare) No.2*
> *Connell* (Meath) No.3*
> *McCullen (do.) No.4*
> **both these headed me in dogma since we entered Theology*

So you see, that the only effect of not killing myself was that I got 4th instead of my usual 3rd place. Some two mistakes, one rather unfair, brought me down a bit in the important subjects, but the secondary ones stood to me, like Church History and Scripture.

R. MacC.

P.S. I'm sure the Bishop is delighted with 3 places out of the top 4.

Richard at his ordination

It is interesting that Richard uses the classical phrase " the drunkenness of yesterday's joy", because one of the items discovered tucked away in a book after his death in 1977, was a certificate of membership of the Pioneer Total Abstinence League, dated 3rd November 1905, and signed at Maynooth by. P. Coffey, Promoter. He had been a Pioneer for 72 years, but often dispensed a drop of whiskey to his guests.

A very short curacy followed ordination, as a supply priest in Dunboyne Parish and then in MountNugent Co.Cavan from 16th August 1909., 'to take Fr.Gerrards place until he is able to leave hospital.' The next appointment for Fr.Dick was as 'Professor' of Greek in St.Finian's College in Mullingar, in September 2009.

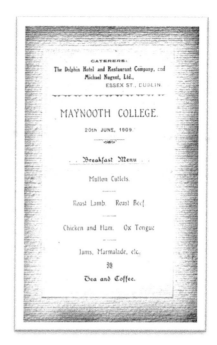

Maynooth Fare

Although not as frequently, Annie continues her correspondence.

18-10-08

On receipt of p.c. I proceeded to search your pockets and a solitary lead pencil was all I discovered. Now I deduce that you got to the train on time, raised some cash, and eventually found your way on the road from Oldcastle to MountNugent, safely. You would need a heavy overcoat on these chilly nights.

Paddie looked very comfortable in his frieze, which did not seem at all too heavy. He is going to 41, Leinster Street, thinks it too far from the Mater and devoid of company, so likely to change soon. Anthony thinks he will soon write an Irish letter to you!

There was an office in St.Mary's today for J.Woods, Stameen. Mr.Parr was here buying wool and very enthusiastic about lucerne. He had just returned from a polytechnic trip to Switzerland. As he is now 78 years, he believed he was the oldest in the party, who climbed one of the mountains there. He means to try Norway next time.

Best love, as ever,

Mother.

23.10.09

I enclose certificate in blue envelope. You may expect Mary's list in a couple of days. Paddy told James that there is a great struggle between McArdle and Blayney for the N.U.I. appointment. Paddie intends to compete for a scholarship there very soon. For Relieving Officer in Stamullen district, to replace Joe Mooney who died last week. There are 20 candidates, including Frank Moran and J.J Corry. The latter has a very good chance.

Let me know if you received a small parcel from the Ballinrobe nuns. The house in Salmon is growing up like a mushroom; the contractor had six masons at work yesterday. I hope that you are getting on well with the rising generation, and that your rooms are getting into shape.

Your father went to see the Institution in Belmont, Waterford and found it an ideal place in all respects except that they don't take anyone under 18 years of age. The Superior gave the address of a House of the Order in Louvain where children are recived. Fr.Doran mentioned a place near Clonmel. Your father made enquiries at the Parochial House there and it was nothing but an Industrial School. He is convinced that the only place in Ireland is the Stewart which is impossible....

Having researched the country, Pat and Annie moved swiftly and having obtained a place at the STROP in Louvain at a cost of £24 per year, they set off in May with Hal to his new home. Annie gives a detailed account of this expedition in her correspondence with Fr.Dick.

En route to Belgium

'They took him to sleep in a room next a brother, which has a window into it. When we went to bid him goodbye, he had been rummaging a dresser as usual, and lying in bed again. He did not mind only asked Father was he going on the Mill. We had a letter since, saying he was accustoming himself to the place, eating well and sleeping well; amused himself singing and walking slowly in the garden. They promised to take his photo and send it to me. I hoped to go back again to see him but your father decided it was better not, for him and us.

Well they directed and sent a messenger with us to a comfortable plain hotel, the 'demi Lune' in Ghent. The city is very old and interesting built on numerous islands connected with bridges. We were at mass on Sunday morning in the old church of St.Ba with a beautiful May altar and seated with prie duex chairs throughout. The shops were all open and we were in the fish and vegetable market. All the milk and country produce was coming in, in cars drawn by one, two or three dogs, and the city scavenging collected in similar manner. Your father was so much interested that I was afraid Mickey and Turley would have sets of harness brought home for them. The wooden sabots are in general use. Paddie provided me with a phrase book and necessity made me remember a lot of my old French so that we had no difficulty all the time in that direction. Your Father was Chancellor of the Exchequer and raised the indignation of countless porters by bestowing a couple of centimes with a lordly air, as if they were sixpences. We were in the Church of St.Etienne, where Choir Priests and Congregation were singing the 'Veni Creator' previous to High Mass at nine o'clock, as I thought I would never again hear it sung at the Sunday in Maynooth.

We then went to Brussels, which is a lovely new white city with long wide straight streets with six rows of big trees. The only old thing was the Cathedral of St.Gudula with tombs of Kings and Queens. We went to the Senate House Park, saw the Palace, stayed a night there and went to the Exhibition which is unfinished, but on an immense scale. Then your father enjoyed the peep he got at Belgian farming, the small plots, and thickly populated country we passed through on our way back to Ostend. They have some hills in Brussels, one big one called a Mountain, from which the water is supplied, otherwise the country is as flat as the Commons of Duleek.

He was rather disgusted to see the industrious Belgians observing the Whit Monday so faithfully as not to work in the fields. The country folk seem to speak in Flemish as they call it, in the cities, near all speak both French and Flemish. We crossed to Dover in an awful fog being 3 ½ hours late. On coming to London, we found they were to bring the King from the Palace to Westminster Hall .

Through the good advice of an Irish Policeman who thawed on hearing the brogue, we secured a splendid view of the procession, they went through Westminster Abbey and Cathedral, National Gallery, St.James Palace, Marlborough House, Coutt's Bank House, Parliament Houses, National Liberal Club, Trafalgar Square, Pall Mall, The Strand, Mooneys and lastly, the Freeman Office. We stayed the Night there, broke at Crewe for Hereford and went out to the Convent in a motor. Father Delhaise gave your father a bed and enlightened him on all Belgian laws, departed next day, and reached House (after taking a two hour survey of Shrewsbury) at seven o'clock on Friday morning.

I hope you will be able to make arrangements to see Hal in vacation, as somebody must see him before Winter, and there are special facilities this summer, on account of the Exhibition.

With reference to Teresa, she is going on very well. Mattie has taken an apartment belonging to the hotel at Bettystown for the sale of highclass groceries and provisions alone, and she is the presiding genius assisted by a little boy, and she is still staying in the same house. I had a couple of letters from her, in the very best of spirits.

On 8th June 1910 Annie continues her tale of Hal's exile ....writing to Fr.Dick.....

You have taken a load off my mind by intimating your intention of going to Belgium, as I could not face the long winter without some member of the family seeing Hal. Mary is very anxious to go and (goodness knows she deserves it after putting in such a long time minding the poor fellow) and your father would like her to go and will defray her expense if it will be possible for her to accompany you. He thinks the trip through the country would benefit any of the boys at any time and would be money well invested, but would prefer to let Mary go under your care. I would not like to ask him this year to pay for two of them, unless it was absolutely necessary.

About the route, when I first announced my intention of bringing Hal myself, it was intensely scouted out. We got terms everywhere and compared them and Paddie tried to join in with a pilgrimage to Bruges and Whit Excursions. I don't like long sea voyages and Hal would be quieter on a train journey. We would have a drawer-ful of literature and Mary will provide you with anything you require – promptly!

PS. In two weeks, we expect that the carpenters will be gone and plasterers installed in Salmon.

Returning from the nearly complete Salmon house, we know that Hal remained in Strop for over four years, with the Brothers of Charity. Annie writes to Richard on 27th November 1911 –

'Only I have so much occupation, I would feel very lonely, as Mary has been in Salmon since the Treasure left.'

'The Treasure' – Hal

Perhaps because of his status as Professor of Greek and various travels to Britain and Europe Fr.Dick must have decided to upgrade his wardrobe and falls back on Thomas McCullough, Tailor and Outfitter of 23, James Street, Drogheda and I have found a receipt for the sum of four pounds and five shillings, for the provision of a Frock Coat Suit and an extra pair of pants, to order, paid on January 16th 1911.

Another journey of his within the country was to visit his Father's first cousins, the Miss Sheridans, who were Mercy Nuns in Ballinrobe, Co.Mayo, a busy market town which was often visited by McCullens purchasing cattle or sheep. Sr. M.Elizabeth writes to Fr.Dick from the convent on 14th November 1913;

My Dear Cousin,

It is time to thank you for your kindness in coming to see Mag in the summer. She is now very well (T.G) only for a slight mark over her eye. The Sisters were disappointed you went so soon. They had the schools prepared for a visit, and when they heard you were gone, I won't say what some of them said. Next visit must be longer and sooner. You should send Anthony down before he leaves Mullingar; How is he getting on ? Rev.Mother thinks you should spend a week down west, with our good kind priests and nuns and lovely scenery. It would be a lovely holiday. Sr.Mag and three others drove out to see the pigeon hole this summer and went down to the very bottom.

I met Fr. Mark Hannon a few days ago and he got thin but is looking very well. I also met Fr.Cunningham he told me he met you , but was sorry you could not have more time together. He spent nearly all his holidays in Ballinrobe, as his sister was very ill. Fr. John McDermott P.P. Balla is in a dying state, he was a former curate here and we liked him very much. He was in Dublin for the operation, but it was very unsuccessful. He may only live a short time. Say a little prayer for him sometime and also for your humble servant.

I was glad St.Finians won something at the Drogheda Bazaar – fancy your Father's Prize to go there. Our school attendance is not so good, about 240 the most. We go a very nice Postulant on the 15th August, trained in Carysfort, she is from Ballyhaunis. Joined by Rev.Mother, Mother Peter, Mag and all in kindest regards –

Your fond cousin, Sr.M Elizabeth.

The Convent at Ballinrobe

In January 1919, she writes once more because Sr.Mag is approaching her Silver Jubilee and inviting Fr.Dick to ' run down to Ballinrobe, you can get petrol galore, now that the War is over'. In this letter we come across the only reference I have seen to her Father – Mr.Sheridan – who had been the widower of Mary McCullen, who was a cousin of Patrick (The Boss). Sr.Elizabeth describes him as 'a great old Warrior to be able to come so far', when he visited during that previous summer. Patrick Sheridan died in September 1919. Sr. Elizabeth herself died in December 1927 and Sr.Magdalen on 8th February 1933, and I have written in more detail of their lives in 'My Dearest Annie'.

In August 1914, War broke out between Britain and Germany. Annie wanted Hal back to Belmont as soon as possible and was not given to waiting for events to unfold themselves. A letter from the Brothers of Charity counsels 'patience and confidence in God for the best outcome...' This was written 20/10/2014 ; ' I am surprised not to have an answer to my letters, all is quiet in Ghent...we can only wait...'

Annie was not for waiting and eventually established a line of communication through the American Counsul in Ghent, and the British Foreign Secretary. After a lot of diplomatic preparation, Fr.Dick and James set out to get behind enemy lines and bring Hal home. The priestly garb probably helped the operation, and James was well used to the diplomacy of the Scottish and West of Ireland sales and fairs. This must have been a formidable duo. However, it took until August 1915 to get Hal home. Too Late. Just before War broke out Annie had been advised to take a total break for her health sake and had spent July and August in Kilkee, Co.Clare at a House called Rock Lodge, East End. A series of letters back and forth followed, which I have catalogued in 'My Dearest Annie'. The reproduction of one of these is an example of how Mary took over the domestic scene, and also acted as News Reporter to her Mother.

Beamore

My Dear Mother ,   *August 4th, 1914*

You must forgive me for not writing on Sunday, but James came down and I did not like to start writing as John and Anthony went off to the football. Martin Knight came over on Wed. last and took out three sections of honey. He says the bees are doing well in the new hive, that they have a queen but that he will leave them the rest of the honey for the winter. Miss Jameson of Delvin was married last week to Capt. McDonnell of Kilsharvan, while Miss Jameson of Platten is getting married today, to Farrell. I am told the date of this marriage was anticipated owing to the mobilization of the forces. All the Navy Reserve men left Drogheda on Monday morning. A good many went from Paddy's district (about Francis st.) and a great number from Clogherhead.

John is very anxious to know if his Rev. went to Tralee on Sunday for the football. Smith of Colpe did not go. Please tell us if you are going to remain in Kilkee for the entire month. Candidly, I'd advise you to, because nothing round this side will do you as much good, and we are getting on very nicely as it is. The post is going now so I'll have to wind up.

Love as ever, From Mary.

Annie returned to Beamore at the end of August 1914 but her condition did not improve, and so she set forth to Kilkee once more at Easter 1915 in order to find a cure, in the Atlantic breezes and a place of rest. This time she resided at Pink Lodge, from where she writes to Paddie on 9th April 1915.

Pink Lodge,

My dear Paddie, *April 9th, 1915.*

It is too soon to report progress, but I am told I look much better. The waves were tremendous yesterday, but that hasn't prevented me going out each day since I came here. It is well I have a cotton ball and crochet needle to occupy my time during the showers or I might be tempted to carve my initials on the furniture but I am very comfortable and have the undivided attention of the hostess. Have the recruiters and the V.C. left town yet?

There were two German young men staying in the house last July. On their departure, the hostess asked if they'd return next year. Their reply was, "You'll never see us again Ma'am." So I suppose they don't mean to invade this coast.

There were two porters, with brass labels on their caps to meet the train at Lahinch but I saw only four probable trippers alighting and none carried golf sticks. The porter who met me and carried down my luggage was anxious to know how long I'd stop; on getting an evasive reply, he remarked that he supposed "as long as the money 'd last". As they speak in a very loud tone, and this was coming along the street, it was decidedly awkward.

Goodbye,

As ever,

Mother.

A return to Beamore followed where she remained until 17th May 1915, and then Eccles St. Hospital for a colostomy to be done. This procedure precipitated toxaemia and Annie died on Sunday June 20th 1915. Hal returned in August of the same year, and died in March 1916, at the age of 22 years.

Mary had been the major carer for both her brother and her Mother, at different levels of involvement from 1901 to 1916. This enabled Annie to continue her correspondence with other members of her family, notably Fr.Dick and Paddie, who had graduated in 1910, obtained the Stamullen job in 1911 and then went to the Dispensary job (No.2 District) in Drogheda in February 1913.

Annie writes on 29th February 1913.....

My Dear Richard,

I now forward the umbrella and a couple of other things...

On the St.Mary's Bazaar – the last dance was described by one who was there as being like a mass meeting.... the ladies tickets were issued free and they are in the majority. The favoured ladies of that stall were honoured by the presence of Fr.Norris and the Pastor.

Paddy is very confident of plain sailing tomorrow and that he will again be elected unanimously. The attendance of the 32 guardians the last day frightened all opponents; as McCullough said – he did 'not know where they were coming from'. Only for the influence of the Archdeacon some of the Guardians would have gone to Parr had it come to a division. It is said that one member was at the Station going to Dundalk to the Louth Council, and when he saw the numbers, he returned to add to them.

The candidate has ordered a hot luncheon of three courses at the Central for about forty. Parr says he thinks he might not contest it with him. Mary received the paper this morning. M.Taaffe is getting bigger, his appetite has returned again and he is making up for lost time.

As ever, Mother.

PS. One election came off unanimously. All the supporters turned up at the entertainment. The Laytown houses were bought at £540 by Miss McKeon; W.F. McQuillan bought the other two £840 and £650.

'Mode of Transport by Catechist'

CHAPTER 7: 1916 - 1929

MARY'S NEXT MINISTRY

Within that traumatic period of seven years, Fr.Dick was ordained and was on his fourth posting, having been made Diocesan Catechist in late 1915, Dr.Paddy had qualified , gone to Stamullen and then Drogheda, Salmon House had been completed, Annie and Hal had both died, Anthony had returned home to farm and the Insurrection of 1916 had happened, and its immediate after effects with death sentences and imprisonments. The World War was continuing since 1914, and Joe, the eternal optimist, got married in September 1916. All of the 'Dramatis Personae' in the family saga can be seen in the Wedding Party Photograph. While Pat is the exception who is missing due to his still being in a state of mourning for his wife and son.

Mary can be seen in all her finery in the middle, to the right of Fr.Dick. She had just spent fifteen years as a Nurse, Childminder, Housekeeper in Beamore and Salmon, correspondent to many, wages clerk and personal assistant, social representative and a cyclist in five counties. A multi-tasker par excellence....what next ?

Mary (centre of midlle row) at the wedding of Joe and Sissy in 1916

If the previous decade had been tumultuous, worse was to follow, certainly at National level. The World War continued until 1918, the certainty of Home Rule faded, the central role of the National Irish Party moved to Sinn Fein, the War of Independence lasted until the Truce of 1922, to be replaced by a Civil War, Independence for 26 counties and the experiment of Nationhood.

During the Black and Tan reprisals, Pat had his horse shot dead on his journey to Salmon, while he survived, Houses were raided in the search for arms, guns were abandoned in the flight for freedom. Beamore, Beabeg and Crufty were not to escape from all of this – Henry hid his valuable gold watch in the ashes of the fire while his house was searched, and various family members often disappeared 'over the fields' just ahead of blood thirsty raiders. The uncertain nature of the new Free State meant that accounts were kept in Derry and Newry as well as in the New State – purely for practical reasons of course, since all was held in pounds sterling.

Mary must have been kept quite busy during that decade, attempting to follow the advice of her aunt, Mother Anthony,

> ' To look after your dear Father and the boys; help them all you can, dear Mary, and always attract them to the home circle; for their sakes, try and be bright and cheerful.'

Fundraising Stamps

Apart from the political turmoil, and her own efforts to 'look after' the household at Beamore, two other significant events took place, in September 1922, Dr.Paddy married Eva Austin, and in October 1923, James married Annie Grimes. By this stage James had established himself at Salmon and the Doctor had purchased a residence and surgery at 33, Lawrence Street, Drogheda. Joe and Sissy were well established at Hartlands in Clonmellon and were also farming Diamor. They had five children in their first eight years of marriage... Nancy (b.1916), Bawn (b.1919), Mary (b.1921), Paddy (b.1922) and Thomas (b.1924).

In February 1921, Fr.Richard was appointed as a Vice President to St.Finians College, and a month later, became President, in place of Fr.O'Farrell. At the age of 36 years he was in a position to instigate positive change in an Institution which he had experienced at all levels. While Mary had less letters to write to her brothers, she still had a huge range of correspondence to various nuns all over Ireland and the world, to maintain. From the point of view of the world of letters and documents extant, two very significant developments happened, in the early 1920's. Eva's arrival into the family brought a kindred spirit who wrote letters and also kept them in bundles. Her first child appeared on the scene on 23rd September 1923, and he was named Patrick John Oliver, better known as Oliver, who grew up with a deep understanding and respect, for the written word.

Several interesting details emerge from some of the documents. The Doctor's House in Laurence Street was purchased for £800 from Coopers, a family who were very well known to the folk at Beamore, because of their several land holdings at Cooperhill, Mount Granville and Beamore. An eccentric 'Samuel Cooper' had fired his gun in order to discourage young Dick McCullen in the 1880's from taking a short cut through the Cooper fields where my own house now stands. A ruined gable still boasts the title of 'Sam's Castle'. The property market in Ireland was a depressed one in 1920's, and the sale of number 33 was carried out by private contract. A deed of costs from M/S Smyth and Son Solrs covering the period from April 1922 to October 1926, has one tiny fascinating addition where on 9-4-1923, a case was heard at Drogheda District Court, in which Guard Breen summonsed Dr.McCullen for driving a motor car without exhibiting a drivers licence', a fine of five shillings, with two shillings 'costs' was imposed.

Samuel Cooper

Returning to Eva Austin herself, a short history of her own background would be of interest. She was the fifth daughter of a farmer from Beechville, Beauparc, who owned a fair bit of land in Co.Meath. Peter Austin had no son however, and when his daughters (older ones!) quizzed him on a name for the new arrival, he reputably growled – 'Another girl ! You can call her what you like!'

Picture sent by Eva, of herself, to Anna Dolan in 1914

This piece of advice was sufficient for the big sisters to decide that the new baby be called 'Eve' after the mother of all mankind. One way or the other, a son did arrive to Mr and Mrs Austin, some years later, who was called 'Peter.' Eva went to school at the Siena Convent Drogheda where my own mother spent some years until the Nuns decided to become contemplative, and moved their teaching operation to Portugal.

My mother's sister, Anna Dolan was a classmate of Eva Austin, and Mary McCullen went to Loreto Navan with Rosita Austin.

Eva moved to live in West Street, Drogheda where her uncle had a business , as a grocer, wine and spirits merchants at no's 10-11, and she married P.D. McCullen at the age of 25 years. They had four children, P.J (Oliver, b.1923), Richard (b.1926), James (b.1928) and Mary (b.1930). Apart from rearing her children Eva was a very charitable lady who was involved in all kinds of committees to help various causes and assist Parish activities and also got through a voluminous amount of correspondence with the relations, in-laws and friends. Needless to say she was an avid Bridge Player and could have made a life occupation as a Detective if she had chosen to do it.

Then there were the unknown acts of kindness, away beyond the call of duty, like the lemon soufflé delivered in a glass bowl for Ann, following the birth of one of our children. For us, as children she was always warm and welcoming and very interested in the lives of small boys. A visit to the Doctors House was often associated with spatulas in throats, cough bottles and infections, so she provided the kindness and distraction needed to recover from the gruffness of P.D. ..... My father had once broken his arm and was in some difficulty in cutting his meat and using a knife and fork. Eva came to the rescue and suddenly P.D. remarked – ' Let him get used to doing it himself; he'll have to learn!'

The early death of Paddy at the age of 64, in 1952 was a huge blow to her, but she kept on going with the aid of her housekeeper, Kathleen, and lived to the ripe old age of 89 years (d.1986). Once when I quizzed Monsignor Richard about his sisters-in-law, he sidestepped me nicely, by his summing up – *'All my brothers managed to marry nice girls.'*

Eva was often seen by those McCullen brothers as a delicate one, but she managed to outlive all of them. In 1976, when we called for Grace's obligatory Communion visit she delayed the photograph of herself and Grace saying – 'Wait until I turn round to show my good side!'

Aunty Eva (her good side) with Grace and Ann McCullen in 1976

Five of the letters to Eva in the 1920's survived, and show the close, newsy relationship between Mary and her sister-in-law. The first of these comes from a market town, about twenty miles south of Manchester. Perhaps herself and Anthony were visiting Aunt May – Mother Anthony of Padua – for her silver jubilee as a nun, and had decided to see another part of England?

In understanding the letter, it is useful to know that 'Fred' was a nickname given to my father, John, which faded from use, except by James, in after years. A 'knut' is a jocose form of 'nut' meaning a fashionable young man, and the 'drummer' would be young Dick at the age of two. 'Queen Alexandra' is a McDermott from West Street.

Claremont, St.John's Road, Buxton

My dear Eva,   *13th July 1927*

You may guess in what a haven of respectability we are anchored when you learn that we are staying at the house that is next to the parish church while on the other side of the road are the public gardens and the Opera House. Thanks so much for your letter, it is a great thing, thank God, that May feels better, give her my best regards. How is Fred getting on with the hay making? Everything seems very late, as they are only cutting the hay now, which is usually made up before the end of June. A Manchester Lady staying here tells me that Mr. Cook, the miner's secretary was recently at the Hydro, while the Duke of Devonshire is staying in his agent's house and taking the waters with the ordinary people!

Anthony went to B'head yesterday morning before the registered letter came. However, he registered the contents and sent them on today. Since coming, we have seen a great deal of the surrounding country. One day, we went by bus to Matlock and then on to the town of Derby 38 miles making 76 for the return journey!! The entire country seems very hilly, so that even where there are industrial towns, you only see one a time so the landscape seems cleaner than that of Lancashire.

On Sunday it was amazing to see the buses not only from Manchester (25 miles off), but from Liverpool which is about 100. However, the highbrows belong to 'Ramblers Clubs' and walk across the hills with knapsacks on their backs, and the males with their coats off and their shirts sleeves turned up at the elbow. What will happen if that fashion strikes your Drogheda 'Knuts'?

Every day this week, I got my ankles massaged by Nurse Murphy, a native of Aughrim, south Wicklow, who has lived here for twenty years. She tells me there is one Irish Catholic doctor here, Dr.Troy, a very nice man. I am glad that everything has turned out so well in West Street. Queen Alexandra must be ecstatic.

You must be greatly relieved that Nursey is coming back, one active young man is a problem but a second who insists on playing the drum is a tragedy. Joined by Anthony in best regards to you all, believe me, dear Eva,

Yours affectionately, Mary

MF in 1921 – World Traveller

My dear Eva,

Beamore, Drogheda, Co.Meath
Monday 18th June 1928

I am posting you today's paper with the names of the newly ordained priests and also the deaths of Fr. Gilmor and Mrs Owen Walsh, Fr. John McCullen came home with the Beabeg people after the ordination and took part in the St.Mary's Procession. Fr. Gilmore was a nephew of the late Sister Xavier on the Dublin Road. He was a class fellow of John's and also of Fr. Conway. Fr.Conway seemed greatly moved by his death and spoke yesterday at mass, of his great loneliness.

Of course, the inhabitants of Duleek St. may have an unduly high opinion of St.Mary's, but the only regret expressed after the Procession last evening was that it did not go up to Sunnyside and so score one over St.Peter's!! Two of Maggie's nephews, one aged seven, the other aged four took part in it. Yesterday morning John went off to Cork. Amongst others taking part in the excursion were John Curran (the first ex he was ever seen on). Mrs Macken's neighbours, Messrs. Fagan, Owens, Barrett etc. When John went to Queenstown, he went out in a tender which is as long but not as wide as a Drogheda Steamer. It sailed into the Atlantic for an hour and a half and cruised round some of the larger liners.

In agricultural matters, the most startling news is that Mr.Miley has been 'fired' out of Cairnes. Father was greatly amused at the possibility of 'Mother's ' making Mr. Stafford Prime Minister in his place. You will see that Dolan was very successful at the Island Bridge Regatta on Sat.

The Milehouse – Home of Fr.John

20th June Wed

Yesterday I spent three hours in Bryanstown and was just leaving when Mr, Mrs and the small Miss McDermott drove into the yard. Cecilia Markey left £1000 to Nurse Gillespie who has been over the years in Naul minding first Mr. And then Miss Markey. The fortunate lady is from the north of Ireland and was trained in Vincent's. Mrs P.McDermott and Aidan are now staying in Kanturk so that she must be still under par. The Meath farmers went to Galway yesterday and not a drop of rain .

On account of your buying a Hugh Walpole book, I thought it was a strange coincidence that Mrs Macken was very enthusiastic about a book of his 'The Wooden Horse' dealing with Cornwall which she had from the Library last week. Queen Alex said the only newcomers to Creaser's for June are Broadberry's, the rubber stamp people and a Dublin family named Roche.

Yesterday the cold went away for the time being and the air is genuinely warm though the paper warns us about unsettled weather ahead. Are you too much removed from insular surroundings to be interested in the fact that a horse bred by J.J. Maher and trained by a W.Meath Boyd-Rochfort won a race worth £1000 in Ascot yesterday. Most probably I'll be in Drogheda tomorrow or Friday and I will tell you about the treasures in Laurence St.
Best Regards, Mary

The reference at the letter to 'Bryanstown' on 20th June update, would be a visit to Aunt Macken's house, halfway between Beamore and Drogheda. In letter number three, Mary is staying in Hartlands, with Joe and Sissy, and their five children. Eileen Rooney is a cousin of Eva's.

Hartlands, Clonmellon
30th Aug 1929

My dear Eva,

Some time ago I asked Miss Crilly to get some of Benziger's Illustrated Books, the same as what Olly has, as I thought Eileen Rooney would like them. Please try if they have come and if so give them to her. The country around is looking lovely. This morning we explored a part of Co.Meath which I have never seen before, which increased (if that were possible) my regards for my native county.

The youngsters here are very energetic . Tom tells me that he'd, love to dwive a twain' ? not merely an engine and is is able to show which road goes to Dublin. Fr Duffy is carrying on energetically in Oldcastle though everyone takes it for granted that he is booked for Tullamore,

Yours, as ever, Mary

Having returned home to Beamore, the next missive gives an example of Mary's generosity where she sends off fifteen shillings, a substantial sum at the time, to support Eva's plea for the charities, the Sienna Convent, and Linden Nursing Home in Blackrock.

Beamore, Drogheda, Co.Meath
23rd Oct 1928

My dear Eva

Many thanks for your note yesterday. We were at Tea when it came and I made a charge to open it, shocked the others by spilling my tea in the effort. I am sending out the balance of what is due on the rug, also five shillings for Sienna and ten shillings for Linden. Sissy sent a very interesting account of her travels. Mrs Hennessey of C'pollard was on the Pilgrimage. She is either a sister or daughter of Joseph O'Connor of Naas. There were a number of them on it, one of whom has died since coming back. Its a good job that you can exist after the Retreat, I am sure Fr Francis's friend, Lady Bellew, must have got a shock at her niece's accident . That Miss O'Brien must have had great courage.

Enclosed is an account of Jas. Ginnell. He was from Delvin, a younger brother of Laurence's. Some of them were at school with Mrs Melia, Laurence m. Alice King, Jas m Cella and one of the younger Ring sisters m, the Mr Farrelly who owns the mansion house of the Sheridans where Dean Swift used to stay. Mr Ginnell seems to have been more energetic than Mr B McNamara thinks the natives of Delvin are,

Best Regards, Mary

The final letter of 1928 is written to celebrate the arrival of Jim in Laurence Street on 20th October 1928, and at the end of a torn page, Mary bemoans the fact that she 'has no news!' The Reader can judge this statement....

Beamore, Drogheda, Co.Meath
6th Nov 1928

My dear Eva,

You may imagine how glad I was to hear that you and the latest arrivals were all right. I suppose you were very glad to see Olly on Sunday. John was greatly amused at his remarks on the journey.

Father was speaking to Mrs.Macken on Sunday, when she was down at last mass. He was surprised to find her look so well. Miss Cunningham was visiting her friends at Mornington last week, so you may imagine the people about here do not believe in sinking into early graves. Mr Edward Malone, Harbourstown, had bought and has already cut down some of the sycamore trees at the Cross of Beamore from Mr.Rooney. They are to be shipped and made into the sale of clogs for Lancashire millworkers. Olly and his Dada have been here 'for only a few minutes', as Olly says. His Dada says there was plenty of silver at Miss Rourke's auction and that it was very cheap.

Maggie tells me that there is consternation in Duleek Street today about the milk supply. Miss Reilly and Mr McEvoy do not feel able to comply with the corporation edicts about cement mangers and do not intend to sell any locally, so I suppose you will all get the bottled stuff now !!

Do you remember some times ago, the others were talking about having bought some cattle from Mr. English, Julianstown ? Previously, Mr.E was noted for his cultivation of cherries and all sorts of early vegetables. Well, yesterday, the new Mr Markey set all Rockbellew except one field . Mr.English took on good deal of it, so we may hardly expect a new sort of cherry or tomato from him from this out.

John tells me that Louth Juniors including your Joe Byrne beat Sligo in Croke Park on Sunday, so I hope you will feel elated. I thought that perhaps Joe and Sissy might come up after they had rested themselves but they did not stir out since. Lady Butler is staying in Gormanston and has Dr.Hunt attending her. Give my very best love to Rosita and tell her I have a barrowful of improving literature for her – a study of Jane Austen and all Jane's works except one. Father is in great form and was in Rockbellew yesterday. Olly seems quite satisfied with 'the little baby' knew its name and all. I am very sorry I have no news, I'd want a visit to Bryanstown to produce that but I send you and his young majesty my very best regards.

Mary.

Eva and Paddy's four children – Mary, Jim, Dick and Oliver. c1933

CHAPTER 8: 1930 - 1939

TROUBLED THIRTIES

The shadow of uncertainty brooded over the decade at home and abroad. A great depression took hold in America, Hitler rose to power in Germany, Mussolini in Italy and Spain was engulfed in a civil war. In a new Ireland, after less than ten years of self government, Fianna Fail with Eamon deValera at the helm, were voted into power with a majority of seats in the Dail. This latter event would give Aunt Mary cause to cover her head with the newspaper when he spoke on the new Radio Eireann. Anthony married and left Beamore, while 'The Boss' and John battened down the hatches on farm economic activity in Beamore and Clonlusk. Mr de Valera flexed his political muscles by refusing to continue paying Land Annuities on Irish Land to the British Government, who retaliated by imposing severe tariffs on livestock exports from Ireland to the United Kingdom. The stalemate which resulted from 1932 onwards was called 'The Economic War', and imposed a severe hardship on the whole population, particularly the farmers. Cattle markets collapsed, and the animals were kept over, in the hope of a change, sometime next year, or the year after.... or even for more years.

The government dug in, and imposed duties on exports from England to Ireland. Original 'Sinn Fein' policies from a different era would win this battle, so we could protect our own Industries and produce what we needed within the country. This would create jobs and save money...

However, rates still had to be paid to the Local Authorities, regardless of Farm Incomes being up or down. Various campaigns to 'pay no rates' provided a spark to form Farmer Organisations which eventually took serious hold with the formation of Macra na Feirme in 1947 – the melting pot from which came N.F.A and I.C.M.S.A. In 1934, the countryside was in a discontented state, and local elections were due. 'Dev' responded by bringing in a series of measures to ease the anger, and the hardship. These included the following measures –

- o Farms below £20 in valuation (circa 20-50 acs) would be allowed a rate rebate,
- o Free beef would be provided for urban dwellers,
- o A premium of 10 shillings and sixpence would be paid for every calf slaughtered,
- o Notices appeared from the Department of Agriculture with this message – 'Farmers, eat your duck eggs – sell your hen eggs'.

At that time, life was much simpler than nowadays with imported goods and multiple choice. Thus, money had only to be found for rates, tea and sugar, tobacco, and fuel for cars, motorbikes and lamps. Government strategy then encouraged the setting up of the Sugar Factories, under Comhlacht Siucre Eireann, to make sugar from beet, and tobacco growing to provide a homegrown version. All other foods were to be produced on the farm.

James and John became expert butchers and bacon, rashers, sausages and mutton chops were produced from a rickety table inside the kitchen door. Quarters of pig hung from the hooks on the kitchen ceiling, well salted ! Enough salt kills all bugs....

Eucharistic Congress, O'Connell Bridge, 1932   Commemorative Badge from the event

Mary had some domestic help in Beamore, and managed to escape to Salmon, to Hartlands and even to special events like the Dublin Eucharistic Congress of 1932, which was for many, a highlight of Ireland's growth as an Independent Nation.

Sixteen letters survive, all written to Eva. As usual they cover a multitude of topics, perhaps with more emphasis on land sales in a depressed market. The first missive describes Bellewstown Races amongst other events.....

Beamore, Drogheda
My dear Eva,   *4ᵗʰ July 1930*

Many thanks for your letter. Unfortunately nearly all yesterday's paper was burned this morning. Father drove up to Bellewstown on Wednesday. He did not want to stand or walk about, so he drove the trap in over the west side of the course. There he was joined by Mr Cluskey of Ladymoor whose land comes up close to the course. Mr C is first cousin of Al McQuillan – their mothers having been Healy's of Kilmessan. Some times ago, Mr C went in for breeding bloodstock but then he got tired and handed them over to his neighbour young Mr Wall so F. Got an amount of inside information that should last him a good while.

Yesterday I went up with him and waited in Ennis's till Annie and Jas came. The attendance was hardly as good as the last time I went – seven years ago. Mona Larkin was there looking very handsome but thin Someone said that Lady Lambert had the old Lady Mc Calmont with her. Joe and Sissy were there with Gillics. You will be amused to hear that I tried both Tote and Bookies and lost with both!! I heard that Doc Murray and Mrs got six winners on Wed, while I do know of two people who each put on 2s/6d with a bookie on a dead snip, then put 2/s on an outsider with the Tote – lost the cert and each drew 54/= on the outsider. So much for the skirts of happy chance!

The Glen is now in North's ad so none of our merchant princes have invested. Mr and Mrs P.Murray left for Oberammergau on Friday. Minnie Reilly said the two Mr and Mrs P. Austins were at the races. Mr and Mrs Behan and Gertie McNamara and some other Drogheda people were there but there seemed to be no country people from Co.Louth and hardly anybody from any distances in Co.Meath. A bus ran from Duleek for 2/= return fare. Before noon there was heavy rain and thunder but afterwards the weather held up. Father was left gasping when he learned from your letter that artistic people are discovering Clogher and finding it 'so different and unsophisticated'.
You see he knew two generations of the McEvoy's the owners of Mrs Collier's house. Annie said she expected if nothing unforseen happened, she would accept your invitation for today.

The tour you have selected seems very interesting. If you care for horrors, not in real life but on canvas, you can see in the Brussels pictures gallery some works by David who sketched some of his scenes at the guillotines during the French Revolution. The Brussels collection I think has his painting of Marat after Charlotte Cordez had stabbed him and similar slices of real life or death rather. Some time ago, you bought at Sir Jas Murphy's a book with some very fine illustrations of the Rhine scenery. When you come in to Laurence St. You go through it so that the reality will be more interesting.

Within the last few weeks, it was positively startling that such a number of Father's contemporaries died. On that account I was very glad that he stirred out to Bellewstown. From P's account I learned that you have discovered the different layers of social strata that forms parochial life in Clogherhead. Hoping that no boulders may break loose from the aforesaid strata and fall on top of you or of the angel children, I remain,
Yours affectionately, Mary

Six weeks later, Mary is in Salmon, and keeping watch on the Strand Races at Laytown.

My dear Eva,

Salmon, Balbriggan
22nd August 1930

Many thanks for your letter. I did not write when you were wandering as I was afraid my letters might not hit your hotel in time, but I did chance sending a paper to Aix-la-Chapelle. Jas drove down on the holiday to Beamore and brought me back here. The weather has been broken for the past few days with unusually high wind for this time of the year. Annie was at Laytown races on Wed – weather very stormy. Joe, Sissy and Gillics were there. Others present were Count McCormack, Mamma Cummisky and her daughters, Phyllis Fulham and the Gallens, Mr and Mrs Larkin and Dr and Mrs Murray. I forget how many winners the latter got. Kitty and Dorcas O'Sullivan were at school in Loreto with me. K is now chief domestic instructress with the Dublin Corporation. Two brothers were engineers with the Dublin Corporation, one of them rising to be Chief Engineer, but both died young. You will see by the Irish Times that McDonnell's holding of Parkmore in the Glens of Antrim is to be sold.

Yesterday, I went to the dentist, I came home by G.N.R bus to Skerries, coming through Rush and seeing all the market gardens. From the glimpses, I caught of Mr Kelly's Whitestown, it might be perhaps rather formal in its layout for your friends who are seeking nature at it's sources but an ordinary person would think it was very pretty. The change from the ample surroundings of Linden to Temple Street would be disagreeable for an ordinary person much less for a native of Co.Meath. Julia will have to bring all her super-natural qualities into play. Next week, I intend making a charge on Aunt Macken (D.V)

If feminine Co.Louth is moving towards beauty parlours, masculine Co.Meath is getting down to bed-rock. Capt. Boylan is selling plants, Mr Plantagenet Hastings – Howard- Stafford – Jenningham-Caddell-Illytid-Nicholls is lorrying eggs and fowl into the Dublin hotels, and one of the younger Mr.Markeys of Rockbellew went to Mrs.Ward Cooperhill to pluck fruit at 1-6 a day, after he had finished making hay at 2/= for Joe Stafford. You need not mention the matter to grandmamma Markey, but the humour of it should appeal to your mother. Albert Reynolds of Garristown was judging horses in Limerick yesterday when he became ill and died R.I.P.

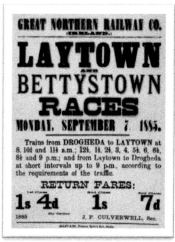

Best Regards, Mary

PS. Your letter was sent out from Beamore, it did not reach me till last evening. Do not ever reveal the activities of 'young Mr.Markey' or indeed Mr.Plantagenet Hastings-Caddell-Nicholls! Within a week the strange lifestyle of the Fingallians is further exposed, and also the Bishop's part in Meath's downfall in football, in 1930.

The Races at Laytown

Salmon, Balbriggan,
27th Aug 1930

My dear Eva,

Many thanks for your letter , I am posting you the last batch of papers as the Drogheda District seems to figure largely in them. Laytown has got quite a number of excursionists for the past fortnight. The new house near Man of War, covered by shells was built by Dowdalls on the farm formerly owned by the late Tom Tolan (Boss). Yesterday Annie and I were in Balbriggan for the close of the Forty Hours. Three of the Morgan children were walking, one in embroidered voile, another in white silk and a little boy. You will see that Fr.Grogan, who told Mrs Brannigan when she came to Drogheda to look up Fr.Nulty has died unexpectedly in Dublin.

Lady Esmonde has been telling the Irish Independent reporter all about the works he did in New York. Even if Mr Kennedy died a catholic, his relatives may have buried him as they wanted. Miss Murphy Buxton, told me of an Irish Catholic married to a Unitarian. The priest attended her during her last illness but the husband had her buried with a Unitarian service. A Mr.Fetherstonhaugh ? from Co.W.Meath has bought from Mr Murtagh of Grange, a very nicely laid out bungalow, just opposite an entrance at Milverton, W.F is a protestant but married to a Catholic, an authoress – what particular line she chooses or what names she writes under, I have not heard yet.

Did you trouble to notice in the Drogheda Independent that Meath drew with Kildare in Croke Park a fortnight ago. A Fr.McManus had been playing during the winter with them under the name of O'Donoghue. Lately , the Bishop decided that priests were not to play. However, a petition was sent in asking for his services for the replay against Kildare. It did not succeed, Meath were beaten badly. Kildare then became champions of Leinster, but last Sunday were unexpectedly beaten by Monaghan representing Ulster, so that their triumph was short lived. Some of the Skerries folks went on Monday to Ashford, Co.Wicklow to a sheep auction.

Mr Synge who stayed in Malahide last year annually sells his sheep that way. Mr and Mrs Healy of Skerries some years ago bought the mansion house of Hackettstown from Lord Holmpatrick. They have found it rather spacious for their tastes and you will notice they are now building an, ordinary sized house just inside the gates.

Best Regards
Mary.
PS. I think that Fr. Called up to Laurence St. Everytime he went to Drogheda, to ask after the little angels.

The House at Salmon

The Letters of Aunt Mary

Back in Beamore, a year later, she gives us an insight into the Honeymoon travels of Anthony and Johanna.

Beamore, Drogheda,
6th July 1931

My dear Eva,

Many thanks for your troubles about the chairs. If you will please finish the job I can settle with Paddy when he comes around. How is the Beechville baby getting on? Anthony & Mrs came here yesterday. They had a very enjoyable time in Buxton, where they met Fr. O'Sullivan. They were home on the boat with Lenehans (Fr. Farrelly's nephew). They had called to Sheffield to see an aunt, Miss Farrelly, who is a sister of Charity there. A community of seven met them, all of whom were Irish and five of whom hailed from the diocese of Meath!!

This week's Standard tells me that the Irish Vincentians are opening a secondary catholic school in the former residence of the Catholic Archbishop of Liverpool with Fr. Paul Cullen as superior.

Your mother or aunt would no doubt do justice to the situation that you describe. Thomas Hardy, if living, could have described it as another of 'Lifes' Little Ironies'. I hope that Dick is now getting used to the air. Imagine when the travellers went to Bartestree. May could describe to them Greenanstown, Clonalvey, the Cross of Cromwell, Clatterstown etc. How's that for Co.Meath patriotism, seeing that she is in Bartestree since 1896?

Father seems very well now (D.G). He drove to Mass yesterday and drove out to Drogheda this morning. One of the priests ordained for Meath this year is Fr. Crilly, a brother of Mr. Larkin's former assistant. It seems that he was born in either Newry or Dundalk but was reared with his mother's people in Westmeath.

The centre pages of last week's Illustrated Sporting and Dramatics News' contained a picture of Mr and Mrs E.F. McKeever leaving the church at Faversham, Kent in a shower of confetti. The lady has been Master of the Faverstown beagles and is a sister to the Mr. Dawes who is married to Miss Mc Veagh, Drewstown,

Best Regards
Mary
P.S Have you had time to read anything . Do not let the little angels take up all your time.

Beamore,Drogheda,
Thurs 2nd June 1932

My dear Eva,

Whenever I mention to John that he could drop into Miss Green's if he were down at the Steampackets, he listens without enthusiasm, even if I quote the words of D Drew and say he might not call that a visit!!

Last Friday, I went with him to the Agricultural Show Balmoral, Belfast. Balmoral is about as far from Belfast as Ballsbridge from Dublin. The attendance that day was nearly 30,000, you would remark a great number of Presbyterians clergy with their wives and families, seven or eight Catholic priests but very few Episcopalians. It is some years since I was in Belfast and I thought that the shops in Royal Avenue and the other principle streets looked grubby. Of course, the closing of the ship-yards must make a great difference. My principles would not allow me to buy anything except some Catholic papers, which interested Father greatly. One of them had a paragraph about the closing down of Gray's factory, Glenavy which is between Goragh Wood and Armagh. Some years ago he knew the Grays' who handled their stuff from the states of raw flax to that of beetled linen. The works supported a population of 1700, so that the stoppage must leave that district very poor.

Your Dutch friends will be interested to know that Mr. M_____ has taken part of the Marsh holdings and put there in cold storage for the Congress, fish fowl etc. One of the Mr and Mrs Williamson books, the 'Bator Chaperon' describes a tour by motor boat through the canals of Holland. After Holland threw off the Spanish Yoke in 1590, she became very powerful on land and sea. She was at war with England in 1666 and the Dutch Admiral swept the English shipping off the sea, and tied a sweeping brush to his mast to celebrate the victory. About that time the Dutch navy sailed up the Medway close to London. Since that time, they have declined as a great power, although their colonies about Java and the East are still important. After they broke away from Spain, the Catholic minority had a hard time but since 1850 their position has improved while the old dogmatic Protestantism has grown weaker. Catholics are now about 30% of the population and mostly in the south beside Belgium.

On Sunday after Ollie, Jim and their dad had gone, Anthony, Mrs and the Misses McCullen arrived. They were all in good spirits and we heard that the young ladies now weigh three times what they did ten weeks ago. Be sure to send some post cards to Salmon, Hartlands and Kilnew and I am sure R. Anne would just love if you sent her one to Beabeg. I am glad the papers reach you so regularly,

Yours, M.

PS. The Derby has been won by a rank outsider.

Anthony, with the twins – gaining weight!

The weights of the young ladies refers to twins, Nancy and Maura, who commenced life at 2lbs each. R.Anne is cousin Rose Anne, in Beabeg.

My dear Eva,

Beamore, Drogheda,
13th Jul 1932

Thanks for your interesting letter. We are all glad to know that Jim has 'sheeps' enough and that Mary and he can study hens and pigs at close quarter. Yesterday a boy aged 6, named Kevin Eustace, slipped into the Boyne and was drowned. I am told he is a grandson of the late Peter Lennon.

Of course we got slabs of information about the Congress the Sunday we went to Hartlands. I forget if they went on Thurs or Fri nights, but they drove on Gillic's car, with the children on Sat and also drove on Sunday to the Mass and heard the Benediction on a loud speaker in Kells. Last Sun, they came here by the early train with Mary, Paddy and Tom. When we had just finished our tea Jas, Annie and the Misses McC arrived. Jas, Annie had driven with Derhams to the Congress Mass. Then Jas walked in the procession where he found himself beside Leo Drew.

While Annie drove back with the others and heard the Benediction over the wireless in Skerries. Anthony said he went to Bellewstown on the Thursday, but I think everything in it was on the dull side. We have been very busy making up hay, and have had no rain since Sunday week (D.G) though there seems to be a change today. I don't know whether John would tackle to drive through the Wicklow Hills but I would just love Father to see Glendalough!! Did the journey down take you long?

The Diocesan Retreat took place in Mullingar last week. Sissy tells me it is being followed by an enclosed retreat for the Conferences of St V. De. Paul. As yet, we have heard nothing of the whereabouts of the Rev R MacCullen.

Maggie tells me that on Sun evening she cycled by Beaulieu and Baltray to Termonfechin, as it would not be so crowded as Laytown or Bettystown. Last week's Universe had a drawing of the ruins of Trim by Peter Anson. This is the convert whom I told you about. He has already done sketches of Glendalough, St.Doulagh's, and Armagh. The Ansons are a great Navy family, several of them having been admirals as I told you before.

Your fellow guests seem to be of very diverse religious outlook; mixed marriages are dreadful . The others are in the hay fields but I presume that they would join with me in sending best regards, M.

Beamore, Drogheda,
14th July 1932

My dear Eva,

Yesterday about three in the afternoon, there came about two thunderclaps and a steady downpour of rain, which lasted till about mid day now. The rain was so heavy that I did not ask anyone to post the letter I had written to you , till Maggie was going home. A great deal of rain fell in a deep calm with only a shade of thunder, not the storm you speak of.

Your letter is very interesting. Some years ago the Catholic Truth Soc of England put some articles under the title ' How I came Home' by well known converts describing their reason for joining the Catholic Church. I am writing this day to C.T. Soc, Abbey St., asking them to post on your catalogue so that perhaps you or the ladies might see the name of something, that would answer. Sometime ago the paper reviewed a book by the convert Rev.Vernon Johnson, Bob Law's cousin. It is called 'One Lord One Faith' and has since been brought out in a paper edition by Sheed and Ward, probably for 1/=. The Rev. C.J. Mac Gillvary is now a Catholic chaplain at Cambridge. He was an Anglican clergyman and went to Palestine Arabia as a missionary. When he saw Anglicanism, Orthodoxy And Rome in close contact, he saw that 'Rome' was right and has written a book on his spiritual progress. I think the title is ' To Rome through the East'. He has also written 'Fr. Vernon and his Critics ' and the True Church'. These are often advertised in the Catholic Papers. Then prayer can do a great deal.

I am very glad to hear that May has been able to go home. By the way, where do you go to Mass now and what is name of your parish ? You ask about the family of Howard, Earl of Wicklow. They claim to belong to the family of the Duke of Norfolk. At any rate the first of them married in England a Miss Hassels sometimes in the 17th century. After his death the widow and her son came to Ireland. She married her cousin who was then in occupation of Shelton Abbey. Her son bought the estate of North Arklow from Butler, Duke of Ormonde and became President of the college of Physicians. After a couple of generations had added to the family wealth by becoming judges and Anglican bishops , they obtained an earldom in the 18th century. The present Earl married a sister of the Duke of Abercorn. Her aunt, the Marchioness of Blandford who is still alive is brought into ' Lothair' by Disraeli. In the book Lothair stays in the Church of England and becomes engaged to Lady Corisande but in real life, the Marquess of Bute became a Catholic and married a Catholic.

A previous Earl of Wicklow who died in 1869 had no sons but seven daughters. They seem to have nearly all become Catholics and married Catholics. Joe and S told us on Sun that Fr Hart and Fr Forde had got parishes but which got which I cannot say. Fr. Hart is a very Jewish looking person. I saw him at Tom Lynch's wedding,

Best Regards, Mary

PS. I hope you thought of bringing 'The Parnell Movement' with you,

Post the Eucharistic Congress, Mary embarks on an intense spell of writing with two long letters and a précis of Disraelis book 'Lothair'.

Lothair

Lothair is the 4th Marquis of Bute but Disraeli departs from life in two instances. The hero goes to fight for the unity of Italy, is wounded at Menbana, is nursed by a heroine whose name I have forgotton, and at the end of the book marries Lady Corisande. In real life, Lord Seymour, heir of the Duke of Somerset joined Garabaldi's volunteers and died of wounds received in Italy . An Englishwoman, Jessie White Mario was an enthusiast for the unification of Italy at that time I think that she married an Italian named Alegrhetti.

Lord Seymour's mother, Georgina Sheridan, had been the queen of beauty in the Eglinton Tournament. She was a granddaughter of R.B. Sheridan and sister to Lady Dufferin and MrsNorton. Lord Bute became a Catholic, and married Gwendoline Fiztalen Howard, cousin to the Duke of Norfolk. Lady Corisande (in real life Lady Alberta Hamilton) married the Marquis of Blandford, son of the Duke of Marlborough, she was mother to the late and grandmother for the present Duke. The Cardinal was Cardinal Manning. The Duke and Duchess were the Abercorns through their London house, Crecy house was really Stafford House owned by the Duke of Sutherland. The 3rd Duke of Sutherland is sketched as St.Aldegard. Mgr Catesby is Mgr Capels who lived on till 1912 or thereabouts. He was an Irishman, the son of a coastguard and was very successful with converts in the 1860's and 70's. When Bute did get married, Dizzy was a guest and Mgr Capel gave the address. Lady St.Jerome was Elizabeth, Lady Herbert of Lea, who lived till 1910.

Mr Phoebus was Frederick Leighton, son of a Scarborough doctor. He afterwards became P.R.A was created a baronet and a peer. He was the only painter to be made a Lord, as well as being a painter, he loved all sorts of beautiful things, and his house Leighton House, Kensington is now a show place.

Beamore, Drogheda
14th July 1933

My dear Eva,

Many thanks for your letter. I hope that Dick has now become accustomed to the air and is enjoying himself. Did you get any sort of a handbook on the district? Mrs Gannon, Kiltallaght, was buried on Monday in St.Peter's New Cemetary. You will no doubt be glad to hear that although John did not call at the North Strand that he went to the funeral which he said was very large!

When we were in Hartland's on 29th June, they told us that Mary was to be confirmed in Matlock on 15th July. From the Catholic papers, I see that the Bishop is to give confirmation and also to be present at Mass in Padley. When I was in Buxton the Catholics organised a pilgrimage to Padley, formerly the mansion of the Fitzherberts and the scene of Bensons 'Come Rack Come Rope.' It was then disused but has since been bought by a Catholic priest, and is to be used as a chapel.On Sunday, Theresa Dowdall was prayed for , as having died in Paris R.I.P. Fr Donegan is in charge of the parish, as the others have gone to Mullingar for the annual retreat. Since last week's thunder the weather has been warm or mild but not as dry as before. They have not yet finished the hay.

Fr.Duffner is saying Mass in the Aug., so I suppose Fr. O'Sullivan has gone on holidays. I wonder who would the Christian Brother be from Kells. Have you come across any Meath priests ? In yesterday's paper, I saw the death of a Miss Carney, Fitwilliam Square. Is that Mrs Gogarty's aunt ? It was very funny to read about the people who married 'in' in each generation. Do you ever get talking to any 'farmer' people? John's great regret, just now is that the lads are not here at the hay-making. Tell Jim that another calf arrived this week. Some time ago you were talking about Highfield House Rathgar and neither of us could think from who the Lyons's had bought it. One of the days I was down in Hartlands, Sissy said that Alphonsus O'Farrelly had sold it , so I was thinking that the name seemed familiar.

Best love to all, Mary

Matlock was a school for girls, run by the Presentation Order, where Nancy, Bawn and Mary were sent to Boarding School in the 1930's.

Matlock School in the 1930's.

Beamore,Drogheda
21ˢᵗ July 1933

My dear Eva,

Last evening Paddy came round with a fine salmon. He had no local news, Father Dick has not turned up since the Retreat, so I suppose that he is carrying out fresh improvements in the college. Did I tell you before that Miss Reilly, North Quay, is entering the Indian provinces of the Loreto order? She was telling Mrs Anthony that she is the first postulant to go from Ireland for the last three years. The weather has got fine again and is quite warm, in fact we would seem to be on the edge of a thunderstorm all the week, but the clouds sheers off just when it seems due to explode.

Your will see that Mr Manning who bought the house from Mr Henly has died. He was an R.I.C pensioner who got a job in the Brewery. Is it not a strange thing that in about twelve months time that someone should have died in these four houses – Mrs Carroll, Mr Manning, Brendan Dwyer and Miss Brunskill. Fr.O'Sullivan has not yet gone to Dublin . Of course, the inevitable remarks have been made about 'The Eloquent Dempsey' and 'The Real McCoy'. Last week, I got an invitation to the Centenary Celebrations of Loreto, Navan, which I did not accept. There is no necessity to make any comment on the firing at Casserly's house, but I remark that the standards are placarded. Again.

A section of our army is camping on the strand near Termonfechin. What the local farmers think when they hear shots being fired from an anti-aircraft gun against an aeroplane, 10,000 feet up, I do not know! John is very glad that Jim has come across someone who can appreciate him, but that will only make it all the harder for him to settle down to the routines of Donor's Green, when he comes back. Except for 'utility' purposes, I have not been in the motor since 29ᵗʰ June, when we were in Hartlands, neither have any of the Hartlands or Salmon people been here. I heard that Sissy was in Lough Derg this week.

Best Regards, Mary

PS. It is a pity that the tide has turned from Lisdoonvarna but now with motors people won't stay a month in one place. Bolgers used to be a great place some time ago.

At the end of August, Mary is sampling life in a hotel in South Dublin, and studying the occupants.

Telephone 113
Pier Hotel, Dun Laoighaire, Co.Dublin
29th August 1932

My dear Eva,

Rosita and Teresa came down last evening and told of their experiences at the Slane celebration. There are about twenty people staying here, three all year rounders (Mrs McBeth, the very Protestant Mrs O'Farrell, the youthful widow and Mrs Kennedy grandmother of the juvenile tennis champion, Miss Olive Poole.) Besides these old Miss Campbell is again here and a number of birds of passage.

The township authorities certainly planted flowers everywhere for the Congress and the place still looks lovely. Some thousands of us went to the wharf on Saturday to meet our returning Olympic warriors. Before the boat came in, we could distinguish them some miles out at sea as they considerately wore their green jackets and stood at the rails of the fore part of the ship. Then we cheered all our public men as they came along Cosgrave, the present Cabinet etc. Suddenly someone said 'There's Alfie' and he seemed to get as much applause as everybody put together. I intend to go home on Wed (D.V),

Best regards, Mary

I have allocated four letters to the year 1933, three by date and one from the references in it to the chattiness of Olly! All are written from Beamore.

Beamore, Drogheda, Co.Meath
Thursday 28th June

My dear Eva,

Many thanks for your letter. Yesterday I called to Laurence Street and found everyone in great form, Olly was very chatty, telling me how you had written to Nursie, Dick was in great humour beaming on me then he thought of himself and turned very shy, taking hold of Nursie's hand for protection.

The daily papers are not worth sending this week, as they have nothing except stuff about General Nobile, and an alleged mutiny on an Australian ship. However, you may expect the Drogheda paper as usual.

Sissy wrote during the week to say that she was not coming up to Bellewstown next week, as she has not gone beyond just driving to Mass. Annie, James and Miss came here last evening, and gave us a full account of the Hamption auction.

The attendance at it was immense and the furniture fetched high prices. The stuff was good but merely a residue and somewhat on the large size.

James McCullen

About 60 Jesuit scholastics are staying in Gormanston castle. They have bicycles and cycle to Skerries, Drogheda etc. W Lenehan came home last week. Fr Norris has got one lung injured and I am told will have to leave Ireland. Fr.John McCullen called round and gave us all his blessing. Our temporary bishop, Fr D. Flynn was up in the Dublin Road for the election of a Rev Mother. Colomba got the job again. How unfortunate that your sister should be appointed to Blackrock and not to Cappagh, Finglas. There she could keep in touch with Co.Meath by way of the passing hay carts. Lancaster diocese was formed a few years ago by taking a slice from Liverpool. One of the Blackpool P.P.'s Fr.Cahill is from Meath and Dr.Pearson got some 'white hopes' from St.Finians lately.

John and Anthony are going tomorrow on an excursion to Portrush. Yesterday I met with Mrs Symmington and congratulated her on Clare's good fortune. The wedding is taking place early next year. You may imagine how soft the weather has been for the past week from the fact that nobody in the district except Cairnes has any hay cut and that Father has been reduced to sitting inside reading a book called 'The Private Palaces of London by Mr. Berefsord Chancellor!!

It is, I admit, a handsomely produced work, which was published at £1-1= (I bought it cheap from a library) but it is not wildly thrilling.

Joined by all in best wishes to you both, I remain,

Yours affectionately, Mary

During the summer months in 1933-34, Eva spent time in Bundoran in the hope that Dick would be better able to cope with his asthma. He would have been aged 7-8 years.

The reference to 'Maggie' being instructed to look for a railway guide, is recognition of Maggie Kelly (1910-1994), Coolagh Street, who spent a lifetime as housekeeper with the McCullen in Beamore, and to whom the Boss presented a gold sovereign to be made into a broach, on her marriage. Mary always held her in high esteem.

Beamore,Drogheda
25ᵗʰ July 1933

My dear Eva,

You will be glad to know that the letter you speak of came here on Wed. Interested though you were in it, the excitement was nothing to what we felt yesterday morning when the card came from Jim. Father was very anxious that it should be answered without delay. So John sat down after dinner to write his reply. The papers have a great deal to say about the B.M..A in Dublin .

The visitors seem to be having the time of their lives, but may have to go for a rest cure when it is over. The old railway guide here says that the mail leaves Limerick at 4.35pm and reaches Dublin at 7.40pm but lest there should be a change, I have asked Maggie to look for a railway guide which I intend to post to you if it can be got.

Father Dick has not come near us, But Fr.Conway told Father on Sunday, that Fr.Nulty was to join Fr.Dick this week in a stay at Carna in Co.Galway. He stayed there some years ago. On Sunday, Father and John went to the funeral of Capt. Jas Lyons R.I.P. It was very large.

The summer before Paddy was married, when Father and I were in Galway, we went one day by steamer to Ballyvaughan some of the passengers were going on to Lisdoonvarna to stay. Another day, we went on the steamer to the Aran Islands, while another day we went up Lough Corrib as far as Cong. We seem to have got very much better weather than yours.

Yesterday the sky was covered with dark clouds and every one felt that a thunderstorm was due. However no rain fell till about 10pm when it rained heavily for an hour and then stopped rather than cleared off. There may have been hotter single days, but I do not think that this part of Ireland has ever had such even warmth sustained though day and night, as we have since the thunder. It amuses me to think of the summers before last year, when we used to put in a big fire every evening!!

Today's 'Irish Times' has a medical supplement with articles on the Dublin hospitals. Both Temple St. And St.Vincent's are written about. Where is Sr.Ignatius taking her holidays this year?

Last week Mrs Fitzharris told me that 70 Holy Faith nuns are staying in the Skerries Convent!! Her sister who is Rev. Mother of H.Faith Celbridge, is among them and came on Sat, with another nun to Drogheda to see the head of O. Plunkett. This ink bottle is a dose. It is a non-spillable one but there is a pocket of air underneath the ink which makes it come out in blobs,

Best Love, M

The following letters are unusual, in being written in pencil and from the hospital in Eccles Street, Dublin. Mary slipped on wet salt outside a shop in Shop Street, Drogheda in 1933, and broke her hip. This was the cause of her limp and built-up shoes on one foot afterwards. These letters would have been written around April 1933, dating them by the death of her cousin Mary Jane Moore, who is buried in the Moore family plot in Donore Old Graveyard.

'Barnville' would be the surgeon who was a member of a well known Dublin medical family; and the P.S at the end of the letter a sign of how protective Mary had become towards her father, who had passed his eightieth year. Despite this , he was still 'The Boss'!

During her absence from Beamore, Nancy was sent from Hartlands to housekeep in Beamore, and then Bawn came to assist her. Their piano playing and re-arrangement of pictures in the house was stopped by the Boss, on the grounds that it would be too much levity for the men working in the fields. This piece of 're-education' for the Matlock Ladies was never forgotton.

32 Eccles St, Dublin.

My dear Eva,   *Friday (April '33?)*

Poor M.J's death came to me as a great surprise. She had been so ill so many times before that I thought she would come through again. The blow to Annie will be very great. Tell me if you see Capt. Denny Lyons at the funeral . About forty years ago he proposed to her, but she would not have him. The poor thing never had the constitution of Annie and during her life must have suffered a lot. When she was young she was accounted to have a good voice and had it trained at the R.I.A.M. Perhaps her connections with Miss Snow in the Augustinian Choir and with old Miss Tighe in the Aug. Altar Society were some of her most real pleasures. R.I.P.

Today Barnville took out the stitches and took off most of the dressings. He said that it would not be too long till he expected to take away the splints!! Of course we all congratulated each other!

Best Regards, Mary.

PS. I'm not writing this home as I have <u>never</u> given any details to the Boss.

32 Eccles St, Dublin.
Saturday

My dear Eva,

On Sat Rosita and Theresa paid me a very nice long visit. Yesterday I had Nancy, last evening Joe, and today James. Of course, I have Mr. Barnville who seems, if anything, a shade breezier and brighter each time and who in the intervals of telling me how perfectly lovely Portmarnock was on Sunday, says that he is quite satisfied with the way I am going on!! At any rate, I can do my hair and wash my face and pour out my tea, so I must be on the mend.

Therese was telling me of the perfectly wonderful radiologist they have in St.Vincents in the person of a junior Miss Dan Brannigan, her elder sister is now with a Harley Street Doctor and engaged to be married to a young doctor, son of a very wealthy doctor. How are your domestic affairs progressing ? Is Kathleen back yet ?

One of the Clarendon St (Strict) Carmelites is a patient on the corridor. Remember me to all particularly Jim & Mary (ask them to pray for me) and with best love to yourself,
I remain, Yours affectionately,
Mary

The reference in the next letter to full grown men coming to help at 'Mangolds crop' is a sign of the widening unemployment in the economy of 1934.

Beamore, Drogheda
15ᵗʰ June 1934

My dear Eva,

Yesterday I forgot to send for your Drogheda Independent, so that Sunday must pass before you read Austin Marry's oratory at Mornington!! Father has been sitting outside the door nearly every day since Sunday and yesterday and the day before walked over to the mangold fields. He was starting over there just now , after his dinner, but as the air is closer and warm, I induced him to sit down instead. I am glad that Kathleen is getting better.

The warm weather has brought out the crops so well that John has eight extra helpers at the mangolds. Sometime ago that used to be a job for boys and girls from ten years upwards, but it is now sorrowful to see full grown men coming to it. Of course it is greatly to their credit that they are willing – at anything. It is quite possible that in your first day at Bundoran you may not have noticed in the paper that Miss Eithne Pentony was beaten. In the first round of the Irish Ladies Golf Championship. If your feelings on that - account were lacerated, let us hope that they were healed later on, when reading of the triumphs of Miss Clarrie Tiernan of Baltray.

John was at the funeral of poor Tom McAuley R.I.P which was very largely attended. He thought it was no use going up to Laurence St. As the young men would be at school. I am glad that Jim managed his letter!

By the way, John saw Queen Alexandra in Drogheda that day – she evidently thinks she can do something while you and Mrs Arthur Moore are off the map!!

A very long time ago, Fr Dick when coming from Lough Derg broke the journey at Enniskillen and went to explore the district. Then the time that he and Joe were in Rosse's Point, they went somewhere to a hotel kept by a Protestant in either Leitrim or Sligo (would it be Dromaheir?). There were three or four Jesuits staying there, one of them being Dr Dillon Kelly whose father was a doctor in Mullingar.

Best Regards,
Mary

Two more letters, both to Eva and from Hartlands occur. The first is undated, and the second seems likely to have been written in December 1939, as she refers to the 'hospital' being now opened. On December 8th 1939, Our Lady Of Lourdes Maternity Hospital was opened. The first baby delivered there was a boy, to a lady from Pearse Park, Drogheda, who was a patient of Doctor Paddy. Mother Mary Martin drove back from Dublin to be present.

Hartlands,Clonmellon,Co.Westmeath
Dec 1939?

My dear Eva,

Many thanks for your two letters. I am thankful to Fr.Willie Doyle for having found the beads, and intend to ask him to look after Ollie and to help Annie to get stronger. VV .Everyone is talking about the weather being so trying, so it is a pity that Paddy won't go away from it, all now that the hospital has been opened. I do hope that Vin Gogarty may get better. After Queen Alexandra, I shall be so glad if this improvement keeps on.

Bawn in pink and Mary in white looked very well last night going to Ballymacad? Dance. As usual it was held in Sylvan Park. Thanks in anticipation for '70 years young'. I am putting together a present for you, which I do not intend to send you till after the shouting and the tumult? Dies after Christmas and you have time to sit down and read it. Some time ago I bought the Christmas number of Country Life, which had the first chapter of our article on Badminton House, Gloucester. I then ordered the number with chapter 2 and hope to send them on to you. The dower house of the family, Troy House, Llangollock was sold in pre war times to May's nuns who have set up a monastery there.

By the way, is Mrs Prehy of Greenhills, whose death is announced in last week's Drogheda Independent, a sister of the late Drummer Kenny V.C. This year, Fr. Tallon reminds the Clonmellon Christmas turkey market which had lapsed some years ago. People were agreeably surprised that more than100 birds in and sold. It is a great pleasure to read in the Daily Independent, then tributes paid by the late Mr Ryan to his medical Man Dr John McNamara of Kensington.....

Hartlands, Clonmellon, Co.Westmeath.
3rd April 1940

My Dear Eva,

By this time I hope that you have rested from your holiday makers and are meditating a trip to either the Marine or to Salthill!! 'The Ladies' came home this morning from the hockey dance in great humour as everything had turned out well D.G. There were two hundred people present with men in the majority. The committee bought the ham, but milk, cakes etc were brought by individual members.

This week's Universe announces the death in Rome of Miss Hayden. She was a sister to Mrs Anthony Scott and kept a pension. A Scott's second daughter Josephine lived with her and married an Italian, named Paroli, who was gentilnomo to the later Card, O'Donnell and now to Card Mc Rory.

Mr Taylour was the old man who left his money to Jemmie Wilson and his farm at Gigginstown to Miss Wilson. He left nothing to his cousins, the Parrs. He was not the Johnnie Taylour whose place comes to Castlepollard-Mullingar Road and who bred 'Drinmore' and Drintyre and who was a contemporary of Father attending fairs.

I am sorry to see of the Archdeacon's death RIP. Today a letter comes from Marie McCullen Los Angeles with an Easter Card of great brilliancy. She broadcasted over the radio in an Irish Hour on St.Patrick's Day,

With best regards to all, I remain, Mary

Both of these letters refer to Fr.Willie Doyle, a Jesuit Priest Chaplain, in the British Army who was killed in the 1914-1918 War, and was revered as a saintly man. Mary often prayed to him for assistance in finding objects, or granting supernatural favours. Saint Jude is the patron saint of impossible cases. In this same bundle of letters of late 1930's, appears a list of book titles, which look like a recommended selection by Mary. It gives some indication of the wide spread of material that she managed to encompass.

- *Potterism by Rose Macauley. Published by Collins 2/6*

- *Sheila Kaye-Smith writes about the South of England. Cassells published all her books and 'Johanna Godden' by her, deals with the life of a girl left an orphan with a younger sister, how she runs her farm on Romney Marsh and the misfortune that befalls her.*

- *'Little England' is the study of a farming parish outside Hastings during the war.*

- *'The End of the House of Alard' is the tale of the post-war break up of a Sussex County family.*

- *Stephen Leacork, publisher John Lane, The Adventures of the Idle Rich etc.*

- *Barry O'Brien's Life of Parnell and Life of Lord Russell of Killowen were both published in Nelson's shilling series in pre-war times. They would probably be more now.*

- *Connolly, born in New England state of Irish Catholics fishing stock. Seems to have served in the U.S.A Navy. Nelson's published two books of his short stories 'Running Free'.*

- *J.Boyle O'Reilly (1846-91) born at Dowth, near Slane wrote 'Moondyne' published by Geo. Routlegde. His Life by Jas. Jeffrey Roche is worth reading, if it can be got in any public library. Some of his poems are fine.*

The decade also brought great sadness, with the drowning of Paddy in the small lake at Hartlands, when ice broke under him, in February 1932, and the death of Pat the Boss in 1938, aged 86 years. Two years earlier a new Patrick arrived to Johanna and Anthony in Kilnew, and as War was declared between England and Germany in Sept. 1939,

John in Beamore caused some surprise by getting married to Dolly Dolan in St.Peter's Church, Drogheda. He was aged 49 at the time, and his bride the eleventh child of thirteen born to a former Mayor of Drogheda, John Dolan, and his wife MaryJane McQuillan. Mr Dolan was a native of Termonfechin.

The Irish Press

The attached cutting appeared in our issue of................ *September 22* 193.9

McCULLEN-DOLAN—The wedding took place in St. Peter's Church, Drogheda, of Mr. J. McCullen, son of the late Mr. Patrick and Mrs. McCullen, Beamore, Drogheda; and Miss Dolly Dolan, daughter of the late Mr. and Mrs. John Dolan, Brookville, Drogheda. The ceremony was performed by Right Rev. Mgr. McCullen, P.P., V.G., Ceananus Mór (brother of the bridegroom), assisted by Right Rev. Mgr. O'Callaghan, P.P., V.G., St. Peter's, Drogheda; Very Rev. Nulty, P.P., V.F., St. Mary's, do., and Rev. M. Rogers, C.C., St. Peter's. The bridesmaid was Miss Anna Dolan, sister of the bride, and Mr. J. Lynch, cousin of the bridegroom, was best man.

There is always some item of interest to you in "THE IRISH PRESS"

Marriage Notice of John and Dolly in the Irish Press 1939.

A selection of the McCullen Patricks....

The altar boys, John with Pat, in Beamore.

'The Boss'

Pat of Mile House with Mary Keenan

Paddy from Hartlands

Dr.Paddy

Frances Ball with Paddy (Kilnew)

CHAPTER 9: 1940 - 1945

WARTIME

This a short six year space, but fraught with the fear of war and invasion, and gradually severe limitations on travel. When John married in 1939, Mary was invited by Sissy to come and live in Hartlands with Joe and herself, whose household was starting to diminish with the impending marriage of both Nancy and Bawn. There is an unusual generosity attached to both actions. Mary was now fifty-seven years of age, and had lived in Beamore for most of that time, apart from the few years spent in Navan at boarding school.

In some sense, she covered her retreat with caution, in that 'Auntie Mary's Room' remained her space in Beamore, whenever she wished to return, and continued to hold her 'things' until John himself died in 1967. Mary Collins confirmed to me in latter years that the invitation to come to Hartlands came from Sissy's generous nature. Perhaps because of being exiled in Clonmellon or due to travel restrictions, more and longer, letters get written!! There are twenty five missives during the six years almost all from Hartlands, mostly to Eva, but also to Oliver, Jim and Mary, in Laurence Street.

Hartlands

Since she was always very conscious of equal treatment for her nieces and nephews, all nineteen of them, it is very likely that many other letters were sent, but have not survived. In order to understand fully the pervading atmosphere of the time, the Dunkirk evacuation happened in 1940, Dublin, Julianstown, Colpe and Duleek were bombed between May and December of 1940, and refugees were arriving in Ireland and England, Europe and Northern Ireland. Foods and fuel were rationed and continued to become scarcer as the war progressed.

The Meath Chronicle announced in January 1942 that the paper size would be limited to four pages, because of a shortage of newsprint, but May wrote more and longer letters!

The first of these is to Oliver, who was then a boarder in Clongoweswood College, and the second to his mother, Eva.

Hartlands, Clonmellon, Co.Westmeath
17th Feb 1940

My dear Ollie,

By this time you have probably accustomed yourself to grappling with the chilblains, early rising , Lent and other things which make the after Christmas term the hardest of the year.

Your friend, Jack Heeney, who is such a good shot and who has been for some years in the Parochial House, Kells was married after Christmas to a girl from Kells. The elder Miss Farrell from Milltown joined the W.A.T. and has gone to the training camp at Newhaven Sussex.

Your mother tells me that you intend speaking about aristocracy. Well on that point , Ireland is unlike most places. Most of the people who claimed that title are descended from what corresponded to the Black & Tans in 1650 or 1690?, while Dean Swift said in 1710 that the Coalporters and labourers of Dublin were largely drawn from the old Catholic gentry. At the present time it may be said that while an aristocracy usually provides people able to carry a policy as capable administrators, but the originating forces as often as not may come 'from an outsider'. Whether diplomacy which apart from a few exceptions is still largely administered in the British empire by people who may not be wealthy but who might be described as 'gentle folk' is more successful when managed thus than in the American fashion where the Ambassadors are usually very wealthy men who have subscribed to the funds of one party and the lesser employers are usually people who have worked for a political party is a matter for discussion. Tom is farming very energetically, almost all the ploughing is done, but the seed is not put in yet. Joined by the others in every good wish, I remain,

Your loving Aunt Mary.

P.S Poor archdeacon Grimes is now a real invalid with two nurses minding him.

Hartlands, Clonmellon
20th Feb 1940

My Dear Eva,

Many thanks for the Irish Times and the Medical . After getting your letter, I wrote a few suggestions to Ollie, which I hope were useful. The Drogheda Ladies have certainly been in the news lately. Here we had hardly recovered from the news of the wedding of Miss Elizabeth Blanche Brannigan (the Blanche was the real flattener!) when the Sunday Independent pictures of Mrs F. H Boland (Miss Shiel Kelly, I presume) hit in the eye! The wedding of Mr and Mrs Val Reddin is just the sort of thing that would lead Lily May to give her social and genealogical knowledge to the world.

I am very sorry that I forgot to thank them in Ashbrook Terrace for the Welsh book. About the time it came I had to go twice to the Kells dentist, between making the appointment getting in etc, I completely forgot to thank them for the book. However, I mean to do so now. Strange to say , I have long taken great interest in Wales and was very glad to see so much of it when Annie and myself went to Hereford as we left the main L.M and S line one way and came back another.

Have you been down to see Dick ? I hope that he is alright now. It must be a great comfort to you that Mary is staying on. Tomorrow the family mean to take a break in their Lenten observances by going to the Ballymacad point to point meeting in Crossakiel. Part of the course is over Mc Namara land at Dogstown.

If the day comes fine it would be pleasant but otherwise it would be uncomfortable as I think Crossakiel is the highest point between Loughcrew hills and the sea. This morning when we were down at Mass, Fr. Fallons housekeeper came to tell Sissy of the arrival in Tom Lyons. Young Mr Farrell of Milltown, who had been training at Portsmouth, to go on an air craft carrier had been due for leave at Christmas. However it had been postponed week after week, till at last he came home this morning.

How is Mother Martin doing for recruits? What do her patients think of the hospital ? Poor Janie Carroll ! she never spared herself doing all she could for her family. Some Drogheda hockey players are coming to Kells on Thursday to play the locals which includes Bawn. When next we meet there are some things like the marriage of Mr.Conlan, Dunderry House, to Miss O'Reilly, Balbriggan and also the Cole Gilsenans, which we should talk over – no letter could fully cover these matters.Give my best wishes to Mrs.Behan. Another character who deserves a Chapter to himself is Mr Coffey formerly of the C.I.D Manchester. Be sure to start me on the subject when next we meet. Some one told me that Sir Wm Hickey now lives permanently in Headford and acts as steward. They expect to start the incubator this week with Rhode Island Reds.

Father Tallon has reconstructed the Chapman Rent Offices as a Parochial Hall, but has not yet furnished it. Sissy is President of the Apostolic League and intends to borrow some chairs and open it soon with a whist drive to raise funds, Hoping that you all are in good form,

I remain, Yours affectionately, Mary

Here and there in these letters, there is evidence of journeys to Drogheda, and other exotic places, and even to the west of Ireland to purchase cattle or sheep. This was accomplished by saving petrol coupons, sharing supplies, and the Doctor also had a 'cache' of petrol hidden in Beamore, in one of the old pits used for Brewer's grain storage. A phrase in letter 3 – 'The Salmon People' is like an escapee from a Yeats poem, but in fact applies to the residents of the Salmon House – James, Annie and their three young ladies, Nancy Oonagh and Maura, who would all have been teenagers in 1940. This letter is dated by the activities of the Drogheda Hockey Team.

Hartlands,Clonmellon,Kells,Co.Meath

My dear Eva,   *Tues 24th April*

Some time ago I gave any old nightdresses etc that I had to a neighbour who needed them badly. I hope that Mary may do well in the competitions. So the wish of the Maynooth students is being realised, and they are losing (!).

Dr Dalton gave his first confirmations in Clonmellon yesterday. The neighbouring clergy from Kells, Athboy, Delvin and Oldcastle come in the church, and at the dinner afterwards. In the interval Dick came here. He mentioned that he has been thinking of opening a school at Rosmeen? where Kells parish borders Oristown, and where some land has been divided. He has his eye on a disused Protestant Church in the parish of Carlanstown which he hopes to buy and to take down and to put up again in Rosmeen.

About three years ago, a Dr McBride from the six counties bought where Henry Dyas used to live. About Easter it was put up for sale. The bidders include some other people from the six counties who went to something under £6000 but it was withdrawn as it had not reached the reserve. Most of the Clonmellon people are lonely after Fr Scully. He said that his new parish Castletown, has two churches – one at Castletown, the other at Fletcherstown and a population of eight hundreds. It is nine miles from Kells from Navan and from Ardee. This is so truly rural that it has no village! So the young Fransicans are to be camped at Killiney instead of at Lowther Lodge.

Best Regards, Mary

Hartlands, Clonmellon
Mon 13th June

My dear Eva,

Thanks very much for your letter. Dr.Bowen would get scornful to hear that I sometimes commend your problems to St.Jude without forgetting Fr.W Doyle!! As to the enclosed you feel that it is so typical that no one else could have written it, the contract at second, third or fourth hand with the Admiralty, and the Marlborough family through the Treglas Hotel and her nieces give her such satisfaction and the present and ex M.F.H's of the Galway Blazers on this side of the Irish Sea!!

I had intended to send some books to you and to Ashbrook Terrace but they have not yet come, but I hope to send them soon. I have also a letter from Lissie White and one from Los Angeles but it is better to keep them till some time in January when the ;shouting and the tumult' may have died down somewhat. Meantime with best wishes to the whole of you,
I remain,
Mary

Hartlands,Clonmellon,

My dear Eva,

Here are some letters which came lately. On Monday Joe went with Fr.Tallon to Creakenstown, Bawn and Mary went with Balls. They encountered Jim and P. Austin taking a great interest in everything. Fr. Tallon came back with Joe and spent the rest of the evening talking about the Saturdays and Sundays he used to spend in Cunninghams of Beamore. Last week Joe and Tom went to Athenry and met most of Co.Meath bound for either Athenry or Ennis. They bought twenty five cattle.

Some years ago people used to talk about Mr Ledoux turning catholic, but it does not seem to have happened. Today I heard about the poor Peggy Kavanagh has been operated on for her appendix. I hope that she may get stronger. Mary spends a great deal of time out of doors and is very busy planning an herbaceous border.

I hope that Dick's neck has got better since you wrote last. A fortnight ago the Drogheda hockey team came to Kells to play the local one – which included Bawn and Mary. Next Thursday the return match is to be played in Drogheda. The Salmon people have promised to come here on St.Patrick's Day, With best wishes to you all,

I remain, Yours,
Mary

Hartlands, Clonmellon, Co.Westmeath.
1940

My Dear Eva,

I hope that you have been able to replace Mary by this. On Tuesday we went to Salmon and found Jas like a good Fingallian doing Balbriggan sale and Miss Tolan's funeral. Annie was in better form than I expected considering what the illness of her Uncle means to her.

The Balbriggan Rev. Mother has a sister staying in the convent. She is a Miss Campbell, who lived in France till last August. She teaches Una's class handicrafts amongst other subjects and Una showed us – a belt that she had made from Miss Campbell's teaching. It was raining very heavily when we drove home but that did not damp the ardour of the County Meathians as everywhere on the roads people were going to dances in Duleek, Kentstown and other places. Dr Hanley of Oldcastle is a great friend of Commissioner Bartley's and the Commissioner has just appointed his nephew Dr Cox from Roscommon as locum in Clonmellon.

The enclosed cuttings from the Irish Catholic. Mr Gilsenan was in the Customs. In Drogheda, between Mr McLoughlin , father of the Shannon Scheme man And Mr O'Leary. Mrs G's name was Cole and their eldest son, John Cole Gilsenan was a boarder in Loreto Navan when I was there. He was unusually good at the violin and passed some high grade exams though he was so young.

Afterwards the Drogheda Independent had an account of his death in a religious house in Wales, probably the Capuchin one, where he had been a student. Both his father and mother were very musical and I saw the published copy of a singing waltz ' Gage d'amour' ? of which one wrote the words and the other the music.

How are Jim and Mary getting on ? Poor Jo in Kilnew must be very run down between the care of Paddy and the lack of a maid.

Thanks for the letter from Miss Daly. It is fit to rank with a composition of Mozarts, which Bawn is teaching Miss B.Farrell and which the BBC orchestra play under the title of 'In an eighteenth century drawing room.'

How is your patient ? If Kingstown or Salthill are closed to him, perhaps he might try Clogherhead for a change. Mary has put on seven pounds weight since she left Castlebar. Everyone is in good form, thank God. Hoping that you may soon get a maid and with best regards to all,

I remain,
Yours affectionately, Mary

Sunday

Mr Mohan came here and put up the wardrobes, which has received general admiration. I am glad that Mary got through her part. Jim must be relieved that the rehearsals are over. When does Dick get home? My cold seems to have very nearly gone away, Thank God, but perhaps it would be just as well for me not to do any travelling before Christmas. However, Paddy in Kilnew may regret the departure of the builders, it must be a great relief to his parents. Some time ago, the Guards in Clonmellon got notice that their barracks would be closed. Fr. Tallon and some others signed a paper in favour of its continuance so last week Joe heard that it is to be kept open and with an additional 5800 acres added to it from the Delvin area.

Thanks for the numbers of the Irish Times. Is the Miss Catherine Eleanor Pentony whose engagement is announced, the great golfer? The '70 years young' is a book worth talking over. It is a curious coincidence that one of the Irish Times has a review of a book by Sir Alex Godley, a native of either Cavan or Leitrim. He gets enthusiastic about some of the beauties to be seen in Dublin about 1886 including the Duchess of Leinster, Constance Gore Booth, Maud Gonne, Prescilla Armitage Moore? (now Countess Annesley?) and the Lambarts of Beauparc.

Monday

It is disgusting to find that owing to the Herald Boot fund, Iolanthe etc, that the Daily Independent gives only one picture of Les Cloches, though last it gets first place.

Tom is in bed today with a cold – everyone else seems in good form.

Best regards to all,
Mary

Tom (Thos) at a later date!

Hartlands, Clonmellon

My dear Eva,   *25th April 1940*

Many thanks for your letter – I have written to Dick enclosing some local picture postcards. I hope that you are not feeling tired after the winter and that the visit from Mr Moore, Galway, consoled you somewhat for the absence of Frances Byrne. Just now we are rather short of petrol, as the car has been to Salmon, to Oldcastle Fair and to Dublin during the months. Sissy, the girls and myself were in Salmon, and I was glad that Annie seemed in such good form. On that account, it may be some time before I get to Drogheda. Whenever you see Mona Larkin tell her to present my homage to Queen Alexandra.

The late Anthony Scott, the architect and his wife were from Galway. He came to Drogheda about 1890 in charge of the restoration of Mellifont Abbey then being carried out by the Board of Works. He lived in Paradise Place which had been built and occupied by John Reilly, a Protestant Contractor who built Stedalt for Tunstall Moore.

Did you notice in this week's papers the bequest of a Miss Taaffe formerly of Ardmulchan, whose sister is a nun in the Irish Sisters of Charity? If you look up the 'Landed Gentry' you should see their pedigree. They owned Ardmulchan which they sold to the Duchess of Hamilton. She sold it for Fletcher of Rosshaugh, Aberdeen. About 1900 he started to build the present house. It is consoling to think that the Pope has such an opinion of the Westmeath people that he has made Fr. Coughlan from Castelpollard his vicar in the British Army. Between that and Admiral Plunkett from Dunsany guarding the Nore district, the British Empire should come through all its dangers.

I was sorry to read of Miss Arnolds death. Although the papers have so much about the half million which the Richmond Hospital authorities are getting from the Sweep money , there is no mention of Vincent's or the Mater getting anything. When next you see Eileen Rooney, give her my best wishes. Fr. Richard came here on Monday and spent most of his time talking about the Kells Convent and Orphanage.

Did I tell you before that the horticultural instructor comes here twice to advise Mary about a flower border, a strawberry bed etc? He spent ten years in Cavan before coming to Meath and seems to be a native of Donegal. He must intend to dig himself into County Meath as he is anxious to buy a piece of land and build a house – about Kells – his present rent is £1.0.0 a week .

Since Mary began gardening not only the stars in their courses but the hens have fought against her. Hens are usually much more stupid than ducks, but a few of them have a perverted intelligence which enables them if they cannot surmount the obstacle of wire netting to burrow underneath.

On our way to Salmon we took in Dublin and going by Athboy and Trim. The road is very interesting, passing by Phyllis Alley's poultry farm, different farms of Parr's, Cliftons Lodge and afterwards Trim, Clonee, Blanchardstown, Mulhuddhart and into Dublin by Castleknock and Phoenix Park. Joined by all in best wishes to the whole of you,

I remain,

Yours affectionately, Mary

In the following letter, there is the first evidence of Mary moving to live in Bettystown for the summer months, in that the origin of the letter is Lisheen, Bettystown, and she also mentions renting a Bayview house for August and September.

> Lisheen, Bettystown, Co.Meath
> 5th June 1940

My dear Eva,

Could you get in touch with Mrs N.J Synott, Furness, Naas through Delaneys of Woodlawn or any of Mrs P.Austin's people. Molly McDermott who knew her and also some relative Miss Neterville who lived in Biarritz once described Mrs S to me as typically Irish very generous in contradistinction. I suppose to the distilled parsimony of the old French families.

As both Mrs Rowntree's house had been let from August, I have taken No 7 Bayview for August and Sept from Mrs Lyons, Lismaura. This is the most northerly of that terrace and is one of two old ones, two stories and with five bedrooms.

Hoping to have plenty of your company during the season and with best regards to all,

M.

As the year progressed, there are some positive news, amidst all the reports of war, rationing, shortages and disruption. On 7th August, there was a new arrival in Beamore, a first son to John and Dolly, when Patrick arrived. Justice Goff announced at Slane Court that: *'In view of the paraffin shortage, he would not grant dance licences, in country districts, later than 12 midnight, except to the gaelic league!'*

As a result, he granted the licence to Stackallen branch of the Gaelic League for a ceilidhe until 12.30am.

> Hartlands, Clonmellon, Co.Westmeath
> Monday

My dear Mary,

Many thanks for your letter. We are always very glad to hear from you since Christmas I wrote to your aunt in Hereford and put in the two letters from Jim and yourself as she would like to read them. Mary here would also like if you wrote to her sometimes.

I am sorry that your cat has died. Just now we are looking for a terrier to help the cats kill some of the rats that the extra corn has brought about the place. The Drogheda Independent gave a very good report of the Presentation concert. On St.Stephen's Day two small wren boys came round. Later on we had six bigger boys painted and dressed up as mummers.

Last evening the others went to see one of your cousins – Charlie Fagan. They met some of your other cousins including the Dardises and Dr.Mary Fagan. Dr.Mary does her medical work and also buys and sells the cattle for the farm which she got from her uncle, the late Mr. Hope. The mill is now here threshing the oats.

Thank Jim for his nice letter to me and tell him that I hope to write to him later on, Again thanking you and wishing you a happy new year,

I remain, Your fond aunt, Mary

Hartlands, Clonmellon
7th Feb 1941

My dear Jim ,

Many thanks for the nice letter which you sent me at Christmas. Now that the snow has gone, they are busy breaking up the land, so I suppose that you will soon tackle your garden. Did you ever grow leeks? Just now we are using some that were grown last year. We have also carrots and parsnips.

Dr. Cox of Clonmellon has bought a racing bike for doing his calls. Mrs O'Reilly , who teaches the girls in Clonmellon lives a mile away and could not come in during the snow. As the boys teacher lives in the village, the boys who live near by did not escape school as their sisters. In some places the snow was ten foot deep. It went up to the roof of the ploughman's house, blocking up door and windows so that Jemmie Reilly could not get out from Sunday till Thursday. The roads about Oldcastle were blocked so nothing could get in that way, then the railway got blocked, the electricity got blocked, there was no lamp oil, so the people used candles. The first day letters were delivered would remind you of Christmas as such bundles came – one person got 29. Hoping that your garden will do well this season and with best wishes to the others,
I remain, Your fond aunt,
Mary

PS. Please give the enclosed letter to your mamma.

In early 1941, Nancy from Hartlands, and her husband, Jim Ball of Boherard, had a son, Paddy, and Mary refers to this event at the start of her letters to Eva, on 13th February and 7th March. She also flags the wedding of Bawn and Desmond Drew, on 23rd April.

Paddy, Mary and Frances Ball

Hartlands, Clonmellon, Co.Westmeath
7th March 1941

Dear Eva,

Many thanks for your letter. Now that Nancy is getting better we all feel relieved, as yet she is up for a short time every day. I hope she may not take cold coming home. Bawn went to Dublin yesterday by the G.N.R. Desmond was to join her at Drogheda and she stayed last night at Clondalkin. Last week she and Mary went to see Nancy and then went to the films ' You will remember' in the Regal Rooms.

The Letters of Aunt Mary

Likes the pictures of Stephen Foster 'way down upon the Swanee River' and Victor Herbert, Sam Lever's grandson, it treats of a realman Tomas Barrett who was born of Irish parents in Liverpool used to play a piano in a pub, when a child, afterwards went to Manchester where he became organist in the Jesuit Church, wrote a number of musical comedies under the name of Leslie Stuart and also coon songs for Eugene Stattons etc. This comedes?, then Silver Slipper, 'Floradene' were very popular. According to Bawn, as the script was composed by English people and 'Leslie Stuart' played by an Englishman, they did not get under the skin of the part and represent let us say, what the son of Duleek Gate parents brought up in the 1870's working at the Liverpool ends of the Drogheda boats would be. It would be better to have an Irishman contemporary of his own, write it and an Abbey actor to take the part.

So you are again suffering from being uplifted. Frank Sheridan's mother was a Janie Black- she used to be a dairymaid in Cairnes'. The late Mrs Rooney once said 'Frank is Gardhara like his father, but Jemmie is just like his mother. Jemmie is a printer in the Drogheda Independent and lives in StMary's villas .

I hope that Mary has shaken off her illness. Tell Jim that I look up for his name every Sunday in the 'Sunday Independent'. Your Beauparc neighbours have been very fortunate. Bawn's wedding will probably be on the 23rd April. Her dress and Mary's are made and home here already. Hoping that Dick may soon have fine weather and with best wishes for all,

I remain,
Yours, Mary

Hartlands, Clonmellon
18th March 1941

My dear Eva,

Nancy is in good form, though as yet she is not up all the day, the baby (note - Paddy Ball) is very well. D.G. Your cousin Connie Gilsenan of Bobsville is engaged to John Keelaghan of Moygrehan. His father is a Westmeath man who married into Murphy's of Moygrehan. One of Mrs K's sister was a nun in Kells and another at Mount Sackville, I think Sheila K, the only daughter married one of the Athboy Newmans and lives in Clifton Lodge, which the Land Commission gave him instead of some land of Rotherhams which they divided. The other Miss Gilsenan, Rita is a nurse in the Elphis ?

Enclosed is Dick's letter, you will learn from it that in this degenerate age Fr. Pentony holds high the standard of prunes and prisms.So Lourdes hospital is coming into the news with its first professions that have taken place and its first ball that is to take place! For many years Michael Garry, the herd in Hilltown, has been writing poetry and has published one volume.

Now Michael McEvoy, a grand nephew of Jim Farrelly's got highly commended by Radio Eireann for his poem on a rainy day. This bard is about twelve years of age. He is now writing another poem. Miss Wilson is finding it hard to book a berth to Jamaica to be married to Johnnie Farrell. It is a pity to see of the death of McDonnell of Kilsharvan, Mrs Hunt's nephew.

Now that Walter Guinness is leader of the House of Lords Meath people can recall with pride that Miss Magan of Killyon in 1902 returned a letter received from Lord Iveagh endorsed with ' Miss Magan does not correspond with business people'. Hoping that Mary is in good form and with best wishes to the others,

I remain, Mary

Ps. Remember me to Mrs Behan

The next letter is to the prisoner in Clongoweswood College, where there is a valuable herd of cattle under threat from Foot and Mouth Disease.

2nd April 1941

My dear Ollie,

Many thanks for your letter. The two ladies have the wedding clothes made at home, the cake has been made, so just now there is a lull before the last bustle. The stand still order made by the Dept. Over all Co.Meath when foot and mouth broke out at Dunboyne, was not modified till last week when this amongst other districts was declared open as all the cattle had been brought here from Diamor, when the snow started in January, your Uncle Joe was glad to send some back. The wheat and oats grown here is now coming up D.G. and they are now sowing barley. A local tractor owner, whose machine often works through the night till 4 or 5am and cannot have all his contracts finished till middle of May.

The account of the precautions for your herd is very interesting and every one was sorry for Mr Donoghue of Cloughran whose entire herd was destroyed. At a time when most people have less to spend there is one exception to the rule in this parish. An old catholic family named O'Reilly have owned Ballinlough Castle for hundreds of years. In the 18th century Mr O'R married a Miss Nugent. Later on his family took the name of Nugent and became Baronets. In the 19th century Sir Chas. Nugent let the castle and and land and started training horses in England. He trained three Grand National winners. His grandson succeeded him about 6 Years ago. About two years ago now the young man's stepfather died leaving a large fortune to his wife, Sir Hugh's mother.

When war broke out Sir H shifted horses to Ballinough and started Cramptons, The Dublin builders to restore the castle. That job took 35 men and is said to have cost £14000 but is now complete with electricity. The indoor staff is seven and there are any number of grooms etc. outside. Sir H is a great Nationalist joined the Irish Army as a private and is now an officer at the Curragh.

To cope with the petrol shortage Dr Cox of Clonmellon bought a bicycle and a horse. He fell off the horse on Sunday and broke his collar bone. The Ardcath man whose foot and mouth case was reported on Sunday, was a person who used to have a few cattle grazing along the road, so the beast is believed to have been infected by a passing lorry. Ireland is believed to have been free from f&m from 1884 till 1912. In 1912 a case was reported at Ballysax Curragh a little later, some cases were reported at Swords, and a little later at Maher's of Clinstown, Stamullen. Nothing could be moved within an area of 15 miles. Salmon was inside the area of Swords and afterwards of Clinstown. So that it was blocked for a long time. Some heifers calved and could not be shifted so they had to churn every day. The butter could be stored, but even after they had given buttermilk to the work people, to calves and pigs, there was still some which any one coming for a night would carry away. Hoping to see you all at Easter,

Your fond aunt,

Mary

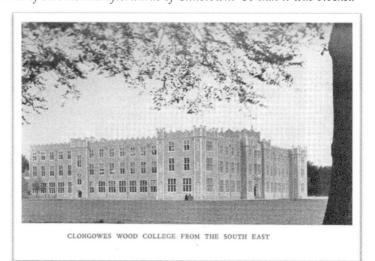

CLONGOWES WOOD COLLEGE FROM THE SOUTH EAST

Hartlands, Clonmellon, Co.Westmeath.
My Dear Eva,   *April 1941*

Many thanks for your letter and kindly offer of coupons. Please do not buy anything for me but add anything you have to spare to the Nursing Fund. Now that your jumble sale is over it is a relief to know that you can say 'My head is bloody , but unbowed'.

So poor Sister A Bobbett in Trim is dead. Lately the death was announced of a Mrs O'Keeffe in Westmeath. She was Miss Cullen of Tara, her mother was a sister of the later Pat Gargan of Newtown, and aunt of the present Gargans. Mr O'K's family had been corn merchants in Wexford. Soldiers are now quartered in Nicholson's of Balrath and also in Oldcastle. So you also are losing a niece ! Imagine three leaving home in such a short time. Bawn expects to go after Easter, as she has a visitor every Thursday and every Sunday, we hear quite a lot of Drogheda news. One item is that Miss Agnes McArdle is having a party in the Baltray hotel.

I hope that P.Austin jun is doing well. The Lord Lothian who died was the great grandson of a Miss Lambert of Beauparc who married Earl Talbot who afterwards was the Ultra-Orange Lord Lieutenant in Ireland in 1820's. Her daughter, Lady Cecil T became Marchioness of Lothian. The Marquis died young. His widow became a Catholic and all her family except her eldest son. Her second son Ld R.Kerr had two sons and three daughters. One son David was killed in the last war. His parents started 'St.David's' Ealing near London under the Sisters of Charity for wounded soldiers. The other son, Philip went into public life and became a Christian Scientist though how anyone who knew anything about politics could think that there are no such things as evil or suffering beats me! He became Marquis of L. on the death of his cousin. His sister, Lady Cecil Kerr has written some lives of well known Catholics.

Again thinking of you and with best wishes to all,

I remain, Mary

Hartlands, Clonmellon
30th May 1941

My dear Ollie,

Many thanks for your letter. For a few days after the wedding (note – Bawn & Des Drew 23.4.41) , everyone was busy getting things back to their old places. At the time a very strong east wind was blowing here, so we were quite surprised that Bawn had got sunburned in Salthill and Achill!

Your comments on the 'inside' of the news – apparently in the 'Standard' is worth remembering. People about here are working 'on the land' or 'on the bog', while the more adventurous are running sugar into the six counties in exchange for tea and flour. The growth for the last three weeks has been wonderful D.G. Just now the men folk are busy shearing the sheep.

There is so much timber about Clonmellon that nearly all the people in the village used to buy a big tree at about £1 for fuel and cut it up in their spare time. This year most of them are supplementing that by working on the bogs about two miles away. One shop-keeper had so little coal that he took out his range and started cooking on the hearth. This smoked so much that he had to have the chimney rebuilt.

Joined by all in best regards and hoping you'll manage your exams.

I remain, Your loving aunt, Mary

There is a gap of almost six months before the next letter to Eva.

Hartlands, Clonmellon, Kells, Co.Meath
Thurs 9th Nov 1941

Dear Eva,

Many thanks for your letter and for Fr John Hanlon's card. Is he a son of the late J Hanlon who owned a pub beside the cattle market and who was married to one of the Maynes. I am sorry that you have had to cope with May's illness, particularly at such a time would Mrs McCann Murphy be available?

And now for congratulations you must be very glad now that Ollie's results are out that he has done so well, give him our good wishes. Thank God that Jim is so well and that Mary is so full of life. I hope that you enjoyed the visit to Maynooth. The weather here was bright yesterday. Tom Lyons stayed in the Parochial House here this week and cycled with Fr.Tallon to the coursing meeting at Killucan. He had a dog running for the Belsize Cup. How he fared I have not heard yet.

You must be greatly relieved that the sale-of-work is over. Foley has bought Radcliffes of Hurdlestown. He bought some cattle here. When he came in to tea, he remarked that Dr.McCullen had not sent him his bill. We were all too polite to suggest that he should write to the doctor for it. He said that Hartigans have sold Clowenstown to Capt. Cliff Nicholson for £28,000. Nicholson farms 1000 acres , mostly in East Yorkshire. Foley has sold him great numbers of cattle at a place called Scunthorpe.

Have you heard that Hugh Brophy is engaged to be married to a Miss Timoney (or Timlin) or some name like that). She is from Ballina and has a sister married to a clerk in the Hibernian Bank Trim. Even more extra ordinary than the price of Fr Marry's dog is a case which Fagans mentioned to us lately. A neighbour of theirs owned a greyhound which had a litter of pups. Before they were a week old and before their eyes were opened she had sold them all for £300. Talk about buying a pig in a poke, but paying £50 or £60 for a blind pup seems to run it close. Sir W. Hickie has left Headfort and the Dowager Marchioness is staying in the Shelbourne so Molly McCann will have to look out for other Bridge partners.

If you want some new place which is not too far away, Would you try Brittas Bay, Co.Wicklow ? For a few years before the War, the Irish Times clientele seemed to go to it – ask Rosita & Theresa about it. I heard them mention it.

This year the Clonmellon Altar Society bought the flowers for Holy Thursday in Headfort instead of going to Dublin. Besides lilies they had a wonderful selection of different sorts of single daffodils. When I was admiring to Nannie, she said that up to this, the Dowager Marchioness not only sent over flowers to Mullaghea Chapel, but dressed the altars there herself. Headfort is in Kells parish, but Mullaghea just besides Headfort, is the second chapel of Carnaross Parish. Fr Joe Nangle is the P.P. Poor Burmah R.I.P. His title was given to him by the Duleek Gates in 1885 or 86 when he joined the British Army and expected to be sent to Burmah, which was being annexed to the British Empire at the times. At the time of the last war he rejoined and told Father that he served under Capt. Hugh Cullen at one time. One of his sons who served in the Near East in the last war was styled 'Baghad' by his neighbours.

Have you heard that the Trim nuns have taken 'Brookside' from Mrs Cooney for the month of August. Although I disappointed you, you will have an opportunity of basking in the Italian Gardens, when you visit M.Gabriel Maher. A grandnephew of Fr M Farrelly Killucan expects to be ordained in Maynooth this summer. He is a Mr Daly from Collinstown and is not related to Sisters Bridget, Vincent, etc.

The account in the Drogheda Independent (Friday 28th April 1941) of the Kieran Lyons wedding makes no mention of clothes or of the hotel where the breakfast was held. They must think that these things have been overdone. How long has Miss Paine been living in Donacarney? Sometimes I wonder how Willie Cairnes's widow is getting on in England since the war broke out. Do Nano Reid's pictures sell well? With best wishes to all in your diminished family,

Your, Mary.

Brookside Cottage at Bettystown

Hartlands, Clonmellon, Co.Westmeath
My dear Eva,   *16th April 1942*

Congratulations from the Hartlands to Mary for her success in Dundalk! Mary came home last night from Dublin after Master Drew's baptism. Young Mr Whaley, whose invalid father owns Bloomsbury, was married recently in the vestry of Kells church by Rev R.J McC . The bride, Miss Barrett, lives in a labourer's cottage near Bloomsbury, and had been a maid in England. Mr McCabes son of the local blacksmith was best man. Although the groom used to preach communism in The Meath Chronicle he turned up with tails hat, frock-coat etc, and the bride wore a long beige gown.

Could you please let me know what would be the price per pound of any tea that you could get for me? I would also like to know what quality you could get as they would like to have plenty here to give to the men when making hay or harvesting. Our men folk are still busy sowing. Thank God the weather has been very dry lately.

Perhaps you may be interested in reading the names of the riders in the Master's Nomination Races at Creakenstown. Joe said it was the best value of all the races, as some of the candidates were big fat Dublin doctors. I notice that Miss F. Murray and Miss V. Dolan were successful at Dundalk.
Did you hear anything about an electrical cooker?

Best regards to all,
Mary

Hartlands, Clonmellon
25th April 1942

My dear Eva,

Many thanks for your letter. I am sorry to hear that K.Rooney has not done as well as you expected some time ago. Please keep the tea in Laurence St till I see further. If I could get enough of extra petrol, we would bring our own car loaded with stuff two or three times to Bettystown in April. If not we would hire a car with a trailer. From previous experience I know that between blankets, etc., our car would want to go at least twice, as we have no trailer.

If possible I will keep the Meath Chronicle which gives scope to Mat Reilly and the artists. Old Melia told Joe that he remembered when Mrs Reilly was married at the age of seventeen. Mat was born when she was eighteen and she lived to be eighty two. Our neighbour Mrs Chill, whose sister, Miss Nally was bombed out of North Strand last year, was being buried in Kilskyre at the same time as Mrs Reilly was being buried in Ballinlough, the out chapel of Kilskyre.

Tom saw your brother in Ballinlough, while Joe went to Kilskyre. Now while eggs are plentiful it would be well for you to buy and crock some. As if meal get tightened up, people may not keep so many hens. I am glad that you have bought the wheat. Is Eileen Rooney now in Portstewart ? I wonder if Bazzie Hughes from Kinnegad (Mother Peter) is still Rev. Mother there.

Michael Foley, the cattle dealer, told Joe that his wife had arranged to go into Lourdes Hospital sometime in May. He is from Bohermeen but had been languishing in the exile of Iona Road till he bought Hurdlestown from Radcliffs within the last two years. Hurdlestown is between Martry And Kells on the west side of the road . Both the road and the river Blackwater turn just there and you see Whaley's place Bloomsbury, on the far side of the river. His wife is a Finnegan from Navan, whose sister is married to Finnegan of Rahood, brother to the late Fr.John Finnegan. Peter Lynch of Oldcastle, nephew to Fr. T.L, the Stamullen chaplain went to work as a carpenter in Belfast a few weeks ago. He is now being transferred to work in a Canadian factory and you must ask me to tell you some day at full length why he went to Belfast first.

I forgot to say that Sweetman, the solicitor, used to live in Hurdlestown. The neighbours said that Mrs S. Got some money when her brother, La Touche died out in the East. At any rate, they bought Tandy's of Johnsbrook with about 30 acres from the herd, who had got it from the Land Commission. The herd's brother, Dr.Lynch of Sandymount is Fianna Fail Deputy for a Dublin area,

Best Wishes to all,

Mary

In April 1942, John Drew arrived and merits a mention, in letter dated Jun 7th of the same year. I arrived myself but gain no reference in the gossip columns! Perhaps by mid October 1942, another John in Beamore was old news

John Drew, with sister Margaret photographed by Mr.Cooney at Brookside

Margaret, with Nancy, Bawn & Pauline Drew

Hartlands, Clonmellon, Co.Westmeath
12th Oct 1942

My Dear Eva,

Since our last talk my time in Dublin was very busy. On Monday evening Sissy and myself spent a very pleasant time in Ashbrook Terrace talking over people and places in Meath and Westmeath with Rosita and Theresa. I was very glad to hear that Kathleen Rooney has got better. Theresa told us that of the seven weeks she had spent in Trim Mercy Convent, when Mother Evangilist was knocked up.

'Nanno' said that Mrs Lyons has set the big thatched cottage that the Murphy Clancy Jones household are leaving, to Vin Smith's son. It is near the bungalow that the Austins used to take, and was at first the farmhouse of the Fanning Family, before Capt Lyons bought the holding. Sissy went through it and says that the grates in the rooms etc are very good but the bank on the south side of the house would cut off the sunshine for the greater part of the day.

Nano also said that the Dublin Publican who was looking about Lisheen was Mr.Brady of Dorset St. Whose mother was Josie Carroll, an elder sister of Mrs Matties and Mrs Davy Sheridan. Mrs Grant, his aunt who lived with him and left him a good deal and he owns 'The Arch' in Henry Street. The previous owner, The late Mr Molloy was related to Mr Molloy of Clonmellon (known locally as Tkiep?)

Did you go to the Lord Castletown Ryan auction . Some of the prices are in today's paper. The enclosed is one of a number of views that Maria McC sent lately with a very nice letter. Her brother, Mattie, is in an officers training camp 250 miles away from them while Geo expects to be called up at any moment. This week's Meath Chronicle has a full account of the wedding of the authoress of 'From Bective Bridge'. Later on I hope to post it to you.

It is indeed comforting to know that her book has been published in Boston and that their inhabitants of the 'Hub of the Universe' now have a chance of knowing the simple minds and unworldly outlook prevailing along that stretch of the River Boyne. About sixty years ago young John Boyle O'Reilly, also in Boston, boasted the Slane Beauparc past in his lines;

> *'How I long for the dear old river*
> *Where I dreamed my youth away*
> *For the dreamer lives forever*
> *And the toiler dies in a day.'*

Hoping that you are now settled down to some really restful evenings and with best wishes to the rest of the family,

I remain, Yours,Mary

P.S Are any of your local ' ragmen' going to buy Nulty's of Newtown, Slane? Willie Taaffe used to have grass taken there for a great number of years. Please let me know if you hear anything about McKennas? And Gogarty's house. If any nuns wished to buy McK's , I would not butt in, but otherwise I might as well have it as anyone else. There is no need to acknowledge this, so all your energy can go ink your letters to Maisie Callan.

Hartlands, Clonmellon, Co.Westmeath
2nd November 1942

My dear Eva,

Many thanks for your letters, enclosure and Irish Times. I hope that by this time you have recovered from your stay in Dublin , and that Jim is feeling the benefit of his. Give him my best wishes. It is interesting to read of the activities of the Lourdes Committee, and even more interesting to read of the taste and discrimination of Mr D Martin. Used not the brothers Adams design some of the fittings for their houses that they built, as well as getting Chippendale to carry out some of their ideas in the larger pieces of furniture?

You were very kind to have asked in Bawn and Desmond for the night of the dance. Did you hear how Mrs Carbery Connolly looked and what she wore? I am really sorry to hear that Dr B is thinking of selling Castletown, because I do not like to see another family losing contacts with their lands, particularly when some of their people had owned it for so long. The natives round here seemed to have all the farms they want but shop keepers from Dublin and elsewhere have been buying land.Of course Carlanstown is not far from Cavan, which should have people with either their own money, or American money to invest. A good deal of the 11 months land about Kilskyre is let to Cavan men. That land went very high this year between £8 and £9 for grazing, but I have heard nothing about Tillage as yet.

Do you notice the advt. of Ivy House, Clonmellon, in last week's Drogheda paper? Mr Coffey, the ex-CID man, sold it in June 1941 for £750 to a returning Yank, a native of Co.Cavan, named Fitzsimons. Two months after afterwards Fitz got disgusted with it, and sold it to a Dublin vet who bought it to use if evacuation were ordered. He has sold it to Wilson, the auctioneer, who is selling it now. Coffey has gone to live about Bray, and posing as a retired doctor, told some other doctor how he had sold a farm for £7500 and that the buyer had resold for £10,000. The other doctor knew Cox, the Clonmellon man, and just mentioned the matter to him . Cox nearly had a fit.

Didn't I tell you that Vin Smith's son has taken from Mrs Lyons the big thatched house that the Murphy Clancy-Jones family have just left. It should be very comfortable in winter time but would be rather dark, with the high bank opposite. Another thing that I heard when at the sea, is that one of the Nicholls of Exchequer St is serving his time in Davis's and that he goes around with McCullochs. Not long ago Fr.Joe Nangle collapsed when attending a parishioner. Dr Lappin was also attending the same person. He turned his attention to Fr. Nangle said that he had either stone or appenditis.

When Fr N was brought to the Mater he was found to have both. Barnville operated on him at 9.30pm and he is said to be getting on well. Fr Scully's dramatic class performed ' Mountain Dew' and a farce last night. As the hall is rather small, there is to be another performance next Sunday, and a matinee for the children.

Capt Naper was buried a pouring wet day. The Marquis of Headfort, Lord Farnham. Sir Jas Nelson, Col Harman and Mr A Harmon wore top hats. Sir Hugh Nugent, who may have remembered that the O'Reilly's were in Ballinlough, before Plunketts or Napers were ever heard of, wore his uniform as a captain in the Irish army. Megville would be ideally situated for a curate's house and I hope that they may have a priest living in Bettystown soon.

Mrs Humphries has certainly beaten Cleopatra, Helen of Troy, Diane de Poitiers and everyone else that I have ever heard of to a frazzle. Imagine a person of her age conquering the new social worlds of royalty and the Automobile Club without either money or male relatives. Did you meet the Princes when you were visiting in Lisheen.

Joe bought an Allis Chalmers tractor last Wed from Reilly's of the North Quay. May God give him good fortune with it. Did you meet poor Maisie Callan this time ?Reading the accompanying paper you will see that the first branch of the Holy Childhood Society in Ireland was set up in Kells convent and that for many years a large part of its income came from a bullock, fed on Brady's lands. Both happenings are so typically Meath.

At one time I had a third volume of Dom Hunter Blair Which I meant to send you if it ever turns up. It is said that both Capt Naper and Lord Headfort were admirers of Rosie Boote, and that Naper then married Miss Trefusis who is a cousin of Headfort's. His grandfather and her grandmother were brother and sister, Thynnes, whose eldest brother was Marquis of Bath. The Trefusis family is of Celtic not Saxon or Norman origin. The old rhyme says; 'By Tre, Pal or Pe so would you know true Cornishmen?'That is names like Trelawney and Trefusis. Just now I cannot think of any Pals or Pens but look up some in Burkes Landed Gentry,

Best Regards, Mary

Hartlands, Clonmellon

5ᵗʰ Feb 1943

My dear Eva,

After leaving you we looked through all the probable houses at Bettystown and Laytown. Brookside is set already for Aug, Simcocks would not set Grove House and would not set St.Gabriel's for the season, while the one empty house of Mrs Creaser Smith's has only three bedrooms. Since then I wrote to Mrs.Lyons saying what extra furniture I wanted her to put into Overstrand if I took it. She has promised to put it in so we must hope for the best.

Of course it is a pity to miss the Italian Garden. If you got some Botticelli-like garments Nano Reid could have painted your family grouped about in the beautiful surroundings. Just think of the interest such a picture would arouse if it were hung in the R.H.A with the title ' A land where it is always afternoon'!

I hope that Mary is getting strong now. So are you losing your PP. What a change for Archdeacon Murphy being in St.Peter's from 187something to 1901, to be followed by Archdeacon Seagrave from 1901 to 1934,

Best Regards, Mary

Hartlands, Clonmellon, Kells, Co.Meath
9th November 1943

My dear Eva,

Yesterday Joe heard from Uncle Dick of Ollie's success. Give Ollie congratulations from us all.

Poor Mrs Savidge. I hope that the rest of her life may be free from trouble. You may remember that Dr Mary Fagan, Charlie's sister used to live with Ned Hope in Garlandstown and that he left her the farm. Another unmarried sister, Rose, lived with her till last year but got a house on the north side of Dublin and went to live there. This summer, Charlie sold some outlying land to Mr McCabe and Dr Mary has got married since to one of the McCabes to the surprise of everyone. By this time you should have recovered from the shock of losing Madam la Marquise, Frances Wafer Byrne. In June 1941, Mr Coffey, ex CID, Manchester and son of a former steward of Chapmans, sold ....

Hartlands, Clonmellon
21 November 1943

My dear Eva,

Many thanks for your letter and the enclosures. Mary's letter is so interesting that I am sending it on to Hereford. It is a great thing that she knocks so much interest and amusement out of her every day life. Joe was very glad to be able to oblige Paddy. Has he got a chauffeur yet ?

Thanks for the information about Jeanville. What good prices residential places like it and Farganstown made! Just now people are afraid to tackle a farm without a house on account of the cost and difficulty of building. Bradleys were lucky to get £3000 for their land. Within the last fortnight, the dowager Mrs Nicholson of Balrath sold a grazing farm of more than 150 Irish acres for £3000. Of course I don't know what sort the land was but Nicholsons would not have bothered to hold a bad farm till now, and farms in that district made from £10,000 to £ 15,000 during the last war. Just now the best buyers for that sort of farm are the people who own lands beside it already. Farms with houses are in great demand still. Both the auctioneers and the newspaper owners must be doing well, the weekly paper never had so many advts.

The Drogheda Independant has given your jumble sale a great puff. After you have finished with the Duleek Gate matrons at the jumble sale, which would be the modern version of St.Paul's. 'Thrice I have fought with wild beasts at Ephesus ' would you think of recuperating at the Royal Marine, Dun Laoighaire. Madame Marquise, will be busy flat hunting or immersed in Buswells. Baltray would have no charms for you, as the evergreen Daisy is not blooming in the Golf Hotel.

Where are the Roantrees going to live? Did you notice in Sat's Daily Independent the advt. of Mr Megahey, Sandycove, which stated that having sold the residence of St.Anne's Torca Hill, Dalkey, He is about to sell the furniture. That was Nurse McCarthy's. Is Mrs Glover remaining on in Drogheda? What would be the amount of a widows' and orphans allowance would she get ? Sometime in Dec I hope to send you £1 for her D.V. and if she stays on in Drogheda I hope to send you another later on. A fortnight ago, a poor lad from Clonmellon, about Tom's age was prayed for. Before the war, he had gone to work in Scotland, was conscripted after twelve months, landed in Italy on a Saturday and was killed the next Monday at Salerno R.I.P.

Some of Fr Scully's difficulties with the males of the Dramatic Society were caused by a triangular drama in real life. We will call his three most active members A, B&C. A and B both admire the same lady. C does not. A was away from Clonmellon for a few days. B arranged with C to hold a meeting of the class during his absence. They gave out all the male parts, keeping the two best for themselves and faced A with an accomplished fact when he came back! I don't know how the females have settled their problems. Paddy's treatment has worked wonders with Tom D.G. His face is 'all clear' now. Mr Mc Ivor's house, Paradise Place, was built and lived in by John Reilly, a Protestant builder, a contemporary of my grandfather's, who had been reared in the Drogheda Blue school. His last piece of work was Moore's of Stedalt.

You may remember that I told you that when 'the Hildegardes' grandfather, Ralph Smyth bought the estate of Newtown Termonfeckin, he got contracts for the building of a house. Reilly and my grandfather put in at almost the same figure, but an Englishman put in at £900 less, got the contract pulled down the old house and went smash.

After Reilly's time, the late Anthony Scott, the architect lived in it before McIvor bought it

24th November 1943

Mr Mc Cabe, the Somax man is a Presbyterian or Methodist from Belfast. After the Dowager Marchioness of Conyngham died, he bought the farm of Harlinstown from her executors and used to stay in the White Horse Hotel since that, he has bought a big place at Tribley, Kilmessan from Mr Cargill, a Protestant who used to breed horses.

This season I do not intend to go to Drogheda before Christmas – as the weather is so changeable. If Mary is giving any books or toys to the nuns be sure not to limit their discretion in giving them away. Remember the poor middle class! Mary here has been working hard at the Christmas gifts. Be <u>sure</u> that your Mary sends a personal note acknowledgement. I never saw anyone who <u>loves</u> getting letters as she does!

Mr Sherlock whose wife and family have lived so long at Robinstown, Kilskyre, is home now on pension from his Judgeship in Jamaica. Before going to Jamaica she had been in Malay. Are county people from Rahan, Offaly – used to be D.L's one of them was a Sergeant at Law. His mother was a Nugent of Ballinlough. His wife is a sister of Miss Cruice of St.Patrick's guild, a daughter of Sir Fr Cruice and Cousin of Mrs Farrell. Did you notice that the Irish Catholic has been boosting our local poetic talent lately – Mr Garry of Kilskyre one week, and the late M.Walsh another ?

Spectator has found that Drogheda has been first in the field to celebrate Balfe. It is a pity that young Coddington is missing. Do transport difficulties keep Sir R Dillon from the 'Gate' now,
Best Regards, Mary

P.S. Give best wishes to yours. Did you notice that since Capt. Lyons landed the deaths in India are going down ?

In November 1943, the Bishop Dr.Mulvaney died and eight farming families from Belmullet migrated to South Meath and Duleek.

Hartlands, Clonmellon,
Sat 8th Jan 1944

My dear Eva,

Thanks from all of us for your presents which reached us yesterday. Years ago MacMillan's was more than a name to me for three reasons – first the blue covered text books used for the Intermediate, then the 'Englishmen of Letters' series edition by John Morley, most of which used to be stocked in the Drogheda Library, and lastly the life of Canon Aniger?, which read in Nelson's series (the same as G.W.E Russell). When Aniger was an under graduate in Cambridge in the 1850's he used to buy books in McM's shop , and in a little while became the personal friends of the two brothers, visiting upstairs. After he had settled in London in the 1860's he kept up the friendship with the surviving brother who had moved to London and wrote some books which the firm published.

Monday
Charlie Fagan and some of his family were here yesterday. They said that Miss Ballesty, sister to the late C.M died unexpectedly. Her niece brought her up breakfast in bed. She talked as usual about things and asked if her niece meant to go out to hunt that day. When some one went up afterwards to take away the tray, she was found to have died. R.I.P.

One of C Fagan's sons is a student in All Hallows, and seems to have liked Fr Ballesty greatly. They were talking also of the P.J Smyths (Dillon). The Mr Quirk who is engaged to Miss Nicollson is nephew of the late P.W. Shaw of Mullingar, his mother having been a sister of the late P.W. For the last month, colds and flus of various strengths have been very general around here. On the 8th Dec about an equal number of both sexes were at a dance in Clonmellon. The next week, there was another dance, but most of the ladies had been laid low with colds and flu and the proportion was four males to every girl. The same proportion held good at a Protestant dance in Rathmolyon.

On Thursday Sissy went to Oldcastle intending to come back the next day. However as she found that her mother had not been well she stayed over. Some months ago I heard that amongst the people who had got infantile paralysis was a Mr. Flood, from Kilbeg, whose wife is a sister of Hugh Brophy's whose brother used to be CC in Trim. His death is announced now.

The threat of war still hung over the Country, and in July 1944, the tea ration of ¾ oz. per week was reduced to ½ ounce, because of low levels of reserve stocks in the country.

Hartlands, Clonmellon
Thursday 27th April 1944

My dear Eva,

Many thanks for your letter, I am glad that you are in such good form after the strain of all your visitors at Easter, you must have been very busy.On Monday I took Mc Donnell's motor and went to Dublin to see Anthony. Mary and Tom came with me. We got to Mount St. Crescent about 2 pm after a time the others went away but I stayed on. Then the others and the car came back and we left after 6pm. When I was there Joan came in and stayed till about 5 oclock when she left to catch her train. Anthony was in very good humour.

It is great that Dick did so well. Joe was glad to meet him the day he called to Laurence St as he has always had a great regard for him. Now that Mary has gone back, I must answer her letter. Now that the grass has started growing, Jim's bullock should do well. A few weeks ago Michael Foley, the cattle dealer, who sold Ivy House, between Hartlands and Clonmellon to a returned Yank, originally from Cavan for £750 or £800. In a few months when bombs fell on Dublin, the buyer sold it to a Dublin vet, who bought it for evacuation. When things got quiet, the vet sold it to Kevin Wilson, who advertised it for twelve months and has sold it at last to Mr Mulhall from Leix for £1100. Mr Mulhall's sister is married to Mr Collier, a brother of the Bishop of Ossory.

Have there ever seen so many places on the market just now ? Last week Joan wrote about the sale of Clatterstown, the price seems very high. I wonder if Jeanville has been sold. Can you remember from whom Mrs Roantree bought it ? I used to hear that the Tiernans were born there and that they branched out into Bro, Dowth and Rathkenny when they got into the Glasgow cattle trade, but they seem to have been declining before 1890 and don't know when they parted with it.

Are there any local billionaires thinking of buying Porter's or Markey's? The Meath Chronicle says that Peter McQuillan has sold his Navan shop to Mr Finnegan. I think that he is the publican bookie who used to stay in Bettystown, and whose wife is a Donnelly from Kinnegad, a sister to Mrs Ambrose Gilmartin, Mrs Roe and Mrs Corry. I hope that Mary has felt strong since she went back to Cabra. Fr. Scully has told us of his troubles in assigning to the members of the Clonmellon Dramatics Class, the different roles of Louis Dalton's play. 'The Money doesn't matter'. It is only fair to say that the males were just as hard to manage as the females. The Kells Operatic Society are learning 'The Gondoliers', the proceeds go to the Orphanage, while the Athboy Choral Society have produced a concert recently.

Perhaps the view of Strawberry Hill may interest you . It is now the training college for English Catholic male teachers and is staffed by Irish Vincentians. Horace Walpole left the reversion of it to his grand niece, the countess Waldegrave.

If you read 'Society in the Country House' by Escott, which I left in Laurence St and also 'Recollection. You will read of the entertainments given there by Frances, Countess Waldegrave, aunt of the late Mrs Gernon,

Best regards to all,
Mary

COPYRIGHT
E 4888

ST. MARY'S TRAINING COLLEGE,
STRAWBERRY HILL, MIDDLESEX.

THE AERIAL
PHOTOGRAPHIC CO.
LONDON

Hartlands, Clonmellon, Kells, Co.Meath
Sun 26th Nov 1944

My dear Eva,

Many thanks for your letter. I hope that you are not too tired after the jumble sale, which I assume has been as strenuous and as successful as ever. Did Dick make any remark about the individual professions in Maynooth or about the routine etc?

Do you know anything about the Dublin girl (I forget her name) whose engagement to young Mr Terrass was announced recently in the daily paper? You will be glad to hear that since Rose, Marchioness, settled into the Shelbourne that Mrs Farrell had been up seeing her and stayed overnight, and that Mollie McCann has been visiting her also! What a pity that Harriet did not live longer.

Monday

How is Jim's bullock getting on ? When Joe and Tom were in West, they met Peter and one of the McKeever's from near Ardee. That time they went to Athenry and Tuam a fortnight ago they went to Ballinrobe. People were very sorry at the death of Mr Larrissey, a cattle dealer from near Athboy. He had gone to Cahir for the fair, got a stroke the night before, was brought home, and recovered but got another in a few week's time, died in a moment. He had been a very strong man and very straight forward and good humoured. He used to handle a great many cattle and bought and sold all the stock for the Misses Chapman of Southill, Delvin, the step-sisters of Laurence of Arabia. Southill has been kept up magnificently so far – seven or eight servants indoor and everything outside to match, but people say now that it is be sold to the Land Commission.

When you write next , please send me the number of Mary Dowling's house in William St. As I would like to send her a Christmas Card.

You make a remark about the coming of the cold weather. Here up to Sat, the weather was damp but very mild, with roses and other flowers in full bloom. On Sat a change came. There was a blue sky, brilliant sunshine, what the thermometer registered I don't know , but it felt like 40 or 50 below zero! That night there was a little snow, enough to show on the Loughcrew Hills. Yesterday there came wonderful sunshine followed last night by a frost which is thawing now.Thanks for the cutting from the Irish Times. 'These things are an allegory'. Just think of the tender hearted Co.Meath person making a pet of a hare which gets killed by a dog belonging to Mr Olahan who is the manager in Armstrong's, the Kells auctioneers and who probably comes from Co.Clare.

The account which Quidnunc gives of the Thomas Moore Society in today's Irish Times is very interesting.Hoping that you have a satisfactory staff and with best wishes to all,

Yours, Mary

My dear Eva,

Hartlands,Clonmellon
Thurs 8th Feb 1945

On pages 244 and 245 of this Catholic Fireside is an article about an eighteenth century chaplain to the Bon Saveur Community in Caen. Congratulations on Ollie's success in St.Vincent's from all here. Yesterday Sissy told me that she forgot to mention it when she was writing to you. Did you hear that Mrs Kelly of Rathmullen has succeeded to the bulk of the money of her uncle, the late Dr.O'Keeffe of Delvin. He retired two years ago and died last summer. His house was bought by one of the Messrs Sherwin from the Naul, whose Aunt, Miss Cully, the former postmistress of Delvin, left one of them Rosmead House, the former residence of the Marquise de la Bedoyere.

Mr Joe Clyne of Delvin , the coursing enthusiast, who is married and had no family, built a private house on the outskirts of Delvin and sold his pub by auction last week. Someone from Galway and someone from Enfield or Longwood were amongst the bidders but it was knocked down at £2900 to a Mr Clyne, a nephew from Clara. What rivals that Tom Eustace bidding for the house in Paradise Place ? You will see by the enclosed cutting that a grandniece of Davy Sheridan has been married to one of the numerous Doctors Prenderville that came from Kerry. One of Davy Sheridan's sisters married a McDonnell from Athboy district. One of her daughters came back to Loughbawn district and married a Monaghan . Another comes back to Loughbawn and lives with her uncle, Jas Sheridan. A son of the late Matt Hand of Millbrook got married to her and lives in Sheridan's. Fr. D Smith, the new P.P of Delvin, comes from Coole not far away and is a brother of Mrs Jas McCann, Athboy. The V.F ship has gone to Fr M Farrelly. The late Fr. P. Flynn died on a Wed. On Thurs morning at 7.30 before the V.G had seen the daily paper, a Kells auctioneer called on him to find out if he were an executor of Fr.Flynn's will. Fr Dick had to disappoint this early bird – he was not .

Just now there is nothing like hazeline lanoline etc to be got from any of the local chemists. If you see any of these preparations about Drogheda please send it on, as I use them on my nose sometimes. Enclosed is a PO for 2/=. Best wishes for your Shrove Tide Whist Drive . I suppose that your house is very quiet now and that your three students have gone. Nicholsons have nearly finished remodelling Balrath. It is very much smaller now but has six bathrooms, any amount of verandas, drive in garages and its own electric plant. Have you seen the Ashbrook people lately ?

Best wishes to all,

Mary

Hartlands, Clonmellon, Kells, Co.Meath
Sat 3ʳᵈ March 1945

My dear Eva,

Many thanks for the letter, the bottles and the 6ds which reached here on Thursday. You might not have bothered about sending back the sixpence. Why did you not light candles with it ? The postal delivery to us is erratic, but the trouble is not locally but due to the fact that the mails for Clonmellon is sorted at Drogheda and sorted again in Kells before coming here. Sometimes it comes on directly, but sometimes it gets caught up in either place.. It is better to leave the cliché 'bottleneck' to the war commentators. You mention having sent on papers – they have not come yet. When we were in Bettystown , Tom went to Dublin one Sat morning and got some form for machinery which he posted in Bettystown at 3pm. The post man took it from the box and brought it to Drogheda alright. On Monday the shopkeeper sent a telephone message asking for the forms which had not reached him. For a few days there was a triangle of telegrams and telephone calls between Hartlands, Kells and Clonmellon. Then Tom went home and the letter arrived in Kells from Drogheda on a Friday, having taken seven days to cover the distance!

What order of priests gave the retreat in St.Peters ? I did not notice anything about it in the Drogheda Independent but everything is so condensed in the papers nowadays that they have to be scrutinised very closely. I am glad that Dick is in good form . Are the Admirable Crichton and Christopher Bean newcomers on the Maynooth stage ? Sometimes ago it used to be occupied by Julius Caesar, Macbeth and Hamlet. Is it because corpses are so plentiful all over the world today that they have lost the power to thrill and that something different must be put on the stage to interest the audience? Give Jim my best wishes and ask him how his bullock is getting on ?

So poor Father Cullen died in Cork and not in Castleknock near the border of Co.Meath! I suppose that it is unlikely that Fr.Dick Macken will leave Australia now. Under the Victorian novels when the hero who was a guardsman lost his money, the first thing he did was to change into a 'line' regiment, as existence was impossible in the Guards, except you had a large private income. In real life too, I read in Lord Castlerosse's book, when the solicitor trustee of the late Lord Athlumney embezzled £100,000 of the client's trust fund, Lord A left the Guards and joined a regiment which was serving in Egypt. However that question will probably not arise for Lt Aidan McD. as with Income Tax 19-6d in the pound, if his comrades cannot all be rich together they can be poor together, to paraphrase the late W.P.Cairnes; Let us hope that the news has trickled through to Queen Alexandra in the other world. Mary knows Mr Burkes garage in Castlebar. Where do the newly weds intend to live? I am glad that you have secured some help and I hope that your eyes are easier. Poor Fr Poland was regretted very generally. I am told that all his curates were greatly attached to him.

Will the late Capt Lyon's house at Mornington be sold? I hasten to add that I have no intention of buying it . The name McDonnell is just as indeterminate as Callan in Co.Louth. By the way did you see that the youngest of the Callans received the tonsure lately.

Congratulations on the victory of the two greyhounds. It is great that Meath can rank as high with dogs as with horses. Clyne's starting place is Delvin, where Joe Clyne lived in the ancestral hall. One brother went to Dublin where he owns a butcher's shop. I don't know whether he is married or not. The other has a butcher's shop in Clara , is married and has a large family, including Fr.Clyne, Dr. Billie, the man in Hibernian Bank, Drogheda, the dealer, and who ever else lives in Clara. Dr Billie acted as locum in Clonmellon and is married in America now. Whelan was bred by Nicholson of Balrath and sold as a yearling to Dr A. O'Reilly. O'Reilly sold him for £1500 guineas to the present owners. The Bective Electric Company (Lord & Lady Headfort and Simon Leonard, son of the late Pat Leonard), tendered for the wiring of Rynanna Airport, but were £50 over their successful competitor – who that was I don't know.

Did Sissy remark that I have taken the Bungalow already ? Someone said that Finnegans have left Seabank and have gone to Duleek Gate. Would that be to one of Larry Walshe's houses ? Did Kitty ask anyone to meet Dr.Lyons at lunch? Do you ever hear anything about Penelope Fitzgerald now ? (I don't mean Pamela mind) Whenever you see Mary in Dublin give her my best regards and hope for her success in drama. Most of the late Fr Flynn's things went dear at the auction in Delvin, one carpet making £40. The total sum was £1200. This is not so much as what the sale of the late Fr.Daly's chattels made at Enfield eighteen months ago. There the goods inside of the house alone came to £1200. A son of T.J Dowdall's Mullingar, has entered the Benedictines at Glenstal, where he had been educated. His other brother is doing law, while the only sister has qualified as an X-Ray operator.

You have heard often enough about the amount of money that has been spent bringing Nugent's of Ballinlough and Nicholsons of Balrath up to date. Last Nov fate intervened to prevent them from showing the splendours of their respective dwellings to the outside world.

When Miss Sherlock of Robinstown fixed the date of her wedding to Capt Harold Barry from Ballyvonne ? it was arranged that there would be a dance at Balrath, another at Ballinlough and the wedding breakfast with 140 guests at Ballinlough to show the Munster people what Meath and Westmeath could stage. Alas the groom's father died on the Saturday before the wedding, the dances were dropped and the list of guests at the breakfast down from 140 to 26.

Best wishes to all, Mary

Ps. Remind me at Bettystown to tell you two stories about Delvin which would take too long to write down here.

In May of 1945, the Germans surrendered, and in August, so did the Japanese. The war was officially declared 'over' on 2nd September. For Ireland, the fear was over, but of course, rationing and shortages continued for several years and the shock of the Economic War, and the 'Emergency' (1935-45) continued. Economics were very much a matter of thrift and of battening down the hatches. Borrowing money for expansion was seriously frowned upon. After all, look what happened to all who were over-borrowed during the 1930's!

The Compulsory Tillage Orders enforced to feed the home population during Wartime, seriously upset the traditional patterns of farming and because of a lack of fertiliser, left land in a poor state. It would take a decade to re-build energy and new confidence. The opening line of Mary's last letter of 1945 about having given away 'any old nightdresses' sums up much about the state of society...very little to squeeze out, for anyone in need

In August of 1944, Peter arrived as third son to John and Dolly in Beamore and both Nancy and Bawn had extra mouths to feed, in Mary and Margaret, during the same period. A long time faithful house-keeper to Doctor Paddy, Mary Dowling, is referred to in the letter of 26th Nov 1944. She is buried in the plot beside the Laurence Street plot in St.Peter's Cemetary. Mrs Brigid Gillic died at Oldcastle on 24th January 1945 aged 82 years.

Aunt Mary with Bridie Gillic

John Mc C with Pat, John and Peter in the snow.   Peter McCullen, with, John and Pat & Snowman!

John, farmer from the early days, feeding ducks in Beamore.

CHAPTER 10: 1946 - 1949

RECOVERY

This is the shortest period of time that we deal with, but it marks the dramatic return of 'cars on the road', food availability , the onset of the Rural Electrification Scheme, and a gradual move to better times. Mary in Hartlands married the local Doctor, Denis Collins and Peter died in Beamore, aged two years. Despite the brief period, fourteen of Mary's letters still survive. She is busy as ever, sending on letters received by her, to Eva, and various, usually religious newspapers and pamphlets. As she was wont to remark; *'The young people of today need to realise....that Mary also corresponded with Nuns in convents all over Ireland and Abroad'.*

Wedding of Mary to Doctor Denis Collins

Since Nuns do not hoard goods and chattels, none of these survive.

Hartlands, Clonmellon, Kells, Co.Meath
Sat 2nd Feb 1946

My dear Eva,

Here are 'Immaculata' and 'Maynooth' when the others have finished reading the letter from India, I will send it back. During the week I wrote to Mona Finegan. Since Monday some mass cards have come to me from about Drogheda, which I intend to acknowledge tomorrow. Did I ever tell you that when A Teresa was boarding in the Convent of St.John of God at Wexford that Tim Healy's only sister, Jane Healy, Walter Callan's aunt a Miss McDonnell from Ardee and a Catholic first cousin of Col Pepper of Ballygarth were staying there also.

A.J. liked the place, but when the order became federated, the Wexford Convent became the Central Novitiate and the lady boarders except those belonging to the Diocese of Ferns had to leave. Those kept were relatives of P.P's of that diocese who had left money for their maintenance when the Wexford Convent was an isolated community.

In last week's Drogheda Independent there is a paragraph saying that Geo IV when visiting Slane Castle in 1821 met the local P.P and gave him permission to put up a belfry in the Catholic Church. There is no foundation for that yarn. In Dean Cogan's history he mentions that Fr.O'Hanlon from Stamullen was travelling as tutor to the eldest son of Caddell of Harbourstown in France sometime in the 18th century. As England and France were at war at the time, it was probably between 1754 and 1760. When Fr O'H and young Caddell arrived at some French town , a great hubbub was going on some English prisoners of war including Capt Conyngham were being badly mauled by the natives. Fr O'H was a fluent French speaker calmed down the crowd and induced them to leave the prisoners alone. Later on when the two governments agreed to exchange prisoners, Capt Conyngham was released. Afterwards he asked that Dr O'H should be appointed to Slane and helped him to put up the belfry.

Enclosed is a picture of Lynn Lodge from yesterday's paper. Here is a family tree as far as I can make out, of the Leavy Family.

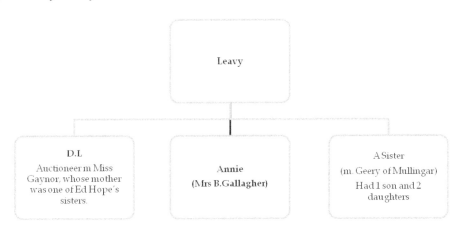

Leavy

D.L	Annie	A Sister
Auctioneer m Miss Gaynor, whose mother was one of Ed Hope's sisters.	(Mrs B.Gallagher)	(m. Geery of Mullingar) Had 1 son and 2 daughters

One niece you will see married a Dr Murphy from Wexford who served some time in the Irish Army. They lived in one of the houses at Bettystown between McDonaghs and the sea and I think he does locums.

The farm that O'Reilly's (formerly of Castle Park Slane) bought from Capt Blount had been bought by him from Jim Brogan, the jockey of Trim. When Anthony was at St.Finians, some of the Mentons were his contemporaries. The priest who was killed last week was curate in the parish of Ballivor. It is one of the few parishes in the diocese of Meath where the curate lives in a separate house beside the chapel of ease which is at Kildalkey. Years ago I drove past the house, a fine Georgian one, which would seem to have belonged to a local landlord and to have been bought afterwards by the priest. From its apparent age it is unlikely that the parish would have been able to put up such a good building at the time. Except in Kilcormac which has a curates house at Mount Bolus, and Oldcastle, which has one at Moylough, I don't know of any other parishes where a curate lives away from the P.P.

Who won the teacloth at the whist drive ?

Best wishes to all,
Mary

Hartlands, Clonmellon, Kells, Co.Meath
18th Feb 1946

My dear Eva,

Many thanks for your letter. We are glad to hear that P.D is better and hope that the rest of you may escape the flu. It has been prevalent about here with schools shut in Kilsykye and other places, but the type seems mild D.G. Last week I ordered some small memorial cards which I intend to send with a note to Costellos, Mrs O'Hagan and the others whose mass cards you have sent me. Will you please acknowledge the card from Mr Paddy Connolly as I have never met him. By the way what is the number of Mrs O'Byrnes house in West St. It used to belong to Jack Gannon.

Everyone said that the Ball in Headfort was most enjoyable with J Lynch's Band. He is a nephew of Fr. Thos Lynch. The Headforts had the house in wonderful trim with rows and rows of pots of flowering plants massed up against the walls. When you read that these came out of heated greenhouses you will imagine what pains had to be taken to produce that effect. The house itself is an 'Adam' House. Our neighbour Mrs Farrell says that the ballroom is the most perfect Adam room in Ireland. Another room which created great interest was 'The Chinese Room'. You may remember that when Sir Wm Chambers, the eighteenth century architect of Somerset House came back from a ship to China, that his drawings of Chinese buildings and furniture made what was called 'Chinoiserie' the fashion in furniture and decoration, Chippendale produced some 'Chinese Chippendale'.

Did you hear that Fr Nulty called to Kells for the V.G and that they drove together to Mullingar to meet Cardinal Glennon. You will be glad to know that the Cardinal was so loyal to Meath and Westmeath as to bring with him to Mullingar not only his own relatives who had travelled from U.S.A but his yankee friends as well. The V.G sat beside the commodore of the aeroplane at lunch, and heard a lot about altitudes, atmospheres and other angles of air travel. About sixty sat down to lunch including the Bishops of Meath, Ardagh, and Kilmore. Dick said that the Cardinal mentioned his connection with the two counties of Meath, Westmeath and spoke of his birth in the natural order in Meath and of his supernatural birth a few days later at the Baptismal Font in Kinnegad Church in Westmeath. The airman was delighted at the Irish Chicken and Ham ('Keep that under your foot'). I don't know if any 'Mullingar heifers' figured on the bill of fare.

The late Mr Greene's grandfather came to Gaulstown almost by chance. A Mr John Cooper, the owner of Cooper Hill died. His relatives who succeeded were two brothers, Nathanial and Henry Cooper. Mrs. Cooper, Nathanial's mother, had married a Greene from Kildare as her second husband and had three or four sons by him. Nat Cooper was of unsound mind and never came to Cooperhill, I think, but the Greene's came there with Henry Cooper, bringing with them from Kildare, the Dollards family as ploughmen. Later on one of the next generation of Dollards married a Dullaghan whose people had been mechanics in Beaumond Mill. One of her sons was a marine engineer, the other the carpenter who married Miss McNally.

Henry Cooper's eldest step brother John Greene took the farm at Gaulstown and built the present house and got married. He was the father of the late Harry Greene. None of Henry Cooper's other step brothers ever got married . They all just lived on in Cooper Hill, but were dead before my time. When H.C was an old man, I remember that I used to be told that Mary Mullen (afterwards Mrs John Ward of CooperHill) was his housekeeper. These Coopers also owned the Balrath farm now belonging to Eddie Delaney. Nat Cooper died I think before Henry.

At any rate sometime about 1901 when I was away at school, Henry died and a Miss Cooper with a widowed sister Mrs Smith came home from New York and succeeded to Cooperhill and Mt Granville. (Henry C had got Mt Granville after 1895 when John C of Beamore had died.) The Balrath farm was sold about or before that time.

I hope that Mary is enjoying her unexpected holiday. Last Thursday we had the family from Beamore accompanied by Anna Dolan and heard plenty of news. During the week I intend to write to Dick (D.V),

Hoping that you all are in good form, Your Mary

Hartlands, Clonmellon, Kells, Co.Meath
4th March 1946

My dear Eva,

Enclosed are some memorial cards. When I write again to Dick, I will send him one. Since I wrote to you last, I have heard that Mr Greene had not become a Catholic when he married, but that latterly he had been receiving instruction from Fr. Nulty and that he died the day before he was to have been received. The nuns at Laytown always gave him great praise for the way he always brought up the children to be baptised and had them attending the Convent School.Since Card. Glennon was in Mullingar I heard from a secular source how Dr.Dalton's entertainment forced Dev to take notice of the other Cardinals designate. Hence Dev stepping into the picture and sending Sean T's car to Rineanna, when Dr. Dalton's car was there to bring Dr Glennon to Mullingar. The other Archbishops were brought to Killarney and now Card. Glennon is being entertained in Dublin. Thank God that we have escaped the 'Flu' although there has been traces of it in the district.

The other brave folks who went to the Ballymacad Point to Point at Crossakiel yesterday say that the attendance was better than ever, and that the top of the hill kept away the strong east winds. Bawn paid us a flying visit but went home from the races. In other years McNamaras used to be there, but of course they were absent this time.

You have heard already how MrAdams who bought Willmount Intends to start a tannery just outside of the town of Kells. He could not get a house in Kells for the manager of the future tannery, he has paid £2000 to Jack Meade for Triermore near Girley. This is a big house with some lands attached for which Meade gave the Land Commission £300 during the 1930's. Formerly it belonged to Rotherams. The Land Comm. divided the rest of the land. The holding is waterlogged and the house seems to be an eighteenth century one, but Meade has done very well out of it, as he sold the timber on it some time ago. He is one of the Meades of Castletown and his first wife, was the only child of Mr Hodgkinson, the electrician who used to live in James's Street .

Have there ever been so many places being sold at the same time in this county? Last night we heard that Mrs Maher has sold the Headfort Arms in Kells for over £5000 to Anthony Conlon, a Kells draper, who stays in Bettystown during the summer. Mrs Maher is an elderly childless widow whose husband had been a vet, who was one of the Mahers of Clownstown.

Sometime ago you heard of the adventurous life of the late Brian Gallagher who bought Lynn Lodge, along the lake outside Mullingar, from Capt. Beardmore Batten. His widow has sold it for £5600 to Flanagan who is in the timber trade. When the deal had been completed, a wire came from some Westmeath person living in Glasgow offering £6000 for it,

Best wishes to all,

Mary

Hartlands, Clonmellon, Kells, Co.Meath
27ᵗʰ March 1946

My dear Eva,

Many thanks for your letter. I suppose that all the people about Drogheda were relieved that even if Armagh is still without an Archbishop that Dr.Lyons was so kind as to do the best he could at the Cistercian Celebrations lately! As to the Medical Missionaries – up to this they have been attending weddings, wakes and funerals, but if they keep on helping at dejeuners, some of the other communities may look for injunctions to restrain their further activities. You will see by the enclosed Cath. Herald that Mrs Lyons Fitzgerald has been heard and seen across the Channel and that Fr Agnellus Andrew has been to Mullingar. It is certainly surprising that such a stir should have been made after he had left the world by a quiet easy going man like Card. Glennon. A day or so before Fr Peter Doyle died, I heard that he suffered from gall stones. During his life, he suffered from ill health.

Did you notice in the paper the death of Mrs Agnes Smith of Roristown, Trim?. She had been a Miss Eivers, a niece of the Carews, the Parnellite MP's, from whom she inherited Roristown. She married Michael Smith, a brother of Willie Smith, the auctioneer. Michael Smith was a widower whose first wife had been the only daughter of Tom Melady of Mount St. A very successful horse dealer. Tom Melady like some like some other great people came from Co.Meath. At first he had a dairy in Mount St. He once told Father that he was content with it , but that his cows took foot and mouth (in the early 1880's) and that he turned to horses then. So Fr John Gilmartin was at Lourdes Hospital for the profession of some one from Milltown Pass.

It is consoling to know that the Hunt Balls at Headfort and the Whitworth Hall were 'different' from the others. Did the Meath Hunt have a Ball this season? In pre-war times it used to be held in Dunsany, but I have not seen any mention of this year. Recently the Meath Chronicle printed an account of the home coming from the East of Col Plunkett, Lord Dunsany's only son. In answer to an address of welcome presented by the neighbours, he said that Ireland was the best place to be at in the present time. That remark from a Plunkett is a novelty. Did you read any of the reviews of Mary Lavin's first long novel ' The House in Clewer St?' One English journal says it is too long. Another is more statistical and says that it is has 380,000 words as against the 350,000 of 'Gone with the Wind'. It could be with an eye on the American market which seems to favour bulk just now ?

Best wishes to all, Mary.

Hartlands, Clonmellon, Kells, Co.Meath
Mon 18ᵗʰ Nov 1946

My dear Eva,

Perhaps these News Reviews may interest yourself and Paddy. I am not sure whether you have seen this Tatler before or not. How does Jim like the office and the Univ. Classes? People are interested in the marriage of Vincent Eivers of Roristown , Trim to Rosemary Fagan. It is said that they had not known each other long and that he proposed to her on their fourth meeting. He had lived in Roristown with his aunt, Mrs Michael Smith who died last April, she had got the place from her uncles, the Carews.

Another brother of his is a V.S lives at Foxbrook Trim and the youngest who studied in All Hallows was ordained this year for Perth, Australia. Tom tells me that he saw your brother, and Joe Macken of Slane at Girley yesterday at Miss Dillon's funeral, Fr.Dick officiated. A few days ago when Mrs Lyons wrote to me enclosing the ESB bills she said that Craigies had stayed on in No.2 Bayview till a week ago, bathing every day! Cooneys have got possession of the Collon House from Woods and are going into it soon. Sir Hugh Nugent has bought a house with about 15 Irish acres of land beside us for an Englishman at £1800. It used to belong to Coffeys, who were Protestant stewards of Chapman One of them, a pensioner from the Manchester, C.I.D sold it from £750 in 1941.

Since then it was resold for £1000 to a returned Australian, who had emigrated from Leix, named Mulhall, who is connected to Bishop Collier from Ossory. Thank God all the corn has been threshed except some that is being left till the spring for seed, and that they expect to bring in the last of the potatoes today,

Best wishes to all, Mary

The reference to Jim liking the office and University classes, is to the start of his career as a stockbroker with Messrs. Dillons, and to the commerce degree he pursued in University College Dublin. Several mentions of memorial cards refer to the death of 'Aunt Teresa Moore' in Dublin in January 1946.

Hartlands, Clonmellon, Kells, Co.Meath
Tues 19th November 1946

My dear Eva,

Yesterday I wrote to you and rolled the letter up in these journals intending to post the bundle today. However, I am adding this postscript first, beginning by thanking you for your interesting letter which came this morning. Some time ago I read that the Gwynnes are descended from a Welsh family who settled in Ireland. I do not know at what time or in what place . If you look at 'Inchiquin' in your Burke's peerage, you will see that a daughter of Wm Smith O'Brien married the Rev. John Gwynne, the Protestant Dean of Raphoe, and Regius Prof of Divinity in T.C.D Gwynne is the Welsh for white, 'Irish ban?'

Mrs Stephen Gwynne became a Catholic when her family were young and brought the children up Catholic. Flanked as she was by so many ministers, she must have been a brave woman seeing that Fr. Aubrey's two grandfathers and two uncles were ministers; it is not surprising that Dick detected a parsonical strain in his manner despite his Jesuit training?

On the other hand, Stephen Gwynne's aunt Charlotte Grace O'Brien , younger daughter of Wm Smith O'Brien became a Catholic in the 1880's and worked to improve the conditions of people emigrating to the USA. I don't know whom S.Gwynne's brothers married or what families they had. If you do open 'Burkes' you will see that a younger son of Wm S.O'B was Protestant Dean of Limerick and a sister of the late R.J. Montgomery of Beaulieu, and an aunt of Mrs Sidney Waddington's.

You may wonder why we are suddenly plunged into the genealogical background of Reverend Aubrey Gwynne S.J. Two of the reasons likely are, firstly, that he has been in regular contact with both Oliver and Jim in Clongoweswood College, and University Hall in Hatch Street, Dublin and secondly, that he was the son of a convert. Conversions were an important part of Aunt Mary's life, and within a short span of time, a letter from the famous Jesuit surfaces, amongst Doctor Paddy's papers.

There is an excellent example of a 'ramble' as my Father would describe it, in this letter, where Mary commences with Una's letter, takes in a sizeable portion of Fingal and South Meath, and ends up with Fr.John Leonard (1865-1933) P.P of Ardcath.

Hartlands, Clonmellon, Kells, Co.Meath
28ᵗʰ Dec 1946

My dear Eva,

Many thanks for your letter and for your gifts – you are great to think of it. I hope that your domestic help problems may be solved by now. Una mentioned in a letter to me that a former class fellow of hers in Balbriggan, Jane Derham is engaged to be married to Jenou Cuntz , a thirty five year old Hungarian, protégé of Mr. Amberlink, the Dutch bulb grower who lives in Rush. The Derhams who are cousins of Annie lives at Balcunnin farm. Their father Andy Derham, who died a few years ago married a Miss Blundell from Dublin, but their grandmother, Mina Gaffney from Malahide (a first cousin of Patk. Macken) and their great grandmother, McCabe from Barnageera were double dyed Fingallians.

Mrs Collins of Moyrath Castle, Kildalkey is being buried today. She was one of the Leavy's of Shanco whose land lies west of Hartlands. Two of her uncles owned pubs in Dublin . When living with her mother's sister, Mrs Darby of Ballivor, she got married to Jas Collins of Moyrath and now leaves three children. She was the same age as Mary here.!! Her husband is grand nephew of the Fr Leonard formerly P.P Ardcath, one of his sisters is married to the McIvor from Ardcath; who has bought so much land. Thanking you again and with good wishes to all,

Yours, Mary

Eva at the Blessed Oliver Stall (second row, centre)

Hartlands, Clonmellon, Kells,

My Dear Eva

Mon 12ᵗʰ January 1947

A few days ago Mary gave me the apple marmalade recipe which I copied out and am sending you now. A fortnight ago when we were in Salmon the talk turned on F.J McCormick. Annie said that she remembered Peter Judge growing up in Skerries where his father was something in the malthouse. His married sisters and stepsister (nee Kierans) lived about Skerries. Mr and Mrs McVeagh of Drewstown (Ismay McKeever) are going to live in Brierly. They have one son and one daughter. People here are busy still getting in potatoes etc.

In this Meath Chronicle is a biography of the Mr Tighe who bought so many farms for his relations – all in Co.Meath. He was born just inside of the Cavan boundary line but Castlepole where he used to send the visitors that Mr McDonnell would drive about is in Carnaross parish, Co.Meath. Harry Dyas's father used to own it.

Apple Marmalade
4 lbs cooking apples (weighed after paring)
4lbs sugar
1 quart water
4 lemons
Put the sugar in the pan and pour the boiling water over it, heat and stir till the sugar is dissolved. Boil about 15 mins skimming if necessary.
Add the lemon juice and boil as fast as possible till set.
Peel, core and slice the lemon rind over them.
Put them into the syrup and stir while the fruit simmers till soft.

Mary & Mrs Beeton?

Thursday 15ᵗʰ May 1947

Today we went to Drewstown auction. The new owner, Mr Fitzgerald, a Dun Laoighaire builder, has men working at the roof already and seedlings growing in the green house. The house is of cut stone, three stories high and has no basement. In front of the porch with three windows on each side, and seven windows on the two upper stories. On the west side are six windows on each of the three stories and a glass door opening on the rock garden. On the east side the drawing room and the two rooms in the stories over it have a round ending the same as yours has, besides that there are three or four windows more in each story of that side. On the north side of the square block is a two story continuation which I suppose is the kitchen etc. There was a demand for nearly everything. Some of the exceptions were stranger. An oak dining room table made for the Duke of Manchester (probably when he bought Kylemore about 1900) was withdrawn at £11. The leather covered chairs to match were withdrawn at £2=10=0. The auctioneer spent more time and trouble over these two lots than over any other but could not get any better bids. Better lots were in very good condition. A large Crown Derby dessert set was withdrawn also a small silver cream jug was sold at £1. On account of the holiday the attendance was very good.

Today a long letter came from Mrs Dowling (Emily O'Reilly) which I mean to show you later on. She writes a good deal about the Grogan Family. Another item that I have for you is a wedding group of Mary's. Maids seem as scarce as ever,

Best wishes to all, Mary .P.S. The Meath Chronicle says that Mrs Ismay McVeagh expects to visit Florida in July with six greyhounds which she will race on the tracks there. The prize fund for some of the greyhound races in Florida deals £1000 per event.

The McVeagh's mentioned in Drewstown had been there since 1780 and moving to Brierly at Duleek has another local slant, not to mention the greyhounds! The last two letters are related to each other in dealing with this topic, so I have upset the chronological order somewhat to pair them.

Our next letter is not written by Mary, but is a good example of how others become sucked in to her historical web , and respond.

University Hall,
Dublin.

Jan. 16 ' 47

Dear Dr. McCullen,

Both Oliver and Jim have given me your message - or rather your sister's message - about the site of the old Royal Castle of Drogheda.   So it is time that I should send you in return a brief note on my reasons for thinking that this castle was on the present Mill Mount - not, as I myself thought when I was in Drogheda for the New Year, near Fr. Nulty's house.

Goddard Orpen, who made a very close study of all the earliest Norman motes and castles in Ireland during the years before 1914, is my authority - and his general view as to the nature and history of these early castles is shared by Leask in his recent book on Nex Irish Castles.   Orpen has a short note on the castle of Drogheda in his "Ireland under the Normans", vol. II (1911), p. 79-80.   But he had made a very much fuller study of the problem in an article which he wrote on "Motes and Norman Castles in Co. Louth" - published in Journal of Soc. of Antiquaries (1908), pp. 246-50.

Having given the little that is known of the history of this castle - which is to be found also in D'Alton's book - he points out that the Mill Mount is the obvious strategic site for a castle on the southern side of the Boyne.   He then makes a careful study (with sketch-plan) of Mill Mount, and especially of the surviving bailey-wall to the west of the mound :-

"The town wall joins the wall of the upper court or bailey of the mote.   This latter wall projects in a curve round the bailey, doubtless following the line of the original rampart, and runs up the a mote, bearing the approach, some 7 feet wide, to the modern fort - which represents the keep, just as may be seen in many English mote-castles.   If there should be any doubt as to where the thirteenth-century castle of Drogheda was situated, this entry (entrance) should set it at rest." (p.249)

In a note on p. 250 he discusses the site to which your
sister refers me ; and argues from a seventeenth-century description of it that this building was never the royal castle - lying
on ground that is too low for a strong defence - but that it is
to be identified as the "Castle of Comfort" or "Old Tholsel",
which is thus described in a document of 1669 :-

"An old stone house lying on the Meath side of the town, at the
foot of the hill, and commonly called the Old Tholsel or Castle
of Comfort, mearing to the way leading to the Bull-ring up the
hill to the Duleek gate on the west ; St. Nicholas's church on the
east ; and the street called the Bull-ring on the north."

If Orpen is right in his assumption the castle
was never rebuilt as a great stone fortification (like Limerick
or Kilkenny etc.), but left in its primitive form as a mote-
castle, since Drogheda was never near enough to Irish attack for
such defensive measures after the first 2 years of the Norman
invasion of this country, then it is easy to see why the memory
of this early castle has faded so completely from the minds of
the townsfolk.   The old castle has simply become the modern
fort or barracks ; and its earlier history, which was never very
important or spectacular, has been forgotten.

On p. 250 Orpen makes the following comment :-

"Drogheda Castle is, in fact, a rare, if not unique example of a
mote-castle used throughout the centuries, with but little alter-
ation in essentials from the time of Hugh de Lacy to that of
Cromwell - or, indeed, seeing that it is still (1908) called a
royal barracks, we might say to the days of King Edward VII."

Jim has had a slight cold, but is on the mend : he is being
attended to by one of our resident doctors, qualified two or
three years ago.   I think we are in for a mild bout of flu in
the house, as this time last year.

Yours sincerely

A. Gwynn S.J.

Clonmellon, Kells, Co.Meath
St.Stephen's Day

My dear Mary,

Many thanks for your letter. It is great that the Lourdes sale of work did so well. I am sorry that nobody from Hartlands was in Dublin on those days. Nancy Ball sent a Christmas card to Dick, so did your Uncle Joe. I sent a card and wrote a letter. How is Mary Dowling ? Nancy and I sent cards to her William St. Address. It will be a great change for the district if the Mosney Gormanston beach is invaded by cross channel trippers. I wonder if the Castle will be sold now.

For the last six years a Panto has been produced in Athboy by local talent. The topical songs used to be written by one of the guards and the books of the different pantos by 'Mr Hexagon (six Athboy people including Fr Irwin CC). Last year some of the references in the songs scored such decided hits that the victims raised protests. This season it is thought safer to have no performance at all. In previous years the Kells Operatic Society had produced a Gilbert & Sullivan works. This time they are trying 'The Geisha' which is to be played early in Jan. I am glad that you liked the cushion that Mary sent you , as she went to a good deal of trouble turning it out. She made one of the same a pattern in other colours for Mrs Collins, Cabinteely. Joined by all in good wishes for the New Year, Your affectionately,

Mary

Editor's Note: Mosney Holiday Camp (Butlins) opened in July 1948.
The Castle refers to Gormanstown Castle, then on the market

My dear Jim,

Many thanks for your letter which came on Christmas Eve. All here are in good form (D.G) and so are the Balls. Although the men folk have not entered any cattle for the Kells Christmas Show, they went there as in other years. They were speaking to Capt.Cullen of Liscarton, who got second prize for a beast over 12cwt. When the cattle came to be auctioned I think that the first prize winner made £66 and the second place made £72. Mary is very busy most of her time is spent sewing on the machine which your Mamma selected for your Uncle Dick's present. On Sat, when in Kells I called to the convent for a few minutes and saw your aunt who looked very well.

Some time ago a woman who emigrated to USA had to leave her daughter behind in Kells oprhanage. In America she saved so much money as a domestic servant that she was able to send enough money to the nuns to buy an outfit for her daughter and also a ticket to New York by air. Accordingly a few weeks ago the young lady went from Kells to Collinstown, then by air to Rinneanna And on to New York. Joined by the others in wishing you a happy new year,

Yours affectionately, Aunt Mary

Apart from the opening of Mosney Holiday Camp, the year 1948 also produced several other significant events. A Meath Chronicle headline of August reads;

'9000 greet deValera at Clonmellon' *'a wild and enthusiastic rush to greet the Leader, fresh from his triumphal World Tour.'*

It is important that we have no written record of Mary's view on the visit of the Leader. She probably took more satisfaction from the events in Leinster House, later in the year, when Mr John A. Costello was elected Taoiseach of an Inter Party Government, by 75 votes to 70, for Mr. de Valera. Not alone was Fianna Fail out of power, but the cars were back on the roads, after wartime and petrol rationing. In our next letter the reference to Eureka is prescient in that it was eventually purchased by Fr.Dick in 1954, and opened as the hub of the new Mercy School in April 1956. The House is quite modern, being built in 1882 for a Land Agent of Lord Headfort. New nieces and a nephew had arrived, Josephine and Helen Drew at Mornington and Edmund Collins, first son to Mary and Dr.Denis.

Helen Drew with Chris Cosgrave and Josephine Drew in 1966.

Maura (Salmon)

Hartlands, Clonmellon, Kells, Co.Meath
Sun 11th November 1948

My dear Eva,

The people here have recovered from the thrills of Fr. Tallons sale and are looking forward to the auction in Athboy Rectory next week. The Rector, who is a Ph.D is leaving Athboy to teach in a college in Egypt. Meantime people are talking still of the very high prices which most of Fr Tallons things fetched. Mr Molloy said that the sale realised more than £2000. I am glad to see that the Drogheda Independent has given your Nursing Association such a good write up. Let us hope that your nerves may be able to stand the tussle on D-Day – 24th Nov.

Some time ago you spoke of the enthusiasm with which Mona Larkin went to wakes. It came back to me when I read that Mother Martin and some of her nuns watched by the bedside of Card. McRory on the night after his death. It must have been hard on the nuns of the convents about Armagh, when they heard the news. Nancy from Salmon stayed here for almost a fortnight and went home on Thursday. What a blessing that the cars are on the roads again.

Thursday

On Tues we went into the auction at Eureka McDonnells must be keeping all the ordinary knives and the breakfast china, as I did not see any of either article. There were a few sets of carvers, some fish knives and dozens and dozens of forks, and of different size spoons. Besides some modern plated ware and one pair of 19th century solid silver candle sticks were some Sheffield plated cake baskets, which did not fetch collector prices. The house at Eureka is beautifully situated, but the grounds are so large that I think that the Parochial authorities did not miss much when Mr Fitzsimmons bought the place. He owns Kileen's bakery and intends to keep the bakery horses in Eureka. He has already sold some land which he owned further out. Have you seen Dick this month?

Dr Colm McDonnell was not at the auction, but his wife was, wearing a very high pink hat, and a very large diamond ring. Her brother in law, Dr. Peter McDonnell and her sister in law, Mrs Doorly of Offaly bought a good many things. Mrs Doorly has four sons and one daughter. The latter is in school in Roscrea. The other, Miss McDonnell is married to a bank man. Mr Devlin. They have no family. In Sat's paper Battersby's advertised a public house in Cross Street.Kells which I suppose is McDonnells. They have been there since 1808. Give my best wishes to Mary whenever you go to Cabra. One of our neighbours who owns a motor went to Longford and bought a pony for his trap the day before the announcement about motors appeared !

Best Regards, Mary.

Hartlands, Clonmellon
Wed 24th November 1948

My dear Eva,

The enclosed letter came yesterday from Miss Gordon. I have answered it sending her congratulations etc. Yesterday I came here after a strenuous week in Dublin. Rosita and Theresa came to tea to me in Hatch St. And I went to them on Sat evening. You may imagine that on these evenings we covered a lot of Co.Meath country. I also saw Emily Dowling and found her as chatty as ever. Nancy Ball and her younger daughter, Frances Margaret, are to go home on Friday D.G.

How did Ada McKeown's auction go? Did you hear that although the jockey off Rooney's horses 'El Capitan' was disqualified last week at Manchester and the stakes given to the owner of the second horse, yet the bets were allowed to stand. It is said that the bookies had to pay £35000.

One cattle dealer who had backed the horse amazed a Little Sister of the Poor who collects at Oldcastle Fair, by giving her a £5 note.

Some years ago I got some booklets from the C.T.S, England, two of which I am sending you. As I had known that Blundells of Crosby were descended from Peppards of Drogheda. I thought that one might say something of them. Since that I have found that the parents of Fr. Beck, the writer of the other, came from Tyrone and that he had been consecrated assistant Bishop of somewhere near London.

Wishing you a successful jumble sale,

Yours, Mary.

Once again, not alone does Eva receive a bundle of Catholic Truth Society booklets, she also receives Miss Gordon's letter, and up to date news on the whereabouts of the new arrival at Boherard, Frances Margaret Ball. The 'Rooney' referred to is most likely, local horse trainer, Jimmy Rooney, whose training stables were adjacent to McCullen's farm in Beamore, and can still be seen to this day, although without horses. Not long after this event, Mr.Rooney lost his trainers licence after an incident of subterfuge, with a horse called Mount Mills, the name coming from the original Rooney Farm in County Down.

Hartlands, Clonmellon, Kells, Co.Meath
Wed 19th Jan 1949

My dear Eva,

By this time I hope that your cold is gone and that your domestic help problems is relieved. Here are some letters from Rosita and from Mrs Dowling.

Tuesday 25th Jan 1949

You will see that Mrs Dowling was interested to hear about the auction which took place before Christmas at Kilcairne Park. For many years it had been owned by Murphys who had a distillery in Navan more than a hundred years ago. Before 1914 one or two Misses Murphy lived there, one was married to General Meagher of the British Army, a brother of Thos F. Meagher, The Young Irelander, and had two sons, Reginald, a solicitor and Mayor M. Of the British Army. The other Miss Murphy married Captain O'Reilly of Rathaldron Castle and had one daughter who is married to M.Drummond.

Major Meaghar who succeeded his aunt in Kilcairne was an English Catholic who had no family, but had two nieces, Misses Crawford who lived with her and one nephew, Fr.Crawford, who is a priest in England. Now the Crawfords have sold the place to an English Family and have gone to live at Dundrum. Here is an item which appeared in Sat's 'Meath Chronicle'; 'The engagement is announced between Joseph, youngest son of Mr and Mrs JB. Moorehead, Tullamore House, Tullamore and Cynthia, only daughter of the late Dr A.B.Kennedy and of Mrs Kennedy, Rathcore, Enfield.' I wonder if he would be a nephew of the late F.W Moorehead who married Miss Brady.

About the time that Anthony bought Kilnew, Mrs Hackett of Killua and her sisters, the Misses Booker sold their farm at Clonleason, beside Girley for £2500. Within the last fortnight it was sold again for £9500. The buyer Mrs Farrell of Lennoxbrook is the widow of an ex St.Finians student, who I think was a nephew of DR Moran of Ardee. Three weeks after the war ended in 1945 he took off from his hospital in Burma where he had been serving in the R.A.M.C when the plane crashed and he was killed. Mrs Farrell has one child. It is said that she is getting married again to a Mr Hawkins who owns race horses and who is a millionaire of course.

Her mother, the late Minnie Matthews who owned Lennoxbrook in Carnaross parish left Loreto, the first year I was there. Her father, Willie Mullen, who married into the places was a horse dealer from Tyrone. Did you notice something lately in the London Correspondence of the Daily Independent about his sister, Mrs Alice Baines, who has been at newspaper work for sixty years, starting in Fermanagh and on to Fleet Street where she is still.

You must be very lonesome for Mary, Best wishes to all,

Mary

Johanna, with Pat Gillic and Aunt Mary   Rosa Lynch with Anthony

The Doings of a thoroughly hard boiled schoolgirl are the theme of Donald Macardle's new novel, Tansy (Hodder & Stroughten 8/6). It begins when the heroine, whose name is that of the book, is expelled from her important boarding school for making off at night to attend the first performance of a play, for which her mother, a successful dressmaker, has designed some of the dresses. Tansy is charming, pretty clever, old for her age – nearly sixteen, devoted to her lovely mother and keen on having a good time herself. Her next escapade is to have a slight collision while driving her mother's car, when it becomes very important to convince immediately the young man whose sports model has been involved in the incident that she is old enough to hold a licence.Tansy, being the most accomplished little liar, succeeded perfectly, and incidentally enchants the young man, whose people have just bought a large house near Tansy's country home. Tansy's talent of lying is called into use fairly frequently now because her mother knows something of Tom's father and disapproves of any friendship between them. Finally a very discreditable story is told and the young people part in sorrow, under a misapprehension, to find a happy solution to their difficulties when Tom is nursed by Tansy is a war hospital.

What is out of the way in this novel is it's author's understanding of the part that clothes may play in a woman's life of the details of running a fashionable dressmaker's salon, of restaurants and hotels in town , and of the unhappy position of children, whose parents are separated.

Hartlands, Clonmellon, Kells, Co.Meath
Friday 11th March 1949

My dear Eva,

On Monday when the Hartlands people were going to Mornington they dropped me at Beamore. Pat was in bed but in great humour and the others were in great form. They said that you had got an 'in and out' maid. Congratulations. They are very scarce about here! I hope that all your family at home and abroad are in good form . Did Ollie meet any of his acquaintances in London ?

Have I told you already of Mrs and Mrs Puldenski and their daughters (10 and 12). They have bought Heathtown beside Sir H.Nugent. It is a Georgian house with 300 acres. Some of the Dyas family used to own it but since 1939 it has changed hands two or three times. Puldenskis have modernised it and put in an electricity plant. As Mrs P has been educated in a Sacred Heart Convent , she asked the Mount Annville nuns to get her a governess to teach the girls until she would send them to school.

Is Jim anxious about the Irish team in Swansea? Some people were surprised that they beat the Scots. The Drogheda Argus informs me that Frankie McDermott has been staying with her respective aunts in Drogheda and Navan, Fancy Aidan being made a BBC announcer! For the last few months a Fr Murray C.S.Sp has been staying in Clonmellon Parochial House. He is a native of Dysart where Fr.Conway had been P.P before coming to Clonmellon. When he came home , on leave from Africa, Fr Conway very kindly asked him to Clonmellon as some of his own people were ill. At one of the masses he gave a long address on the missionary work. When I was in Beamore, John asked if I knew how Eileen Rooney is getting on. Give her our best wishes. Have any of you heard from Ada since she reached the hub of the universe?

Best wishes to all, Mary

Arising from this last letter I am pleased to notice that I get a mention, with my parents, 'as being in great form!'.

This is what the People's weekly says about 'The Univited'. 'A weird and chilling story about an old house and the Cornish Coast is the theme of a new Paramount Film, 'The Univited', which is based on the best seller of the same name by Dorothy Macardle. This film has faithfully followed the novel and it is thus responsible for quite a new departure on the treatment of ghosts in a serious fashion 'The Lodger', 'The Phantom of the Opera', and those various Dracula and Franksenstein films all depend on a blatant disregard of those supernatural agents which are commonly accepted, preferring to deal with horror for its own sake, and warped criminal minds.

The refreshing departures in 'The Univited' would be thoroughly enjoyed even if it did not happen to be a ghost story as well. Miss Mcardle will be remembered for her Irish short stories and especially her book 'The Irish Republic' which contained a preface by Mr De Valera. She played a prominent part as a Republican propagandist during the Civil War, and her booklet called 'Tragedies of Kerry' created a deep and far reaching impression. She has been in England for several years and is at present occupied with B.B.C work.'

According to 'The Irish Catholic' of 27th April. Ray Milland was born in Drogheda and his real name is Jack Millane.

Fittingly, at the end of the decade, Mary does this film/book review of a ghost story. She admits that the work is that of the People's weekly, and deals with 'The Uninvited'. Thus ends Mary's correspondence of 1940's. There is no remaining written piece on her views of the County Footballers success in the All-Ireland's Senior Championship, when they defeated an old 'enemy', Cavan, by 1-10 to 1-6. This was a famous event, as she might say, for true Meathians.

From snippets of memory I can recall her say;

'Well, now, young Mattie McDonnell is very promising – he comes from Stonefield, out beside Pat Gillic's farm..... Christo Hand from Ardcath, one of the Hands...The Captain was Brian Smyth, and then Peter McDermott, the Hegler who was really a Corkman... Paddy Dixon from Ballivor........

......the Dixons were good farmers and the Syddan men pronounce that 'Sudden', Bill Halpenny and Paddy Meegan – they could easily have been playing with Louth. In 1912, the Louth Captain was one of the Smiths of Colpe – Jemmie Smith. He bought Smithstown.... It had been owned by.... Oh! Heavenly Mike, what was their name? Yes! The Bowsie Osborne, he married one of the Ladies with a lot of money, and they did great Ceilings.... Where was I? Oh! Football... The local hero was Dessie Taaffe... he wasn't one of our Taaffes....

She could recall the whole team who had brought glory to the beloved Meath, with an unusual genealogical slant, which most sport reporters lacked in those days, being more consumed with mundane facts, like goals and points. Of course, the year ended with an event of considerable importance, in the arrival of a fourth son to Dolly and John at Beamore. Richard the third had landed, a few month after Joseph Collins, second son of Mary and Dr.Denis.

Joe Collins putting manners on his big brother, Edmund, and cousin Richard, c.1952

TRAVELLING AUNT

Travelling Aunt
Now Towell was a soldier from Somerset,
"But please, Auntie Mary, could we ever get..."
After the Rosary child, let us begin,
There's a few trimmin's, we have to fit in.

Now a Darcy from Platin came from Dunmoe,
"But please, Auntie Mary, this time can we go...?"
Not without sunhats, down to the field of hay,
You could just catch cold in the sun today.

Now Cromwell brought in a fellow named Napper
"But please, Auntie Mary, what was a flapper?"
Well young idle women with nothing to do...
As I said, he settled down in Loughcrew.

Now the Raths have a fish-cart in Clogherhead,
"But please, Auntie Mary, all fish tastes like lead..."
Never mind child, we'll have some in milk today,
I'll make a nice stew, still fresh from the say.

Now the Boss used to go to Doctor Chance,
"But please, Auntie Mary, did you have romance?"
Hush child, I looked after the two men,
They needed cooking and minding, now and then.

Now the bowsies haven't sent my dividend,
"But please, Auntie Mary, can we have a lend...?"
You wish to buy comics or books in the shop,
Of course, here is a florin, watch out for Pop.

Now Taaffe, evicted from Sillery's places,
"But please, Auntie Mary, can we go to the races...?"
Don't be gambling money, watch for Delany,
He will win on the strand, sunny or rainy.

Now Patrick McCullen, weaver, lived in Beabeg,
"But please, Auntie Mary, what's wrong with your leg?"
I slipped one wet day and fell in the rain,
The broken right hip never came right again.

Now Hanrahan's Tinkers lived at the crossroads,
"But please, Auntie Mary, do you give them loads...?"
Hush child, I'm just giving some little aid,

The children are hungry, I need some tins made.

Now Ninch was a fine place when Grimes was alive,
"Oh! Auntie Mary, see the taxi arrive..."
Well, bless my soul, indeed what you say is true,
I almost forgot, I'm off to Kilnew.

"But please, Auntie Mary, tell us family links
Before you go off in the big Hillman Minx,
Despite all you've said, we need to know more,
How did all these ancestors get to Beamore?"

'Travelling Aunt'

by John McCullen, published in 'Jingles of the Harness' poetry collection, 1999.

During this time, Mary would have been in her late sixties and older, and the letters reflect the changes in her lifestyle, and places of her residence. Mostly from Hartlands but also Beamore, various guest houses and convalescent homes and at the sea, in St. Patrick's Square. There is a total of fifteen letters, thirteen of which we can date fairly accurately, and two which require some research and a bit of groundwork. I am placing these two at a time, very early in the 1950's, but perhaps some local folk memory may come to the rescue in the future...

An allusion in this first letter to 'Mary's stay in Kells' looked like a positive date in history, until I discovered that Mary (Laurence St.) went to Kells, as often as she could, apart from a teaching post there for six months. On one such occasion, she was invited by Thos, to attend the Ballymacad Hunt Ball, but the Lenten season clashed with the event, and being resident in the Parochial House complicated the attendance. This was smoothed out by bringing the ball gown to Hartlands on one trip, and then getting dressed up, on another one. A strong attraction for Mary , in visiting Uncle Dick, was the fact that he had a complete library of 'William' books! I have a feeling that the 'V.G' as he was called, had his ears close to the ground and that the escape to the Ball would have been hard to keep secret.

Hartlands,Clonmellon, Kells,Co.Meath
Tues 22nd May

My dear Eva,

Many thanks for your letter. It has been a real disappointment to us that Mary's stay in Kells should have been so short and that she should come out here. Do you remember hearing Mary talk about a boarder in Cabra, whose father came from Westmeath, and was a doctor in England. Mary got a letter from her during the summer holiday of 1943 (?) saying that she was going back to England, and would be sent to the Convent of Poles, Herts. This is, I think an 18th century community set up in what had been either an old palace or a mansion with historic associations. Was the girl's name Groarke?

If so her father may be a brother to the Mr Groarke mentioned in the enclosed advt. They were talking here about his case which is very sad. He had one son who had been out in Switzerland for T.B. He came home, got married to a Miss Mangan from Delvin, had one child, and then died of T.B. As the grandfather is an old man, and the boy very young, they have sold the land by auction and are selling the chattels tomorrow. The land joins Jigginstown which old Taylor left to Wilsons, and Jimmie Wilson bought it. We must remember Dick and his exams in our prayers. Has he got any idea what sisters of Charity are in the college Infirmary. Agnes Fay from Peter Street (Sister Patrick) was there some time ago, but she is in Mill Hill now.

What a number of weddings you have impending! What is the name of Pat Taaffe's fiancé? Imagine Mr Donnelly having to buy jewellery for six bridesmaids! Perhaps it is just as well that Granny Smyth is not alive to get such a shock as that!You may remember having heard that the C.S.Sp were thinking of buying Killua Castle for a Juniorate, and sent Fr McQuaid to inspect. He said that the roof was in bad condition and they bought Kilshane, Tipperary instead. When the state of emergency was declared the govt. took over the greater part of it to accommodate refugees should the occasion arise. They left Hacketts the use of some rooms, and spent thousands in fixing the roof and putting in plumbing (that alone came to £600). Now that the land has been sold in six divisions (it is said by the mortgagees) and the Castle has been sold to Smith's of Lincoln Place for demolition.

The men have been taking it down since Monday. Everyone is disgusted that it has not been used as a sanatorium headquarters even if they put up chalets there as well. I think that this Smith is married to a sister of Geo Kavanaghs. Jim must have been interested to see history being made before his eyes.

Did you ever hear anything about the antecedents of the Mr Terence O'Reilly who died so unexpectedly? Who is the billionaire that got Mr. Vincent Kelly to design such a masterpiece in 1934 and that sold it now when the shrubberies, rock gardens etc have grown up? I must try to keep that advt till august so that M. Evangelist may see what one of her former pupils can do.

I am posting you a number of Catholic Fireside which has a few paragraphs about the Bon Secours Convent in Caen Have the Delanys heard from that nun since the Germans were driven from Normandy. Donnellys have let the Mornington bungalow for the season to Mrs Wilson of Boltown. She intends to bring each of her daughters and their families there in turn. Besides Mrs Johnnie Farrell, she has Mrs Boyd whose husband is a nephew of Allens of Whitefields and a conscientious objector, another daughter is a lady doctor married in Dublin. I think that there are some more. I am glad that Paddy and Dick are getting away early this year. It is nice to go about when the evening are so long. Whenever you see Rosita and Theresa remember me to them. Hoping to see you in good form when we go east and with best wishes to all,

I remain,
Yours, Mary

The name of Pat Taaffe's fiancé was Molly Lyons who came from Navan, and was a second cousin of my own, through the McQuillans, on my mother's side, Pat Taaffe was the famous jockey of the 1950's and 60's. Molly's father and brothers were in a veterinary Practise in Navan, while Mr.Donnelly was from Beauparc, and married Doreen Hardy from Drogheda, a daughter of Doctor Hardy.

Letter #2 alludes to Marie McCullen who corresponded with Mary from Los Angeles, a daughter of Mattie, who emigrated in the 1920's. There is some evidence that Marie was a good storyteller, who was picked up at a bus stop in London, once upon a time, by no less a personage as the Queen, who ordered her chauffeur to drive to Marie's hotel!

Mattie and Marie McCullen in later years

Hartlands, Clonmellon, Kells. Co.Meath
13ᵗʰ   Dec

My dear Eva,

Yesterday Marie McCullen's Christmas despatch arrived, made up of one letter, one snap of herself and one snap of Flossie taken with her brother, Mattie, and one four page Christmas Card. Although frost and snow are unknown in Los Angeles, the two landscapes on the cards were so completely covered with snow and the larger one had such shining icicles that you would think it came from Alaska rather than from California. She said that Flossie and her husband have a nice little place not far from them . George is back from Germany and at home with his wife and son.

Her older brother, Matt is still in the army. He is commandant in an officer's home on the Mexican border. She says that he got great honours, including the President's citation, the Bronze medal for having saved the life of a colonel and other distinctions.

Please do not send me any Christmas present – I would rather that you would give it to the Irish Red Cross. Was Jim duly impressed by the fact that the entries for Kells fat Stock Show were 375 this year as against 225 last year? The men folk were there but had no entries. Mr Fagan must take great pains feeding his cattle. Last June he paid £70 for the prize beast that Michael Byrne bought for £100.

Enclosed is a letter from Bartestree. On Monday another came in which May mentioned that the two Irish postulants who had entered with her, have died. One was a Miss Behan from Dublin, the other was Katie Branagan from Waterunder. As her mother had been a sister to Old Nich. Halligan of Banktown she was a first cousin to the late Andrew Collier and to the Halligans. Her father's sister was the second wife of the late Geo. McCarthy and thus mother to the late Mrs Roche and step-mother to the late Jas McCarthy.

About three years ago McDonnell's sold about one half of their big block of shops in Kells to a former shop boy, named Reilly, who turned his new purchases into a lounge bar, equipped very expensively. Last week they sold the adjoining public house and dwelling house for £2400 to Samuel Bell, a Co.Cavan Presbyterian(?) who owns a grocery shop in Market St. Mr Reilly is married to a sister of Fr.Ryans P.P. Ardcath. She comes from Kilbeggan and was in a job in Kells up to the time of her marriage. Both Mr Reilly and Mr Bell have been very active not only in the white but also in the black market. You may remember that when Mr Reilly's oldest girl, who did a course in Edinburgh Domestic School married Dr McGuinness from Dundalk, there were about seventy people to the reception in a Dublin hotel.

O'Reilly's of Castle Park have bought a farm from Jimmy Brogan, the steeplechase jockey of Trim. People were surprised that the house division of Mrs P Sheridan's land at Bolies made £7500. The farm was originally very much larger, but some of it was sold to the Land Commission while her husband was alive, and she sold another lot to her brother about three years ago. Her only child married a Mr Brogan, an only son whose father owns a butcher's shop in Athboy.

Of course you will give Dick our good wishes whenever you see him at Christmas. I have not been in Kells since the day of the auction in Eureka, on the morning of the show the men folk were out of the place before I got up, and I did not want to be there for such a long day. Hoping that you have recovered from the effects of the Jumble Sale and with every good wish to the others, whether they have reached Laurence St or not already,

Yours, Mary

In the strange way that connections occur, the Nicholas Halligan referred to was one of the joint liquidators of the Drogheda Steampacket Company with Patrick McCullen of Beamore, in 1904. The House division of Mrs P.Sheridan's land at Bolies, which made £7,500, in the early 1950's, became the house which I lived in for three years from 1966-1968 while Agricultural Advisor in the Oldcastle area. Bolies townland has the most spectacular wall boundaries to its large fields, which were constructed as a famine relief scheme, and bankrupted the then owner, Hugh 'the Bow' Reilly, who paid one penny per day to the workers.

Beamore, Drogheda.
Thursday 25th May 1950

My dear Eva,

Many thanks for your letter and cuttings. Nichevo's Description of the stock exchange dinner is very well done. Thank God about Dick. Fr. Shortall is a nephew of Fr.Mc Loughlin P.P. of Duleek. When war broke out he was a student in the Irish College Rome. When ordained he served as chaplain to the British Army in Italy. He acted as 'reader' to Fr.Scully who thought a great deal about him. Joe and Tom Met him in Fr.Scully's.

Different families names Oates lived in St.Mary's when I was young. One was a nailer in Pitcher Hill. Of course the machine made nails have long replaced the 'tenpenny nails' that he made. That means they were ten a penny for one size and dearer for the larger ones. Two Misses Fay lived in the Marsh and had dressmaking rooms upstairs in what is now Joe Reilly's office, 41 Laurence Street. Their elder sister had been married to a man named Oates and had a family. I think that their niece, Miss Oates lives in James St opposite St.Mary's. Henry and the Lynches went this morning to see Mary in Ferbane, Best wishes to all, Mary

Ps. Please add a pair of large sized bed socks to my trousseau.

A reference to Henry visiting Mary in Ferbane, is to Mary Lynch, who had entered the Sisters of St.Joseph of Cluny. She was a niece of Henry McC of Beabeg, and afterwards spent years in Kerala, India.

Beamore, Drogheda, Co.Meath
26 May 1950

My dear Eva,

Many thanks for your invitation under ordinary circumstances I'd be delighted to go to you , but I am still so swayed by the weather that it is safer for me to stay where I am . What a nursery of genius the Marsh must be , first to produce a political economist like Geo O'Brien and now to bring forth what may be described as Professor of Applied Art. Trying to adjust myself to having a cousin Deirdre,
I remain,
Mary

Following the spell in Beamore, Mary moved to Beaumont Convalescent Home in Drumcondra, where she studies her fellow residents. The reference to Professor of Art is to Nano Reid.

Beaumont Convalescent Home, Drumcondra, Dublin.
9th June 1950

My dear Eva,

When I asked you to get some things for me I sent you £4 – here is the balance, with many thanks. Here I am the first inhabitant of three new bedrooms which have been added to this particular house. It has brand new furniture, a parquet floor with rugs and a big bay window. There are fifteen bedrooms here, the boarders vary from young girls to grandmothers and aged spinsters. Mrs Cafolla, one of the restaurant people had a car load of grand children to see her. Old Mrs Hallon, an aunt of Briscoe, the stockbroker, has been secretary to the Woollen manufacturer's association, a young Mrs Gaffney went home yesterday to Co.Kilkenny. My next room neighbour, is a young English woman who married an Irish Dr Harding when he was working in England. Since that they came to Ireland and he is a doctor in Baileboro now. The others I will tell you about later and now for Drogheda Affairs. Has the Alverno been sold yet ?
Did any one buy Mattie Langan's? I hope that Mary is having a good rest after her exams. She need not bother about the bed socks, as I have an old pair. Will write you more later,
M

Matty Langans was a farm and residence of 32 acres bordering Beamore, and was purchased by Michael Convery, from Co.Down. His family still live there.

In September 1950, Maura (Kilnew) entered the French Sisters of Charity.

Sr. Maura Pictured with John, Pat, John and Richard at Cabra.

Beaumont Convalescent Home , Drumcondra, Dublin.
12th June 1950

My dear Eva,

Even though head squares have become quite démodé elsewhere, the most stately dowagers use them here. One reason is that as the chapel is in the centre of all the buildings as we pass it on our way to the dining room. It is more convenient to carry a scarf to put on if you want to slip in than to walk back to your bedroom and put on a hat formally. If you would get me a perfectly plain square, a very dark red would clash least with my blue, I would be very thankful.

Just one other job which you need not hurry about. During the spring I sent a parcel of tinned meat through Connell Dolans to Bartestree. When May thanked me , she said that she would be glad to get chicken and ham. Of course, the shop keeper only takes the order and sends it to the factory, ask if any of the factories put up chicken and ham. If so order it, failing that order something else.

Hartlands, Clonmellon, Co.Meath
July 1952

My dear Eva,

When the bus left Drogheda on the Louth excursions Dolly , Anna, Sissy, Una and myself found ourselves beside Lily McGee and the Misses Halligan. After a time one Miss Halligan began to tell me what a lot she thought about yourself and 'the Doctor' and how she hoped that Dr Le Marqaud would be of help to Ollie. For the greater part of the day we were together – they were very pleasant and unaffected. When someone else talked of having gone through the Newgrange caves, nobody screamed!

The Drogheda bus also brought the two Misses Murphy, West St., Miss Mollie Reid, a Mr Art O'Murnaghan who does manuscript illuminations, the Town Clerk, Mattie Corcoran, the Mr Daly who has what used to be McGranes pub near to Peter Lynch's on the Bull Ring and some others.

When we came to Dundalk a bus pulled out before us on the road . It had Mr and Mrs G Tempest, the Protestant Doctor, some priests, a Mr Russell, who I presume is a son in law of the late Micky Meade and some others, the majority of whom had 'a Protestant look'. Mr Tempest explained the layout of some earthworks. When we got to Armagh we had a very good lunch in the City Bakery Cafe. Then we were driven to the Protestant Cathedral where Mr Paterson, the museum curator lectured first and then showed us round.

When you come back I'll tell you about the other places that he showed us – the Catholic Cath., Navan Fort, Gosford Castle, Bessbrook Village and Deramore House. After having seen Navan Fort we drove back to our tea in the C.B Cafe and then started for Gosford Castle, near Markethill, Bessbrook and back to Dundalk by Camlough and Ravensdale. The outing was great value £1 for members and 22/6 for others.

Tom drove to Bettystown on Sat and drove us back . On that day there was a good deal of lightening from Mullingar to Delvin where some cattle were killed but it did not come near us. D.G. Today a letter came from Dolly who said that she enjoyed the outing. She also said that on Sunday and Monday they had gone to Balbriggan to see Eileen who came back there last week. Are the people staying in your hotel like the guests at 'Tankardstown House'? Is this Mary's first trip to the south west? I know that she has been in Cork already.Looking forward to seeing you in Sept and with good wishes to all,

Yours, Mary

PS. The Platten farm sold by Sillery is 'The Lerrigan' on the south side of the road. Taaffes lived here before Sillery's. So poor Miss Carney has left Laurence St. RIP.

Hartlands, Clonmellon, Kells, Co.Meath
31st May 1952

My dear Dolly,

Please excuse my delay in acknowledging your letter and parcels. Enclosed is £10 for the 'Grassmaster' gadget which I trust may live up to its name. On Ascension Thursday we went to Oldcastle. While the men were discussing cattle Bridie drove us out to Loughbawn where the trees have grown greatly since Joe and Sissy lived there.

Jas. Drove here on Monday evening and took Joe and Tom to Loughrea Fair. He bought a wagon of cattle and so did Joe. Today a leaflet came from the B+I about the Dublin to Liverpool service. I hope to go to Hereford soon. Desmond came here on Wed and said that they had met you bound for Mornington on Sunday. How does Richard like the sea?

Best wishes to all especially to him,
Auntie Mary

At this stage of his career, Richard would have been thirty months old. As far as we know, he did like the sea!

Mary was a life member of the Co.Louth Archaeological and Historical Society, and the letter from July gives us an inside view of the Annual Outing. The Drogheda delegation was certainly a high powered group. The particular outing was of such value and popularity that a large group (62) repeated it in August of the same year.

Bartestree Convent, Bartestree, Hereford, England
Fri 18th July 1952

My dear Eva,

Since we came here the weather has been very good. The 9.50 am train from Lime Street was in Hereford about 12.30 and went to Exeter, Torquay etc to finish up in Plymouth.

Of course we have talked and talked to the nuns and have visited Mrs Painter and Mrs Dobbs twice. Mrs Painter (nee Dobbs) is the convert. Her father had a china shop in Cardiff and one in Swansea. She showed us some fine Royal Worcester vases and an ornament of Staffordshire china made in the Dresden style. Her husband, Capt Painter was torpedoed in April 1918 when coming from Gibraltar with a merchant navy convoy. The other four vessels came through but his was blown in two and all forty people onboard were lost.

Mrs Dobbs, her non catholic sister in law has lived for some time in Penzance with a son who is married now. When I mentioned that the former Miss Parr from Drogheda was married to a doctor in Penzance whose names was Reid, I thought she said that a Dr. Reid lives there.

A Yorkshire Redemptorist, Fr Marram is giving a Retreat to the girls, we go to the evening sermon and Benediction. The nuns appreciated Jim and Dick greatly. May is proud that Dick wore the gothic vestments so gracefully! She says that in England the Benedictines use them a good deal.

Joined by May and Sissy in best wishes to all,

Yours, Mary.

The visit to see Mother Anthony Moore in Hereford would be Fr.Richard's first as a priest. The summer of 1952 was a traumatic time for Eva – Fr.Richard, her son was ordained priest with the Vincentians on Sunday 25th May , and Doctor Paddy died suddenly on 22nd June – hardly a month later.

The First Blessing

Fr.Dick, with Dr.Oliver and Mary

Beamore, Drogheda,

My dear Eva,   *Thursday 22nd April 1954*

All here welcome you home. I hope that you do not feel too tired. The weather held up well for the Pageant on Sat and Sunday and has been dry ever since. The G.N.R ran in special services of buses to each point and there were a great number from Ulster in Drogheda on Sat, some people went on the coal boats lying in the river to get a good view. The floodlit scene at Slane is said to have been impressive. Paddy (Kilnew) and Nancy were in Tara on Sunday night and saw the idols being destroyed.

Quite a number of Drogheda people were married during the week. The Kilnews were in Fairyhouse on Tuesday and said that the attendance was large. On Sat I saw Mr and Mrs Stanley Matthews in Drogheda. He seems very much better. Last week Rosita kindly sent me a copy of 'The Old House by the Boyne' which she had bought in Webb's Crampton Quay, the writer, Miss Blake was from Co.Cavan had been a boarder in Sienna. She married a Mr Sadlier, an Irish Catholic, who became a publisher in New York. Her daughter m. a son of Frank Chadwick who had built The Glen, Mornington. Looking forward to seeing you next week,
Yours
M.F.McCullen

Mount Oliver,Dundalk,
13th January 1958

My dear Eva,

Of course I begin by saying that I hope Mary Kingston is in good form and that I pray for her every day. All the guests here are permanent boarders just now. Fr.Crilly, a retired P.P. Armagh Diocese has worked mostly in Tyrone. Fr O'Hanlon has worked in Texas. Miss Murphy is his cousin. Miss Donnelly, Belfast is a retired science (?) teacher. Miss Kavanagh , a former poultry inspector.

Miss Walshe has given up her place in Greystones since the death of her mother and stepbrother and has lived here for four years. She used to play golf and bridge in Greystones, has brought her own car here, drives the nuns about, has taken holidays in Holmes Hall and knows that part of Yorkshire well.

Since coming here I have not seen my heavy brown coat which had been on a hanger in Laurence Street over the light tweed one. However, if it had been left in the car , Mrs McDonnell will let you know. Later on I will write about the house and district which all....   *..... Unfinished*

Editors Note – Mrs McDonnell (nee Durnin) was a taxi operator who lived at the end of Mary Street and one of the Durnin Family of Mornington and Beamore.

In 1957, Mary would become the eldest survivor of her family, when James, her beloved brother died in June, and his wife Annie died in December.

John Drew, Nancy Long, Desmond Drew and John McC   Kathleen & Teddy Sheridan, Jim and Michael Long

Mount Oliver, Dundalk,
28th January 1958

My dear Eva,

In case that you have not seen the Sunday Independent with its very full account of Miss Wingfield's wedding I am sending it on to you.

On Page 7 are some paragraphs about a Miss Smith from Clontarf, whose father, Hugh Smith is a native of Kells and a first cousin to Miss R. M Smith, who was my night nurse in Eccles St. Mr Smith using the gaelicized form of his name MacGowan(?) has contributed to the Irish Tatler and sketch the articles on historic Irish Houses. This series has been running for years and must have entailed a great deal of research.

Today a very nice letter came from Mary Kingston . When does she expect to leave the Leinster ? Although I have been thinking over the matter I cannot remember whether Westland Row or the Catholic University Church would be the correct place for Miss Kingston's baptism. By the way I had.....

.... unfinished

In January 1958, Mary and Billy Kingston were expecting their first child, Rachel, so would merit extra prayers from Aunt Mary. The letter of 28th January suggests that all went well, and Mary and Rachel were resting in Leinster Nursing Home. Having followed a similar pattern some years previously, I would imagine that St.Andrew's Church in Westland Row would have been the 'correct' place for the Miss Kingston's baptism. Several new arrivals also appeared in Drews – Pauline (1950) and Desmond (1958) and Collins's – Denise (1952), Martin (1954) and Maureen (1958), and a son in Hartlands to Thos and Nora, Patrick in 1959.

Thos & Nora's Wedding

In the following letter, Mary is based in #1 St.Patrick's Square, Laytown and this house becomes the Holiday Home for many of her nieces and nephews over the following decade, including myself. We would spend a 'holiday' week with 'Aunt Mary', and enjoy her cooking. Duffners also rented a house in the square.

The Dowager Marchioness of Headfort was the famous Theatre Lady, Rosie Boote, who married the marquis in 1901. She remained a Catholic, and was a very popular lady in Kells, in the Gold Club, and at Church, crowds came to see her. Rosie had been educated by the Ursuline nuns in Thurles and sent her sons to the Christian Brothers in Kells, and then to the English benedictines. Fr.Dick consecrated the ground on the island, where she was buried and all others, including her husband, were buried at the Mausoleum, at Headfort.

1 St. Patrick's Square , Laytown,
Tues 5.15pm

My dear Eva,

Many thanks for your invitation for Thursday – of course you may expect us (D.V). Two of the Kells Mercy Nuns have just paid us a visit. One was M Gabriel O'Reilly whose sister, Sister Theresa of the St.Mary's 'Mercys' died lately. One of her sisters, Mrs McKenna of Mullagh, Cavan is the mother of T.P McKenna who acts in the Abbey Theatre, in the Ardmore Studios, Bray and takes the part of Brian Kennedy in the Kennedys of Castle Ross. His sister Annette entered the French Sisters of Charity some time before Maura (Kilnew) and was sent to their hospital the North Infirmary, to train as a nurse, since she qualified she has been kept there nursing, Hoping to see you and with best wishes to all,

Yours, Mary

PS. Mother Gabriel said that the Dowager Marchioness of H is to be brought to and to be buried in the family mausoleum on an island in the Blackwater.

Guest House, Mount Oliver, Dundalk
Wed 12th Feb 1952

My dear Eva,

Many thanks for having redirected the enclosed letter from Sister Presentation which came here yesterday. The poor thing has so much to think of that I had not expected her to remember about me at all. Since you sent the sweets to Sister Lua and Peter etc they have written to thank me. I hope that Mrs and Miss Kingston are doing well. When you meet Rosita give her my best regards. What new neighbours have come to the other flat?

Dr Walshe from Navan who died lately used to take Donnelly's bungalow at Mornington, some of the family used to play tennis. His wife is a daughter of the late Willie Smith. Quite a number of relatives of the nuns have been staying here to see them before Lent . A Miss Dickson came a few days ago to see her sister, a young widow, who is a novice. There two are the only converts in the family. Miss Dickson lives in the Wirral peninsula, Cheshire near Hoylake and goes into a Liverpool office every day. She stands 5 feet 11 3/4 inches in her stocking feet and is built in proportion.

When another boarder mentioned how hard it is to get a '7' shoe, Miss Dickson said that she wore a '9' and that a shop in London called 'The Tall Girls', stocked all the larger sizes not only in shoes but also in gloves. She promised to write down the address.

On the Sunday before last some delegates came here to arrange for a Catholic summer school to be held in August at Garron Tower in the Glens of Antrim. This place belonged to a younger son of the Londonderry's but he had it set as it stood, family portraits, furniture and all to McNeills Ltd of Larne, who ran a number of hotels in that district. It was lovely with the original etc. Within the last five years the Diocese of Down and Connor bought it and have set up a secondary boarding school there.

Have the Lourdes hospital nuns many of the upper floors filled now ? I hope that some of the night sisters may be able to to sleep there and not have to walk over to the house in Fair St. A visitor from Dundalk said that a lady doctor McAldin (?) who has a job about Dundalk had arranged to go on Saturday to Lourdes in France. However, her car skidded on Friday night and she was brought to Lourdes Hospital , Drogheda with some broken ribs.

Wed 12.2.58

You have probably seen in today's paper that Lord Bective is engaged to Miss Nall Cain. She is a daughter of Cain, the brewer of Warrington. Her grandfather who died within the last few years bought quite a number of things including;

1. *The property of Brockett, formerly the residence of two Victorian Prime Ministers, LordMelbourne and his brother-in-law, Lord Palmerston*
2. *The peerage of Brocket*
3. *Carton House, Kildare*
4. *The Dublin property of the dukes of Leinster.*
5. *The Wicklow Hotel, Dublin*
6. *Bonners hotel, Tralee*
7. *The Bramshill estate, Hampshire*
8. *Walker's Brewery, Liverpool, etc etc*

Presumably she is not a Catholic. Some time ago Uncle Dick, when writing to me mentioned that he had bought a detached house on the east side of the road which leads to Kells Railway station which he intends to turn into a secondary school to be run by the Christian Brothers. Some of these nuns are doing their medical course in Univ College Cork and others are doing nursing in a Cork hospital .

The budding teachers get their B.A. in Glasgow University and do a training course afterwards in the Sacred Heart College, Craiglockard. Yesterday a short letter came from Bartestree in which Sister Anthony mentioned that 'Federation' had been brought about and that everything was being fixed up before the visit of the newly appointed Mother General from Bitherne, Hants.

This is probably the official name of a convent of the order near Southampton which May had mentioned before.

Thank God I feel quite well,

Best wishes to all,

Mary

Dear Eva,

If you have not yet committed yourself in your search for a wireless please suspend operations till I have seen you on Friday (D.V) and explained why. The only piece of Co.Meath news I have is that the Ballivor farm which the late Mr O'Reilly V.S had bought when he went on pension has been sold by his brother Dr.Arthur O'Reilly to Mr Hugh Gibney. Mrs Gibney was formerly a daughter of the late Mr O'Reilly from Killeen who used to supply you with cream.

Some years ago poor Cattie McQuillan said that while some people ' had seen the two days.' Well this O'Reilly lady had seen the four days'. Her husband owned a shop in Castlepollard. They sold it, went to Canada, came back , had a public house at the turf camps in the midlands, sold it and have come back to Co.Meath now!!

Best wishes to all, Looking forward to Friday,

Mary

Cattie McQuillan was wife of Al McQuillan who ran the large grocery shop in West Street. She had sons Noel, Desmond and Aidan and a daughter Maeve (Lappin), and was my mothers Aunt by marriage. Cattie was originally a McNamara, and related to Eva in her own right. An original Fr.McNamara was one of the founding Vincentian Priests in Ireland.

Cattie Mac Namara with family, and Maryjane Dolan at Brookville.

As the decade faded, Sara Jane Kingston arrived in 1959, the new Agriculture College at Warrenstown was opened, Naper's Mansion at Loughcrew was gutted by fire, and 'the largest ever' meeting in Clonmellon Hall took place on February 4th to protest against a proposal to amalgamate Clonmellon and Delvin Dispensary Districts. Meath footballers had won their second All-Ireland Championship in 1954, and Aunt Mary gloried in the genealogy of the Lenehans of Duleek, since Kevin was on the team.

Kevin with Sam Maguire

CHAPTER 12: 1960 - 1970

SETTLED AT SEA

Having lived in probably ten houses along the seafront of Laytown and Bettystown over the years, Mary knew every stick, stone and shell of the place, not to mention all the people who came there for their summer holidays and each nun in the various congregations as well. If she did not know the nun, it would not take her long to work out who was their aunt or uncle and there they hailed from. Young nephews providing company to her, like Pat, or myself John Drew or Paddy Ball suffered restrictions of social activity as well as being sent to bed early, while there was still action outside on the green or particularly of grief to John Drew, the lure of the swinging boats at the Carnival in Laytown.

School Outing to Laytown Beach, Pat McC at rear, John in middle row, Pat Duffner in front.

My most serious difficulties were in the area of food, menus and cooking. Two examples will suffice. A certain fisherman and his cart of fish was wont to come from Clogherhead to sell his catch along the way through Termonfechin, Drogheda and on to Mornington, Bettystown and Laytown. By the time Mr.Rath would reach Saint Patrick's Square, the horse, the Owner and the fish would all be weary and Mary would take pity on him. She would do a bulk deal and we might then have fish daily for a week.

My aunt always supported the farmers, so it would be cooked in milk. I was a picky enough eater at the best of times so I devised a strategy to avoid the fish. Mary was dutiful to men, so she would serve me, and stand waiting for a command. I would make great show of eating the first fork full and then request salt, pepper, or mustard, whichever one was missing from the table. She would wobble off to the kitchen to get it and I would grab the fish, and deposit it on the inner chimney ledge of the open fire. Gone !

Returning Mary would say   *' Oh, John, you made short work of it'!*
'I did indeed ...it was tasty.'
'Would you like some more ?'
'Oh not at all thanks, I am full!'

I often wondered that she was so gullible after being reared with seven brothers. In the second example, I fared less well. The one dish that I thought was safe from Aunt Mary's Cooking was cornflakes, so I looked forward eagerly to breakfast. Arriving down to the dining room on my first morning, I found Mary with a heap of cornflakes in a large meat dish on the table. She was busily picking cornflakes out of it into my breakfast dish, one by one. Being a thrifty woman, she believed in wasting nothing, so always put scraps and leftovers in a cornflake box for my mother to feed the hens with, at the weekend. Alas ! The empty box had got confused with the fresh one, and so the pieces of onions, rashers, eggshells, potato skins and grizzle had been tipped into the new cornflakes, and then shaken up. The only answer was to sort them out, manually.

I am afraid that my taste buds were traumatised, particularly because her eyesight was poor in one eye, and bits of grizzle in cornflakes are off putting! These incidents happened in St.Patrick's Square but at the time of our first letter of the sixties, Mary was living in Ardpatrick, just over the wall from the square.

Ard Patrick,Laytown
My dear Eva,   *15th March 1961*

Yesterday I heard that Drake Rath in the parish of Castletown, Kilpatric had been bought by Mr Cullen Brophy from Arizona. I do not know what is the price, but probably you may hear that from Beechville. Hugh Brophy and Nattie Lacy had to do with it.

About 1918 the Misses Gargan sold it. One of their sisters had been married to Laurence Ball who settled about Maynooth. The buyer, Mr Mc Ardle native of the six counties owned some pubs and hotels along the south coast of England. He was married twice but had no family. On the death of his second wife, the farm passed to his cousin, a Dr Bradley from about Belfast. He held it for some years and sold it for £60,000, inclusive of stocks, to a Scottish family named Cameron. You may be sure that that they got a good deal from the present owner. Some years ago one of the Navan Loreto nuns lent me a book about Arizona by a Mr Cullen Brophy. The dust jacket gave particulars of his career. Find out all you can but do not quote me please,

Best Regards, Mary

P.S. Have you heard that Michael and Mrs McDermott are home on holiday from New Zealand. They have been to Lourdes and Dublin to stay with various relatives.

In May of 1961, Nancy (Salmon) married Barry Cassin, best described as a 'man of the theatre'. Salmon was soon to buzz with the sounds of children, once more., Anne, James, Philip and Andrew.

Ard Patrick, Laytown
Sat 17ᵗʰ Feb 1962

My dear Eva,

Please read this very carefully and note the change of programme. When I came back here last night I heard that Fr.Dick had written from Kells to say that he would come here to Laytown on Tuesday evening, spend the night here and go from here to Balbriggan on Wed morning. That frees you and Jim from the job of coming round here to pick me up but never-the-less I am very thankful for your offer.

To turn to the subject. This week's Drogheda Independent has a notice about the death of Mrs Bridget Brannigan, Lisdornan. She and her husband came from Seagrave of Dunany to us about 1909 or 1910. He had been a ploughman and she had been children's nurse in Dunany and both were very decent people. The June after they came, a daughter was born who was christened Rose. There were other children too. They left us to go to Jemmie Hoey in Raholland, but whenever I met her in Drogheda on a Sat she would tell me about her family, her grand children and her great grandchildren R.I.P.

Thanking you again for your helpfulness and hoping that the programme may not change again (!!).

Yours, Mary

Mary and her brother, Dick...

Dear Dick,

This issue of the Drogheda Independent has an article about our local Dominicans. Your grandfather told me, that the Dominican nuns were founded in 1717 (?) from Taylor's Hill, Galway. The first Prioress was Mother McMahon, a grandniece of Oliver Plunkett. Their convent was in Dyer Street, the site of which is owned by the Dead Meat Company. Towards the end of the eighteenth century they started building Sienna convent and moved there.

When the nuns were in Dyer St, some of the Dominican priests lived on the Marsh and used to go by boat to say Mass every day in the Dyer St. Convent. That is not mentioned in the Independent article but is mentioned in an article which the Old Drogheda Argus printed long ago which I heard from your grandfather as well as the fact that they lived in Donore.

Other pre-Reformation foundations in Drogheda includes the Carmelites on the site where the Church of Ireland was built in 1810. Some of the local pre-ref Catholic families like Gogarty (Beamore), Cunningam, (Beamore) and Reilly (Duleek St.) were buried there till their families died out. Another religious houses owned the lands from John St, westwards, including all the lands all the Ballsgrove property. I do not know the name of that order. A Dublin man got possession of it, also its property at Killartry, Co.Louth. After his death, his daughter, Mrs Ball inherited both properties. In 1918 descendant Geo de Belle Ball, sold Ballsgrove to the late Bertram Allen Geo Ball left two daughters, who rented St.Josephs's, Laytown from McKeowns. They became Catholics and live in Kent now.

I think that the Fransicans were on the east side of the town that the property went down to the river. Aylmer of Dollardstown got it at the breakup. I do not know the names of the orders who lived on the west side of Shop St and in the Old Abbey. The Trinitarians lived about Trinity St.

Joined by Auntie Sissy in best wishes for the present year, Your Sincerely ,
Auntie Mary

Ard Patrick, Laytown
Tues 9th April 1963

My dear Eva,

Many thanks for your helpfulness to me on Friday, for which I am very thankful. Just now I am remembering your intentions, including a suitable successor to Pauline. On account of the Lenten devotions, it is unlikely that I shall see you this week. Whenever you see Fr.Dick, give him our best regards.

The Michael Fintan Dodd of the enclosed paragraph was the youngest son of the man who designed and owned the Central Hotel in Peter St. Pat Dodd came from Dublin and had charges of Board of Works Schemes about Drogheda . He was the architect who designed the Dublin Road convent for the Sisters of Mercy and St.Mary's Church James St. He also designed the Brown Derby and the adjoining houses for the late Pat Kelly, father of Fr. Paul .He married Miss Curran whose confectionary shop occupied the site of the Singer Sewing Machine Company. He replaced the confectionary house with the present building, bought the adjoining Peter St. Site and built the Central hotel there. The family used to come to school to St.Mary's in my time. They were Packey, Maggie, Brendan, Cattie And Finnie (otherwise Michael Fintan) who was very much younger that I – about the age of Uncle John. Both the parents died young, leaving Joe Curran (Mrs D's brother) and Dan Corry the guardians. The family spent their holiday in Balgeen with Corrys.

Packy and Brendan did engineering in Inchicore and settled in Pittsburg. Maggie went into Clery's after leaving school and went to Pittsburg to her brothers. Cattie became a Holy Faith nun and has died since. Finnie used to take a house from Mrs Creaser Smith. Looking forward to seeing you again and with best wishes to all,

Yours, Mary

Apart from population changes in Salmon, Mary and Billy also had extra mouths to feed, Charles (b.1960), Miriam (b.1962) and John (b.1963) had added to the large rambling house in Mespil Road and Mary alludes to this in our next letter, second paragraph.

The family in Hartlands also increased in the 1960's with the arrival of Joan (1960), Alice (1962), Helen (1963), Joe (1965) and a namesake for Aunt Mary, Mary Frances (1967). In Fair Street, arrivals were Luke (1961), Patricia Ann (1963) and John (1965).

St.Margaret's, Laytown
Sat 25th May 1963

My dear Eva,

Many thanks for your letter, and also for having sent the message through Joseph Collins who came here on Thursday afternoon. Yesterday (Friday) I went to Drogheda, met Dolly and went out to Beamore . Richard's holidays begin on 5th June!! Pat and John's exams start later. Please remember them in your prayers.

Give my best wishes to the Kingstons – I hope that Mary may get a suitable help.

The late Fr Hickey CM, was the son of a man who had a drapery shop next door to Boyer's in Earl St. Old Mr H had a brother who was a Dominican priest and was stationed about Dublin in the early 1900's. He would be an uncle to the Vincentians.

When Edward Reilly's family moved to Dublin about 1892 the youngest daughter, who had served her time in Clarkes drapery got a job in Hickey's. The family used to attend Phibsboro Church and became friendly with Fr. Jones C.M? and it was she who entered the French Sisters of Charity and who died in Hull. In after years Hickey's were replaced in the drapery by Bolger's who I think have moved since to the opposite side of the street. If Michael Smyth and his wife throught they were coming to the real country when they bought Coolagh Lodge, they will have to think again !

Mr. McAvinny, Olga's Uncle, who bought McEvoy's holding, which goes over the lane, to Macken's has been selling building plots on his field at the top of the road from Drogheda. So far most of the houses are one storied, but a two storey house with twelve rooms is being built for the manager of the Singer Sewing Machine Company. As the field is on the top of the hill between Drogheda and Beamore, the views from it are fine. Bellewstown etc. Can be seen from the South, Tullyesker from the north, the Louth and Mourne Mountains on the north east and the sea due east.

Yesterday Uncle Dick came here with Tom and stayed till 6pm. While he was here Oonagh drove down and Nancy and Miss Cassin in her car. Oonagh hopes to move to Howth in August. Best wishes to all and hope to see you on on Friday (D.V.)

Mary

Seamus Phelan (Howth resident) with Ann McC

The reference to Sr. Mary Francis Reilly is to the holy nun who features in a chapter of 'My Dearest Annie'. She died in 1949.

This is the first letter from the new bungalow, opposite the church in Laytown, to which Sissy and Joe retired, offering a space to Mary once more. For whatever reason, the twelve roomed two storey house for the Singer sewing machine manager, Mr. Michael O'Leary, never got built. A large bungalow now occupies the site, and Michael and Monica O'Leary became godparents to Colm McCullen (b.1977).

St.Margaret's, Laytown,Co.Meath
7th August.63

My dear Eva,

As I do not intend to go to Drogheda this week I am sending you some surmises about who occupied Kilineer House from 1900 onwards. After Richard Montgomery of Beaulieu had married Miss Robinson they were tenants of Platten Hall while Wm Jameson had succeeded Casey Connolly as tenants of Beaulieu. Montgomery's left Platten and took or bought some place to the North West of Drogheda which may have been Kilineer, where they lived till about 1911.

Freddy Smith, Montgomery's uncle, had been a tenant of Ball's Grove House from the 1860's till Geo de Belle Ball and his two daughters came back to live in it about 1911 (?). Mrs Montgomery (nee Robinson) inherited Rokeby Hall about that time. She determined to live in Beaulieu, sold Rokeby Hall to Johnnie Clinton, uncle of Mrs Lochrin, paid Jamesons some compensation for the expired term of their lease of Beaulieu and was preparing to go back to live there when she died unexpectedly in April or May 1912 .In that year I was at the Spring Show in Ballsbridge where she was pointed out to me. She was dead about eight days afterwards. Freddy Smith and his family lived I think in Kilineer. After his death his daughters moved to England. After the 1914 war some Englishman lived there who was in the seed business in Narrow West Street. I do not remember from whom Jas Carroll bought it.

Best wishes to you all, Mary

St.Margaret's, Laytown, Co.Meath
Friday 9th Dec 1966

Dear John and Dolly,

For the last ten days I had been intending to go over to Beamore and was waiting for the weather to get settled. However, I had not left Laytown for the last fortnight but am living in hopes!!

Please accept my best wishes for Christmas and the New Year to all of you whether in Beamore or elsewhere. Yesterday's paper had the notices of the death of Philly Dolan (R.I.P). His father had a shop in the house which belongs to Flanagan in West Street. His uncle had a grocer's shop in Laurence Street about where McKeons are now and was married to a daughter of Captain Guinety of the Drogheda boats. Philly Dolan's mother, Mrs Jas Swift and my mother were all great friends of Lissie and Mary Callaghan and used to get their hats etc, in the shop which now belongs to J.Reilly, The Solicitor.

After the golden wedding gathering I ordered copies of the photographs which Vin Duffner had taken and thought that I would have them in time to send them to you for Christmas. However, they have not turned up yet but when they do come I will send them on.

In the meantime with best wishes,

I remain,

Auntie Mary

The Family Group

Back row – Jim Ball, Thos, Nora, Denis, Mary and Des Drew.
Front Row – Nancy, Joe, Sissy and Bawn

St.Margaret's, Laytown, Co.Meath
Monday 9th Oct 1967

My dear Eva,

Many thanks for your letter and R.U.K.B.A a list better for me to get the business dealt with first. The list gives the names of 5 candidates deceased, one of them is Mrs M.A. Cunningham. Mr B Cunningham has got a special annuity. That leaves you free to give votes to Mrs Curran OConnor , Mrs Godfrey and Mrs Bowe. Thank God that Marie Austin had such a peaceful passing and had lived to see her grandchildren.

So you are going to 'Delgany Inn'. When you are, there you may see 'Glencullen House'. One of Dan O'Connell's daughters married a Fitzsimons and had a daughter who was a boarder in Siena Convent, Drogheda in the 1860's.

There were some celebration which my grandmother (1827-1890) attended. When my mother mentioned that Miss O.C.F was a granddaughter of Dan O'Connell, my grandmother who had often seen Dan, remarked 'Wouldn't I know her out of Dan and his potato face!!'

You know that the O'Connells used to claim that they had always been good looking till Dan O'C's father married someone (I forget the name) who had bad teeth and a turned up nose', which she passed on to Dan. But then in-laws can be very critical!!

In May 1916 P.D sent me to Lacy's Hotel Bray, to shake off an attack of flu. While there I hired a push bike and explored the district of Delgany, Glen of the Downs and Kilmacanogue. One day I walked round Bray head into Greystones and came back by train.

It was quite a godsend that Mary Kingston and Mary Ball got in touch in 96. Joe was talking to Billy and Miss Kingston in Mounttown. Uncle John also climbed the hill to it. Bawn and Mary have been so busy, Bawn expecting the people coming home and Mary Collins sending off Edmund and Joseph, that they have not been here lately.

Eamonn Delany's eldest son, Eamonn Jn, is to be married on Wed in Duleek to Alma Wall of West Carn House. Her father is a brother of Mrs Callans, Willie Wall etc. The bride had been an air hostess, who joined the Australian airlines. The Meath Chronicle says that when bidding stopped at £14,500 it was withdrawn and sold afterwards to Mr Moffat of Balmoral (Dublin) Ltd Furniture manufacturers for an 'undisclosed' sum. (What would it be?).

Some time in the 1860's a Mr Lyons-Montgomery of Belhavel Co.Leitrim who had 7 daughters thought that they would be more likely to pick up husbands in the Duleek Beauparc , Drogheda area than in Co.Leitrim. He took a place near Bessbrook Annesbrook area and in due course his daughters settled in places . Here is an account of the after life of these girls;

       i.   *One m. Col Herstemann*
      ii.   *One m. Charlie Smyth and was mother of the 'Hildegards'*
     iii.   *One m. Ralph Smith of Termonfeckin (now An Grianan)*
     iv.   *One married Smith of Annesbrook*
     v.   *One married Ralph Smith of Greenhills (son of St. Geo Smith)*
     vi.   *One m. Gen Cavagnan (killed in Kabul 1880)*
    vii.   *One m. Another Smith or Smyth, I cannot remember*

The Golden Wedding Anniversary gathering was that in honour of Joe and Sissy which was a rare bringing together of the older McCullen family. As is often the case with such events, it was well it took place when it did in the Autumn of 1966 because my father, John, died suddenly in late October 1967. This passing was a shock to everyone since he neither smoked nor drank alcohol.

Dolly Dolan McCullen with Fr.O'Connor

John McC with Fr.Johnson

St.Margaret's, Laytown, Co.Meath
Sat 9th December 1967

Dear Eva,

Many thanks for your letters and enclosures. I hope that Jim is getting better now. It is a good thing to know that Mrs Godfrey has been elected. I must ask Collinses about Mrs Bower? How are John and Mona Rath getting on ? Keep any literature that you have about R.U.B.A for me, there is no hurry about it. The Mr Allen whose orchard at Julianstown has been advertised is a non-Catholic from Roscommon. Would this be the farm from which Lord Gormanston evicted the Fullams and which Mortimer, a Co.Cavan protestant held for a time. In my lifetime Mrs Capt. Brannigan told your father in law that her Fullam brother-in-law had been reinstated. Phyllis Fullam owned it afterwards – she may have sold it.

It is a pity about Lily Magee. I had been wondering if there was anyone about the town like Elsie Swift who could set her two rooms, that is if her health was reasonably good. Don't say that to anyone else!! That £5-5-0 should be very heartening to Mary Lynch, congratulating Mary Kingston having secured a maid and with good wishes to everyones including Rosita,

Yours, Auntie Mary.

PS. Laytown and Bettystown are having Fancy Fairs to pull down the debt. Last Sunday's gathering took £100 gross – that is £80 net. £50,000 seems to be the only figure for premises in Drogheda. Did Stephanie sell her West St. Shop? What family has she besides her sons (Schwers). There have been two cases in which the C of I. clergyman's offers of celebration have been disregarded.

The first was in 1909 when old Joe Osborne was brought from Brighton to be buried in Stamullen when the then Rector, the Rev Mr Preston turned up, the late Frank Osborne of Smithstown, a nephew of Joe's and the father of the late Mrs Coddington stood up and declared that Fr. Davis would attend to the burial. Joe was the second son of the old Squire and had always remained a Catholic. His elder brother, Henry and his younger brother, Frank, had both married Protestants and had their families brought up in the Church of Ireland.The other case was rather different. It happened one Sat, in 1947, when I was staying in Beamore and I was in Drogheda that afternoon when it happened. When Pat and John were at school in the Dublin Road Convent, Pat was in the same class as Robert Kingston (usually known as 'King Robert'). The family lived in Jack Connolly's house. Robert's father had been brought up as a Protestant, had married a Catholic and became a Catholic. His grandfather, a widower lived with them and was C. ofIreland. The grandfather had been taken to Jervis St. Hospital for some treatments.

When there he asked to be received into the Catholic Church on the day before his death. Word was sent to his relatives. The coffin came down on the afternoon train. Rev. Mr. Charles turned up at the station. So did Fr.Laurence Lenehan, PP. St.Mary's. The relatives told Mr.Charles what had happened in Mr. Kingston's last 24 hours.

Saying goodbye again, Auntie Mary.

PPS. Another 11th hour conversion is that of Mrs.Plunkett of Barristown who went to the only Anglican convent in Ireland and became Catholic before her death.

The congratulations to Mary Kingston may have been to do with an added member of the family, Christopher, who had arrived in 1966. References around this time to R.U.K.B.A – the Royal United Kingdom Beneficient Association had to do with how members voted to award private pensions or help gentlefolk who fell on hard times. I think two cases came up annually (?) and were voted on by the membership. This led to canvassing beforehand.

St.Margaret's, Laytown, Co.Meath
Monday 15th Jan 1968

My dear Eva,
All here sends your best wishes and hope that you are getting rid of your flu. The visit from Fr.Dick, C.M. was very welcome – our only regret was that it did not last very much longer!! Enclosed is a letter from Eileen Rooney (Sister Giovanni). It has such a beautiful thought that I am sending it to you rather than trying to paraphrase it.

Thanks for having sent the R.U.K.B.A sheet which I mean to send to Sister Acquinas Boylan of Clara. She says that there is only one family in the parish that would be interested in joining. Most of the people have the factory wage earning mind but if she can get one subscriber so much the better. Mrs Bowe has been elected. Thank God that Mrs Godfrey has got in as well. Have you heard anything lately about John and Mona Rath ?

Later on I mean to write to Mary Kingston who is doing well I hope. So Geo Donnelly is engaged to Miss McEnery , who is a stepdaughter of Denis Gwynn. Where ever you go , you and your relations seem to trip up against the Gwynns. Father Aubrey S.J whose parsonical appearance struck Fr.Dick in U.C.D and who visited you in Laurence St, when his mother was in Stamullen Convent and now his brother Denis, who married then widowed Mrs McEnery.

Did you know that Emily O'Reilly, Geo D's cousin was a nursery governess to the Gwynns in the early 1900's and taught as well as her sister, Sheila who married a Doctor Moorehead who was blind and not a Catholic. Mrs Tommy McCullen is back in Mile House. She had been in Kilkenny where her sister, Mrs Warren died on Christmas Day R.I.P

Do not bother to acknowledge this screed. Mr Jas Matthews residence in the advts was given as 'Mitchelstown'. Well in the 1870's a friend of my mother's from Duleek parish was married to a man from Hoathstown, Ardee.

A priest who had been in Duleek had been moved to Hoathstown district thought a great deal about the then Mrs Matthews, grandmother of the present Jas Matthews. She was niece and heiress of a Jimmie O'Farrell who had a very big shop in Kells. Besides her son, Arthur, she had two daughters. One of them married Roantree. The other married a bank man as well. Was his name Perry and was he stationed in Cork? Remember my good wishes to you all,

Yours, Mary F

Fr.Richard withPope Pius XII and Pope Paul VI

St.Margaret's, Laytown, Co.Meath
Thurs 7th March 1968

Dear Eva,

There is no need to acknowledge this. I hope that you and all the family are keeping free from colds etc. So Joe Carr has been buried in Colpe. Well Well Well and not in Kilsharvan. I have often told you that about 1713 Mr Pearson from Athboy bought the townland of Beamore. He built a 4 story redbrick mansion, something like Platten Hall, planted chestnuts, beeches and sycamores and evergreen oaks. He also built a circular redbrick ice-house which he covered with a two foot thick blanket of clay and grass.

Having done all that, he died leaving the property to his niece, Hester Coghill, who was the wife of Moore, Earl of Charleville Forest, near Tullamore. Hester's paternal uncle was Sir Marmaduke Coghill a judge in Dublin. He had also built a house at Drumcondra, which he left to Hester. This is the original block of All Hallows College. It still bears above the entrance the crest of the Coghills. It is a cock crowing on a hill. Well as Hester had so many houses at her disposal, she set the dwelling house and immediate fields to a North of Ireland man named Coulter .

He grew flax, had it woven and left out to bleach, one field is still called the Bleach. To work the flax he brought people from the north. The people around called them ' The Yons'? as they used some words that were strange to the natives. ' Yon' was their word for 'that', 'Do you see yon house?' meant ' Do you see that house?' Well Joe Carr's ancestors were amongst the 'yons' – the name Kerr is very general in Ulster. Other 'yons' were Maxwells.

Mr. Coulter lacked common honesty so much that when he got tired of living in the big four storied red bricked house which Pearson had built that he stripped all the lead off the roof, sold it and went to live in the big house at the Boyne Viaduct – St.James. After his death when the hand loom weaving was declining, the weavers who lived in huts stuck up against the orchard walls, died out by degrees. Their families went elsewhere. In the 1860's when your father-in-law was able to write, he got the job of writing on behalf of the older people to a Carr, who was a sailor on a steamer in the 'Great Lakes'. One Maxwell who went into Jameson's Distillery in Drogheda, was brought to Dublin, by Jameson's when they ceased distilling in Drogheda. His son worked with John Gore ? in the Temperance Movement of the Capuchins. His daughter was the organist in Church St. In the early 1900's.

Another Maxwell joined the British Army, was an artillery man, who got into Kabul before Lord Roberts, who got a title for going there. Perhaps Kingstons might like to read these items. The 'bog' may have been widened to do form a 'pool' to ret the flax. In Beabeg there is also a big pool which could have been made for the same use. The old P McCullen, whose picture is in Beamore was a master weaver on a smaller scale, usually about 3 or 4 men worked for him. Besides the flax grown in the district , the master weavers about Beabeg used to go down to Granard to buy flax. Each master brought his wife. They travelled in convoy in covered wagons, something like the fashion of pioneers which you see recorded in the Western Films.

After Mrs McCullen (Bridget Hammill) died about 1830, her husband made up his mind to give up the linen trade and devote his attention to bringing up his family of four sons and 2 daughters.

They were; James (1817-1877), Patrick died about 1910, Mary 1882, m P.Sheridan, had 2 daughters, (Mercy Nuns in Ballinrobe), John died in 1880's unmarried, Henry 1824-1903 m Elizabeth Cartin and had 13 children, and Jennie 1892

John McC, with Noel Dempsey launching the heritage trail at Kilsharvan Graveyard, where many McCullen's are buried.

The dishonest Mr Joseph Coulter died in April 1810 aged 98 years and is buried in St.Mary's Church of Ireland Graveyard in Drogheda, with eleven of his children and grandchildren, under a monument raised by his son, George of St.James, Drogheda.

The next letter is an unusual example of the political thinker in Mary, analysing and making a decision. It is no harm to point out that the plan was to change the voting system, away from Proportional Representation to the system used in the British Elections. Back in Beamore, Ruth, born in 1968, and was the first girl in Beamore since May 7th, 85 years previously.

St.Margaret's, Laytown, Co.Meath
Tues 15th Oct 1968

Dear Eva,

You must not acknowledge this – I hope that you all are in good form. Dick must be busy back in Maynooth. If the Duleek nuns could raise the money, it would be a great thing for them to buy the Dowth Institute.

On Sunday Dick Brannigan and Frank Roe spoke in Laytown on the P.R issue. As the system has worked all right since 1922 I see no reason to change and I hope to mark X in the No squares tomorrow D.V. If minorities feel frustrated with no hope as in the six counties there is bound to be broken windows , and bomb throwing, on one side, with repression on the other.

At a general election people may prefer the programme of Fianna Fail, F Gael or Labour and should get a chance. The straight vote has been working in the six counties , plain for all folks to see !People who abstain 1may be personated.

The Mullingar Presentation nuns have bought the house on the ? grandfather had practicing on the north side of Dublin and is mentioned as having attended Lord Edward Fitzgerald. One of Dr John Adrian's sisters was a French sister of charity, the other married John Macken of Clonsword, a brother of Dan Macken.   Their only child , Nan, left her money to the St Vincent de Paul Society. Tina Drew, Mrs Collier, has just called on her way from the dentist. She intends to visit you. Dr John Adrian had the reputation of being a great shot. He used to shoot the 'Long Leg' , a field in Beamore , which harboured snipe, wild ducks, water hens, and plover. As snipe whirls round instead of flying on, it used to be regarded as a great feat to be able to bring down a snipe.

Congratulations on Mr Boland on having been selected as candidate by F G. So Brendan Crinion is retiring after having come out so strongly in his support of Fianna Fail,

Mary F

St.Margaret's, Laytown, Co.Meath
Sat 19th October 1968

Dear Eva,

Many thanks for your letter. I am glad that you have decided in the best choice for the R.U.K.B.A. Would R.U.K.B.A consider keeping Mrs Esther permanently in Duleek? They have done so in other cases. Nora McQuillan is lucky. Thank God that Mary Collins is doing well so far!!

During the 1914-1918 war Uncle Dick used to go from Mullingar every Sun to offer mass in the Netterville Institute. It would be unfortunate if such a foundation which has done so much good from the 1820'2 should come to an end through lack of a convenient bus service, perhaps some institute for retarded people might take it over. So Florrie Ryan was not a 'scattersilver'. Ryans were fromTipperary, I think a branch of the 'Scarteen Family', who kept a pack of hounds even during the times of the Penal Laws. Mrs Power Lalor of Long Orchard Templemore who founded the 'Dispersed Ladies Assoc.' had been a Miss Ryan.

Aristides Onassis seems to have had ' a rag on every bush' before he thought of Mrs Kennedy. Apart from the religious issues , it is surprising that she is bothering about a man whose only interest in life seems to be 'besting' other people. What would they have to talk about? There must be plenty of Americans or English with whom she would have more interests in common. And then her children – growing up cruising – about on a yacht, separated from grass roots of the USA. Poor John F, who cried when his third child died; Cardinal Cushing must be saddened.

Congratulate your nephew, Mr Boland for having spoken out on the PR matter at the Dublin Co. Council, with Taca and all the rest, it required a great deal of moral courage to make such a stand. Of course now, when the result is known, it is easy to open one's mouth but before this, one would be told ' You could not tell when it would come agin you.'

Many people feared that the question was too abstract and that people would not bother to vote but quite a number despite inconveniences did vote . Louth had always a body of A.O.H people who never went Sinn Fein, so that their rallying is not surprising but Meath, who were so bitterly pro Dev during the economic war finds most of the young people in farming societies have no use either for warriors of the 'where were you in '16? School or the young Mr Brendan Crinion who told the public that his division is 60 miles long, that he has not time to be giving everyone the attention that he'd like at present. Perhaps at the next election the task may be taken from him.

Do you read the reports of the sales at Doncaster and Newmarket. Well Doncaster was started some years ago by Arthur and Willie Stephenson with a third partner. The Stephensons were farmers (not county people) in Westmeath. Uncle John said he used to see Willie Stephenson carrying his saddle into Oldcastle station to cross to England. He never was a first class jockey, but always had a great judgement about horses and has trained Derby runners, one for McGrath and has made Doncaster sales a success. Years ago when Uncle Anthony had land taken at Gormanston, a daughter of Sir J Arnott and her little boy was living with Lady Gormanston. She was Madam van Cutsen.

When Anthony and the herd would stop to go through the fields, young Van C would put on wellingtons to join them. He is training horses at Newmarket and had got hold of some very rich clients. He gave absurd prices at the Newmarket Sales lately.

Best wishes to you all,

Mary

Much of Mary's charitable work was hidden – the correspondence in the next two letters is an example of a 'thank you' note!

St.Margaret's, Laytown, Co.Meath
Wed 11th Dec 1968

Dear Eva,

This note came from Miss Gordon today. Thank God she is being cared for. Please do not send me anything for Christmas or the New Year – the same applies to Mary and the others. If you send a few bob to the Itinerants Fund, it would help to put a roof over someone's head. Some years ago when the late Fr McQuillan came to Ireland, he visited Laytown and went over his old home, St.Anne's.

If by this time you have recovered from your travels in South East Ireland, please tell me more about your experience they should have been interesting. Who benefits by Gabriel Brock's money – poor Miss Hipwell.

c/o Rev Mother, St.Patrick's Ward, Our Lady's Hospice,
Terenure, Harold's Cross, Dublin
10ᵗʰ Dec 1968

My dear Miss McCullen,

Many thanks for your welcome letter and enclosed. I was delighted to hear from you. The day I received your letter. I was moving here and at present I am very tired as my health is poor. If you are ever in this direction do call in to see me. Of course the coming here was the best for me. As I will get the best care.

With best wishes to yourself and Mrs McCullen,
From Anne Gordon

Father McQuillan was a son of Willie McQuillan, an uncle of my Mother. He was a Carmelite Priest who worked in Rhodesia, for many years. When John died in October 1967, he left no will, believing that his Father's will dealt with lands he had inherited, but were only his 'for his day'.

This position caused a substantial death duty bill and uncertainty for his wife, Dolly, and family. Eventually, an unusual deed was drawn up, by which all the descendents of Pat McCullen would sign away their legal claims to such lands, in favour of Dolly. This they all generously did.

 However a great deal of research was required by Dolly to ascertain the facts of title of the various pieces of land. Who better to know the peculiar details of each holding than Mary.

The next letter speaks for itself.

St.Margaret's, Laytown, Co.Meath
Mon 15ᵗʰ Jan 1969

My dear Dolly,

Here are all the particulars that I can remember about the different pieces of fee simple land which is scattered about. I hope that it may be of some help to you. All here send you best wishes for the New Year and hope that your household may escape cold and flu. Mrs Anna Jordan is at present in Lourdes Hospital. Do not bother to acknowledge this,

Yours, Auntie Mary

Pat McCullen, Beabeg was born in 1783 and died in 1861.
In 1816 he married Bridget Hammill and had four sons and 2 daughters.

The only ones to concern us were James McCullen, Beamore and John St. and Henry McCullen, Beabeg and John St.

Both were builders. He married Elizabeth Cartin. He had been born in 1824 and died in April 1903 and had a family of 13.

James McCullen (1817-1877) married Ann Taaffe in 1850. She died after the birth of her son, Patrick McCullen (1852-1938).

Patrick McCullen married Annie Moore in Feb 1881. She died in June 1915. They had seven sons and one daughter. They were:

> *James McCullen, born Dec 1881, died in June 1957.*
> *Mary Frances, b.1883*
> *Rev. Richard McCullen May 1885*
> *Dr Patrick Dominic born 4th Aug 1887, died June 1951.*
> *John Alphonsus, Beamore born Sept 1889, died Oct 1967.*
> *Joseph, Laytown born Sept 1891.*
> *Henry Vincent born 1894, died March 1915.*
> *Anthony Joseph, Grennanstown born 1898.*

Of the Land League Campaign for three F's, Fair Rent, Fixity Of Tenure and Free Sale were met partially.

In the 1850's James McCullen bought some fee simple land in the townlands of Bryanstown, Boyanstown or Legavoureen is separated from **Beamore** *by the stream know locally as 'The Bog'. The townland is very large. It starts at the Dublin Road, opposite to Stameen and Colpe and goes over to the Platten Road on the west.*

About 1858 Jas McCullen bought **Clonlusk** *in fee simple. I think that in his will that he left fee simple lands to Patrick McC and his heirs male. If Patrick McCullen had no sons but had daughters they were to have the use of the lands for their life but on their death, it was to go to Henry McCullen, Beabeg or his male descendants.*

Patrick McCullen (1852-1938) had seven sons. In 1903 he bought the farm of **Salmon**, *Balbriggan in the name of his wife. He built the present house and most of the farmyards. His eldest son, James McCullen was given the place, where he went to live and the tenacy was transferred to him, I imagine, that the entail in the fee simple land of Clonlusk was broken.*

Salmon, had at least three times the acreage. He also suceeded to a life interest in a trust which had been set up for the benefit of Henry Vincent McCullen, in 1910. When Henry Vincent died in 1915, the income passed to James. When James died. Fr Richard McCullen inherited this , but he has transferred this to Dr Oliver McCullen, who is the eldest son of the late Dr. Patrick McCullen.

In 1930 the fee simple lands of **Kilnew,** *Stamulen was bought for Anthony Joseph McCullen, the youngest of the family.*
During Patrick McCullen's lifetime Mary Frances was otherwise provided for.

As the bulk of his assets had been distributed during his lifetime, I think that the only items in Patrick McCullen's will would have been the Clonlusk and Beamore lands and the Bryanstown holdings – some of the Bryanstown lands was fee simple – some was held from the Drogheda Corporation.

In later years, John McCullen paid £300 to the late Patrick McCullen , Mile House, High Road, Drogheda for an isolated field at Bryanstown held in fee simple. This field had been bought by the bachelor Uncle Patrick McCullen who had the Mile House Farm and who built the present Mile House. His nephew, also Patrick McC, had lived in the Mile House and was the eldest son of Henry McCullen who lived in Beabeg. This P McC was married and had three sons.

The two elder died in the 1930's. The youngest Fr John McCullen, a curate in Meath Diocese sold the farm to his Uncle Henry McC, Beabeg for £1500. Fr. John died in 1951.

Henry McC married Agnes Woods, Stameen, who died on the birth of her first child. This child died within a fortnight. Henry McC's youngest sister, Katherine, married Cornelius Lynch of Eagle Lodge, Platten Road, Drogheda. As well as the land at Eagle Lodge, he owned a farm at Bolies, Duleek. He died in 1927, having named three executors, one of them was Henry McCullen. His widow Katherine, died about 1939, leaving three daughters and a son, Conor Lynch.

When Henry McC died in the 1950's, he left the Lynch family the Mile House Farm, the Beabeg farm and 70 acres joining Beabeg, which is in the parish of Stamullen, and was sold to him by Markeys of Rockbellew.

Conor Lynch lives in Eagle Lodge. Mrs Thos McCullen, the widow of an elder brother of Henry lives in the Mile House. She has the use of it for her life. Mrs Berrill, a sister of Conor Lynch lives in Beabeg with her husband. They farm the lands at Beabeg. An unmarried sister stays sometimes with friends in Dublin , while the youngest of them all, a Cluny nun who has been in India since her profession got 6 months leave from Kerala last August. She has divided her holiday staying with various relatives and has gone back now to Mount Sackville where she has to stay till she sails for India in February.

John with Conor Lynch, 2003

As James McCullen's inlaws., the Taaffes suffered from the insecurity of tenure and had been evicted twice through non payments of rent, just because the different landlords decided to occupy the land themselves.

Taaffes who had some capital were burning lime on the Crufty part of Hoey's farm. When Sherlock, the landlord took over their holding they moved to 'the Lerrigans' now occupied by Owens, it is due south of Mount Granville, on the south side of the road . They burned lime there for two generations supplying amongst other places the Church at Mornington, Hilltown House for Boylans etc, as well as farming.

Then Sillery, the landlord took up the holdings and came to live there. Taaffe had to move again – this time to Newtown, Duleek. There, their son in law, James McCullen built their present house and farmyard .

James McCullen (1817-77) took the holding at Beamore on a lease . he built the present house and yard. He intended to buy any future land in fee simple for security. (it was not till 1881 that the demands of the Land League were partially granted.)

Payment to Charles Parnell and the Land League by Patrick McCullen in 1880.

Lourdes Hospital, Drogheda
Friday 25ᵗʰ April 69

Dear Eva,

As the heating plant in Ardcath church is not working you had better clothe yourself as warmly as possible before you climb to that artic region tomorrow . I hope that Dolly knows Before you come down again try if Daltons History of Drogheda mentions anything about Ignaitius Peppard or Pepper who fought a rearguard action in the Drogheda Corporation after the Battle of the Boyne in 1689 had beaten the Catholics and led to the Code of Penal Laws.

Best regards to you all at home and abroad, Yours, Auntie Mary.

The reference to Ardcath Church has to do with the wedding of Paddy Ball and Marie Gogan, which took place on the 26ᵗʰ April in that year.

Room 4, Lourdes Hospital
Sunday

Dear Dolly,

One night last week Jim came from Laurence St to tell me about the good news which had come that day about Richard. That next night Jennie came and added further details. Thank God.

The strain on all of you for the past few weeks must have been trying. Give him my congratulations.

With best wishes to you all,
Auntie Mary F McCullen

Richard connects this congratulation with passing as exam in UCD. This letter is written in a wobbly script and lines are unsure, so her illness in the hospital was certainly a handicap to the great corresponder. Mary spent the best part of a year, in the Lourdes, which was some reward for the massive support to the MMM's, over a thirty year period. Fittingly the final letter comes in March 1970 concerning the arrival of Grace, daughter of John and Ann.

Room 4, Lourdes Hospital
March 1970

Dear Dolly

Congratulations on the safe arrival of the new little girl in Beamore. Best wishes to all. Thank God,

Yours, Auntie Mary.

CHAPTER 13

HISTORICAL SNIPPETS

There is universal regret that 'someone' did not discipline Mary, to write down more of the oral history, and folklore, which she carried in her head. Oliver did make a valiant attempt, and actually got as far as typing up some of her specialist lectures. A few of these survive, some typed and some written by her own hand, on old jotters or 'sums' copies. Much of the McCullen Family History now available to us came from Patrick (1785-1861) who was Mary's great grandfather, and lived in Beabeg, the small townland, adjacent to Beamore.

Snippet 1 - Linen, Mills etc

Linen and the weaving industry were particularly important to Drogheda in the late 1700's and into the early 1800's. Patrick himself was a weaver, so the first piece we record is on this topic, but does digress somewhat to end up in a Brewery.

> *For handmade linen as well as the locally grown flax used, some went to the Fair of Granard and elsewhere. All these journeys had to be made by road, in covered wagons. Three or four wagons usually made the journey together. I think that it took four days. My great grandfather (1783-1861) often brought his wife.*

> *The standard length of the web was 90 yards. No chemicals were used to whiten them but they were spread on a field which was known as 'The Bleach'. Many fields on farms keep the name still, although no weaving has been done for the last 100 years.*

> *Amongst the master weavers were Chester of Cartown Manor, Chester, now Chester Walsh of Williamstown, Castlebellingham. John Magrane whose house at Stameen formed the nucleus of the present Stameen Hotel. It was known as 'The Forty Acres' and sometimes ironically as 'Cotton Hall'. After Magranes death, the property was sold to Wm. Cairnes (No.1) who enlarged the house and added to the acerage.*

> *The Misses Magrane moved to Fair Street, where they set up a day school. To give the pupils a good knowledge of French, they brought in a Mr Magill to teach French. Mr Magill was born in Rouen, where his father, an Irishman had been British Consul. He married the younger Miss Magrane. They had two sons. The elder Wm became a priest, served for a time as a chaplain in the British Army and afterwards in Dublin Diocese. At the time of his death he was P.P of St.James's Dublin. His younger brother, Frank, went to sea and became Commodore of the Leyland Line.*

> *The mud wall thatched houses still inhabited at Coolagh St all have their kitchens built very large so that they could hold two looms. The master weavers had in some cases six storey warehouses always called 'Calendars'. One belonging to the Ennis family (later Tiernans of Annaville) is still standing at the back of their former West St shop. Mr John Owens, who lived in the private house which Mr Thos Brady turned into a drapers shop, had one on Bachelor's Walk.*

> *In the first half of the 18 hundreds, a steamdriven weaving factory was set up near Narrow West Street by Mr Flynn. Other members of his clan seem to have had mechanical interests as well. His cousins (?) Richd Flynn invented the first winnowing machine for cleaning corn which he made in Duke Street.*

He afterwards moved to Skerries where he worked the windmill which is still standing. Through his daughter his property passed to Ennis of Clonard who owned flour mills, bakeries etc.

A Mr Oates also started a steam mill. Somebody started Mell Mills which was owned in the 1890's by a Belfast firm. The manager was Mr Hull, whose daughter Melissa used to take first place for All-Ireland in the Intermediate exams with a few gold medals thrown in. She was a student of Victoria College Belfast. A Mr Mullen was also employed in the Mell Mill and had a family who attended the CBS after years, one of them came back to Drogheda as a Fransiscan priest. He died in Drogheda about 1922. His memorial plaque may be seen outside of the Fransiscan Church.

About the 1840's John and Richard Gradwell who had come from Preston joined with John Chadwick in building St.Mary's Spinning Company. Beside the mill in the Marsh, they also built houses for their workers. To get a good supply of flax, they sent their ship, commanded by Capt. Michael Reilly Scarlet St to France and to Riga. The Marsh Mill closed about 1900, some time after the death of Mr John Chadwick of Eden View.

When Gernons of Gernonstown Co.Louth had their property confiscated by the Cromwellians, it was given to Daniel Bellingham who changed the name to Castle Bellingham. They came into Drogheda and opened a Brewery in West St (south side). About 1830, they bought Athcarne Castle near Duleek. When they ceased to brew I cannot say. Mr Hugh Harbinson , from Co.Tyrone came to Drogheda as a representative of Musgrave's, the Belfast heating firm. He decided to settle in Drogheda and opened a iron monger on the north side of West Street in a house which is now being replaced by Ulster Bank. When Gernon's house became vacant, he moved over and opened there.

John Jameson, the Dublin distiller, had a distillery and also a malting house in the premises now owned by Preston (Grant). After a time they ceased to distill but kept on malting till the 1920's (?) when they sold the malting works to the Castelbellingham & Drogheda Breweries.

The Flynn (Flinn) family mentioned, who lived in West Street and Skerries, have a burial plot in Kilsharvan, and also the oldest 'inhabitant' of the graveyard, Mary, who lived to be 105 years. This year (2013) a descendent of theirs, from the USA, visited Drogheda in July.

Kilsharvan graveyard with the church in the background.

Snippet 2 - Chadwicks

Mr. Gerry Martin of the St.Vincent de Paul Society wrote to me in 1996 to exchange notes on the Chadwicks and compile a record and recently, I have been in correspondence with Barbara Cookson, a descendent of Chadwicks in England, who wished to find out about the Chadwick Connections in Drogheda, and where the family had lived.

Before 1800 a Chadwick had married a Miss Drumgoole. The Drumgooles were an old Catholic family who had been active on the confederate side in 1641. Their mansion in West St became an hotel, The Imperial, and was taken down to make room for the present Post. The last of their family, John Drumgoole was a tenant on the Massarene Estate, was an active Land Leaguer and lost his farm the time of 'The Plan of Campaign in 1887. Wm Ennis, Clonard, Balbriggan was related to the Drumgooles, through his grandmother, Miss Flynn, had some interest (titles) in the West Street house, till Stanley bought.

The French Sisters of Charity had made two attempts to set up in the British Isles, one in Dublin. Both of them failed. In the 1850's Father Nugent Dardis was a Fransiscan priest in Drogheda. His family had come from Balgeen, beside the townland of Dardistown in Drogheda. They had a distillery in the entry in Shop street where Morgans occupy now. When Miss Dardis died Fr Nugent Dardis inherited £6000. As bound by the vow of poverty, he could not touch it, but he obtained leave of the then Pope to enable the Sisters of Charity to set up a community in Drogheda. Mr John Chadwick's three sons at the time moved out of Harpur House and the Sisters of Charity moved in.

At that time the then Primate Dixon Lived in a large house in Fair Street which had been built as barracks. When Primate Dixon? Died in 1867, Fr.Kieran P.P. of Dundalk succeeded him. As Fr Kieran was greatly attached to Dundalk he made Dundalk his mensal Parish and appointed an Archdeacon in St .Peter's instead of an administrator – Archdeacon Gossan, Archdeacon Tierney, Archdeacon Murphy and Archdeacon Segrave. The Sisters of Charity then left Harper House and moved to Primate Dixon's where they have been since. After Fr.Dardis's death a window to his memory was put up in the Fransican church behind the high altar. During the alterations in the 1930's it was replaced by the present one.

What the original name of Harper House was I do not know. It was occupied at one time by George Harper, a Drogheda timber merchant who moved out and built the present Kilineer House. His wife was a Miss Ball of Ballsgrove, a sister of Mrs Shepherd of Bettystown House and an aunt of Geo. De Belle Ball who sold Ball's Grove in 1918 to Bertram Allen. Geo. Harper had no family. His executor was Jas. Cooke who lived in Harper House afterwards, was married to a sister of R.B. Davis who afterwards went to Dublin and became Chairman of Arnotts.

John Chadwick of Harper House had three sons, one Jas (born 1813), a student in Ushaw became the first bishop of Hexham and Newcastle in 1850 on the restoration of the Hierarchy in England. When a student , he wrote several hymns including 'Angels we have heard on high' which is sung at Christmas time. Frank Chadwick built the Glen which was sold to Alan Cairnes, two of his sons became lawyers in England and partners in the firm of Fooks, Chadwick and Arnold of London.

Another son went to Canada and afterwards to U.S.A . He married a Miss Sadlier whose father owned the publishing firm of Sadlier, New York. His mother in law (nee Blake) from Cavan had been educated in Siena, Drogheda and wrote a number of best sellers including 'The Old House by the Boyne'.

John Chadwick II married a daughter of the owner of Eden View and had one son whose wife was a Miss Woodlock from Dublin . This son lived in Bayview, now owned by Mr Kenny (Chemicals). His only son F.A Chadwick was P.P of the Church of the English Martyrs in York City, facing York

Minster, which is occupied by the Anglicans. When John (Johnnie) Chadwick II died about 1896 Eden View was sold to Christopher Tighe for £3000. Two unmarried sisters lived with their parents at Eden View until their father died about 1894, they moved to live in Bath. When St.Mary's Church was built in 1884, one of them Mary, painted the Stations of the Cross. One of the Woodlock helped found All Hallows College and became Bishop of Ardagh, afterwards. Two other daughters of John Chadwick became nuns – one joined Poor Clare, in Cavan – Ballyjamesduff, the other the French Sisters of Charity and she died at Mill Hill, well over 90 years. The Chadwicks are buried in the Cord Cemetary, Latin inscriptions.

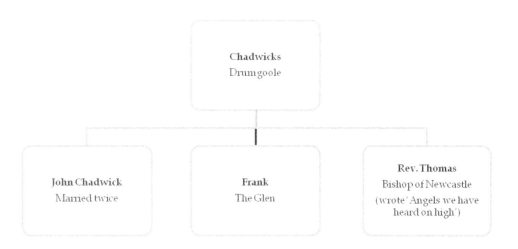

Chadwicks
Drumgoole

John Chadwick
Married twice

Frank
The Glen

Rev. Thomas
Bishop of Newcastle
(wrote 'Angels we have heard on high')

Snippet 3 - Kellys

The most common name in Graveyards in County Louth is Kelly, so Mary F offers some help to anyone trying to unravel the complicated genealogy of the Kelly's around Piltown and Painstown. Here are some items about Kelly's who farmed most of the lands from Colpe to Julianstown.

Another Kelly lived at Mile House and had 2 sons, both of them were sea captains. One married a sister of the late Peter and Tom Connolly. He sold Mile House in 1861 and settled in USA where the Moore's (Annie McCullen's brothers) and other sailors used to visit him. Once they were at a christening where they drank the toast of 'Geo Washington Kelly'. This Kelly's brother, Michael Kelly moved to Scarlet St., Drogheda and married a Miss Crawley from Dyer St. He sailed for Chadwick's to Riga and to the Belgian ports for flax. He had 4 sons and 2 daughters.

*They were **Tommie**, Capt of a ship out of Liverpool which was lost with all hands of the African coast in 1876 or 7. **Paddy** on Cork, Liverpool, Antwerp service torpedoed in 1914 war, operated on in Mater hospital to move torpedo pieces from his brain and lived till 1932. Another son , Capt on service New York to Naples. m his 1st cousin Miss Crawley and had one son. He lived till the 1930's.*

***Johnnie**, youngest mate on Drogheda boat died young. He had one son Michael and 2 girls. The widow settled in Philadelphia, you may remember her two daughters, Daisy and Minnie who stayed with Mrs Larkin. Capt. **Michael** Kelly had 2 daughters, Annie McDermott , Lily married Mark Simington..*

A third Kelly family lived on the Narrow Way which passes Piltown on the north side and joins the Bettystown Road at Bettystown House. This Kelly married a Miss Moran who owned a farm near Garlow Cross. He had 2 sons and 2 daughters. Wille Kelly lived on the Narrow Way with one sister. She died before him. The older brother and sister lived at Garlow Cross. She was a very able woman. When Willie died she got Edward Reilly, Larry R's eldest son to set her farms.

He used to walk over every Sun to see the Bettystown land. When they were younger, these two Miss Kellys used to visit in Scarlet St., Mrs Macken told me. Once after Willie's death , P.D. was called to attend the surviving Miss Kelly and he suggested to me to tell Mrs McKenna to tell Cosie McDermott about her cousin, as items in her district it might be to her advantage. I did so.

At any rate Mrs McC, Mile House succeeded to the Narrowway Farm. However'Big Pat' just slabbered away everything and she had to sell the farm to Toner (a brother of Mrs Downey) after 'Big Pat's' death.

Second marriages seemed to be very general.

Mary Anne Campbell's mother married one of the Greenes and lived with her daughter, who was married first to Ed. Kennan and secondly to ' Big Pat'. The McC's had been neighbours for centuries to Greene's and Kelly's but the only relationship was with Fr. John's mother (Mrs. Keenan McCullen).

Pat McCullen, with Mrs Keenan McCullen

The Kelly Family Tree as documented by Mary F. in her snippets.

Snippet 4 – McCann's

During the Liquidation of the Drogheda Steampacket Company, one of the people who worked very closely with Pat McCullen was James McCann, a noted Nationalist. Two of the family were M.P's, living at Simmonscourt, Dubin and Staleen, Donore. There is a railed McCann burial plot in Kilsharvan, unmarked with any name, because he was so famous in the early 1900's. The last Mill operated by the family was the Victoria Mills in Newry, which was sold in the 1980's and the Owner moved to Australia.

Some time in the 18th century a man named McCann from the 'White River' Co.Louth came to Beaumond near Duleek and built an oatmeal grinding mill which was worked by power from the River Nanny. Other branches of the same family set up mills in a different parts of Ireland. They were McCanns of Tuinaleack, Co.Longford. McCann's of Channonrock, Dundalk. Jas McCann, M.P the stockbroker came from there.

Jas McCann M.P for Drogheda in 1850 had a flour mill in Drogheda and lived in Staleen. He also owned a bakery in Drogheda and had, I think, a mill at Kilcarne.

The Tighe family lived near Beamond. In 1789 the McCann family built the mill at Beamond and the present dwelling house (now Jenkinsons).

A Mr Tighe was employed at the mill, had a large family which included Christopher Tighe, Eden View, Michael Tighe, West St., Mrs Reilly whose husband had a bakery on the south side of West St, further west than the Post Office, Mrs Commins, whose husband was a farmer in Monasterboice, Co.Louth. Miss Tighe who had a dry salter shop in partnership with Mrs Cluskey from Duleek. This Miss Tighe always had an interest in public affairs.

When Parnell, Dillon & Davitt were jailed and the Land League declared illegal in 1881, Anna Parnell started the Ladies Land League, Miss Tighe became President of the Drogheda Branch. She found a kindred spirit in Fr James Anderson O.S.A, a native of Drogheda who was stationed in Shop Street., Drogheda. Miss Tighe also worked at the Augustinian Alter Society etc. To come back to Christopher Tighe he had some connection with Kilcarne Mills and when living in Drogheda he started a bakery in John Street, Drogheda and lived in the adjoining house which had been the dwelling of Thomas Carty in 1840 , the first Catholic Mayor of Drogheda since 1689. Mr Tom Lyons lives there now. (Now demolished).

Mr Christopher Tighe opened a shop for his bread, meal etc on the Bull Ring, Drogheda. He married Miss Jane Courtney. There were four or five families of Courtneys about the town, all dry salters. A great number of small sailing ships needed provision like salt fish,bacon, etc.

A cousin of Mrs Tighe, William Courtney, who became a doctor joined the Indian section of the R.A. MC, and served with a native regiment. This carried higher pay than the ordinary army services. When he retired he settled with his sisters in The Crescent, Clontarf. One sister married Mr Strong, related to Husseys of Weston, Co.Dublin, an old Catholic family. The other two were unmarried.

Clr Tighe was a partner in the North City Milling Co and started a number of Drogheda young men in various branches of it. Their traveller in the Connaught area was Mr Jas Reilly, son of a life long friend, Mr A Tiernan, some of the neighbours from Balmarino and others owed their start to him. In 1895(?) Mr C Tighe bought Eden View Stameen from the family of John Chadwick and moved from John Street to it. .

When the Tighe family moved to Eden View, they maintained the garden to the full extent. At the local flower and vegetable shows not only outdoor plants and fruits were entered, but melon and other glass house products appeared. To come back to Mr Tighe's business interests. About 1893 the Mr McCann of Stameen sold his retail shop in West Street to Mr C Tighe and settled in England. Mr C Tighe had four daughters and a son, the youngest of the family, who died in his father's life time. Mr C Tighe took a keen interest in the Nationalist movement of his time.

With Fr W P Kearney, CC St.Mary's, Fr James Anderson, O.S.A, the late Peter McNamara, John Dolan of Sunday's Gate and others he helped to found the Drogheda Independent.

There was a close connection between Tighes and McCullens. Tommie McC (Mile House) of Beabeg was working there as a sales representative, and apparently was thus nicknamed 'The Bun'. At some stage, he went off with young Master Tighe on an overnight spree to Liverpool, and when they returned, Tommie got the blame for leading Master Tighe astray, and was sacked.

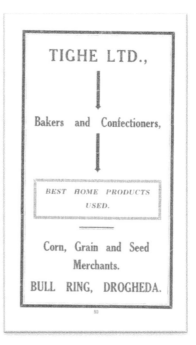

Snippet 5 – More Kelly's

A family named Kelly who lived in a large house in Fair Street for a couple of generations, employed a number of weavers who did their work in their own homes. A younger son who became an Augustinian was Prior in Shop Street. His brother, Mr.John Kelly, who visited Lourdes, after a serious illness, erected the present pulpit afterwards as thanksgiving. Mr Kelly lived for another thirty years. Mr. John Kelly's only son, James, joined the Irish Contingent formed by Mayor Miles O'Reilly of Knock Abbey, to fight for the Pope in the 1860's. Mr Kelly's nephew, Fr.James Anderson O.S.A, a friend of John Boyle O'Reilly, often visited Drogheda, and was attached to John's Lane Priory, Dublin, at his death in 1903.

Quite a number of local young men joined the Irish Papal Brigade, including Peter Carroll-Greene from Manimore, one of whose sisters was the Mrs Finnegan of Shop Street. Others were Mr.Heeney of Oldbridge, always known as 'the Pope Heeney' and Mr. Maguire from Monasterboice, who was titles 'Pope Maguire'.

Kelly's of Fair Street gave the present High Altar to St.Peter's. After John Kelly's death, his widow gave the present High Altar to the Augustinians in Shop Street. Her other gifts to the Parish included a sum of money to found a hospital. Archdeacon O'Callaghan bought the Mansion House built by Hardmans, and started the institution which became the Lourdes Hospital.

Mr Faulkner, who came from Beabeg, made sails in his place on North Quay, next to Mr.McGovern. His only daughter married Thomas Greene, who carried on the business. Mr Greene was Mayor in the 1860's. His only son, John, was the Borough Engineer. Mr.John Greene settled in Newry and is represented by a descendent, who was attached to the British Embassy in Paris.

When St.George Smith of Green Hills died in 1873, aged 86, worth £500,000, he was probably the weathiest person in the district. His interests included the flour milling concern of Smith & Smyth. Where his partner was Ralph Smyth of Newtown House (now AnGrianan), grandfather of the Misses Smyth of Newtown. Mr St.George Smith was also Chairman of the Drogheda Steampacket Co. And of Grendon's Ironworks, who were building ships before Harland & Wolff.

At the time of the Famine, Smith & Smyth offered £40,000 free of interest, to straighten out the Boyne, from Drogheda to the sea, but all sorts of objections were raised, and their efforts were thwarted. St.George Smith had a large family, probably twelve, but in 1858, his wife and five youngest children were drowned, when the steamer in which they travelled, sank in the harbour of Cuxhaven, in Germany. Every one was drowned.

Snippet 6 – 'Slavery

Mr Terence deVere White says 'Irish Nationalists did not make all that fuss over oppression, when they were at Westminster, and John Mitchell, who was a whole hearted supporter of negro slavery in America.' Mr White should remember that when negro slavery was taken for granted by many people, Dan O'Connell always spoke against it. Just now I cannot give the reference, but I read that when he got the offer of the support of twenty seven members, connected with the Slave Trade, who undertook to support any measure which he wanted for Ireland, if he remained silent on the slavery issue, he refused the offer. Later on, in Conciliation Hall, he refused to accept help from the slave-owning States of America, greatly to the disgust of Charles Gavan-Duffy. When Gavan Duffy wrote his recollections in 1879-80, he harped on that fact. As to the general attitude of Irish Nationalists towards cruelty, well Phil Callan, a Home Rule M.P. before Parnell, started the movement in the House of Commons to stop flogging in the British Army, which succeeded afterwards.

In the 1880's, the Nationalist Members opposed the Liberals and afterwards the Unionists for their occupation of Egypt, for their actions against the Boers etc. You can verify this by looking up the files of the 'Freeman Journal.' Whenever, news came of a British Defeat, the Nationalist M.P.'s cheered in the House of Commons. Of course, not everyone agreed, but most people did!

John Mitchell supported Negro Slavery. In the 1900's when Swift McNeill was the spokesman for the abolition of flogging in the British Navy, Mr.Edward Martyn said that any Irishman, who was in the British Army deserved to be flogged. Mr D.P. Moran, founder of 'The Leader' objected to the activity of John Dillon in the House of Commons against different aspects of Imperialism. In the 1900's 'Imaal', a contributor to 'The Leader', when receiving a book dealing with the 1880's, wrote-'Those cheers for the Mahdi have cost us dear'.

Just because Irish people thought that Arabi Pasha was right and that England was making Egypt safe for the bond-holders. Reconsider our record, Mr. White !

Here is something that has nothing to do with anything on these issues but is recorded by O'Neill Daunt about O'Connell. In a discussion on the proposition that every man would be able to write one novel, O'Connell was asked what subject he would select. He answered – one about George III and Hannah Lightfoot. Hannah was a sixteen year old Quakeress whom George was supposed to have admired before his marriage. Dan said that he would (in the novel) provide her with a son, who emigrates to America, joins the Rebel Army, and fights for Washington. I don't know how his story would have ended.

An interesting memory was presented to me in 2011 by Mary Ball, who had spent many years as a teaching nun with the Loreto Order. Aunt Mary's gift to her at the start of her career was a bundle of two large books. The first was a 'Life of John Henry, Cardinal Newman 1801-1890', a famous convert to Catholicism and Author of the hymn 'Lead Kindly Light' and the 'Dream of Gerontius' . The second was a 'Life of Daniel O'Connell.'

'The Liberator'.

Snippet 7 – 'Names'

Early gaelic names in Louth included O'Carroll and it's later forms, Carroll, McArdle etc Callan....
Scandanavian names include Pentony, Sweetman (corrupted from Swede-mann), Plunkett, Friary,
Grimes, Hamill, Turtle (corrupted from Turgesius), Thunder, Ledwich (otherwise Ledwidge), which
means a 'man from the island of Lewis'). Some Anglo Saxons came in the Pre-Reformation times like
Goodman, the Dundalk family who were in Co.Louth before 1300, Holdcroft, Marmions have been in
Louth and Meath for centuries, whether they are Scandanavian or Anglo-Norman, I do not know.
Anglo Normans include Verdons (from Verdun), Dardis (from Artois), Devereux (from Evereux),
Barniville or Barnwell (from Barniville), Lacy or deLacy (from Lassy), Nugent (from Nogent).

From a large scale map of Normandy to be seen the names of districts from which some of the local
workshop came. They sailed with William in 1066, and having plundered the inhabitants of England,
moved to Ireland to do the same. As years went on, the French names that they gave to the districts,
became muddled by the natives: Beau Bec (formerly Killossery or Kiltrough) became Beabeg, Beau
Mont became Beamond. It should be Crockafotha, Beaulieu in Co.Louth became Bewly till the 19th
Century.

People who had come eg. John from London, was John de Londres, then Landers, as Norman-French
melted away. From the time of the Reformation, the lands of the district were being confiscated. From
1656, the Corporation of Drogheda manned by Anglo-Saxon Puritans, who held control, until the
Reformed Corporation took over about 1833. These included Leland, Metcalfe, Barlow, Leigh, Balfour,
Tandy etc.

Bertholomew van Homrigh was a Dutchman who came to Ireland, with William of Orange. He got
grants of land about Drogheda, where his descendents lived until 1832, one of whom was the last
Mayor of the unreformed Corporation, and also M.P. for Drogheda, in the British Parliament. He lived
in the house in Laurence Street, which the Hibernian Bank opened immediately after he had gone to
Dublin. The best known member of the family was Esther Van H, daughter of the first Bartholomew,
who was smitten by Dean Swift, and whome he styled 'Vanessa'. She died in Celbridge. Most of these
later planters thought it safer not to live on their lands, and built big houses, in the town, eg Barlow at
Westgate, Leland, who lived at 33 Laurence Street, until they moved to Beltitchbourne in the 1850's,
Leigh, who got Co.Louth lands before Cromwell, and also more lands, in and out of Drogheda, from
William of Orange (1689), built the South Quay House (since replaced by Murdocks).

Towards the end of the 18th and into the 19th century, the puritanic fibres of some of these seem to have
worn thin. The last Metcalfe had five daughters, outside wedlock. After his death, the property passed
to his kinsman, Mr.Leland, who seems to have shared the same outlook on life. Beside the legitimate
descendents who live in Beltichbourne, a large number were scattered about the town, in various offices
and in Cairnes' Brewery. Probably the last of them would be the man, who lived in the Brewery House,
in Mary Street, next to Mrs McDonnells.

John Cooper, who lived in Cooperhill till 1848, left a number of descendents, including a grandson, a
clergyman. This man married a daughter of the Protestant Bishop of Cork. However, the property had
to pass to a cousin, Henry Cooper. Coopers had various social grades. Another Cooper, who seemed to
have a Catholic grandmother, lived beside us in Beamore, and rented an Orchard from Cunninghams.
His Catholic cousin, Margaret Kane, used to come up to our house, on the day of a Station. Two
Coopers were tenant farmers on the farm in Morington, which was then occupied by John Drew I. That
would be in 1840-50.

Another Anglo-French name was de la Hyde, the last male would have been Dr.George delahyde who
lived in Palace Street. He was Medical Officer for St.Mary's at the time of my birth. His immediate

successor was Dr.Wm Bradley Sn, father of the present Dr. W. Bradley. Palace Street and the North side of Laurence Steet had been Church property. After the Reformation, the Protestant Archbishop of Armagh, lived in a house on that grounds.

Besides the people who got larger properties from confiscations, a smaller group of Protestants settled on 'The Corporate Estate' and lived in, and on, the Drogheda Corporation. This Corporate Estate encircled the town. It went round the North Side, including Townrath, crossed the river, stretched around the Platten Road, and came to its southerly point 'The Liberty', a triangular patch beside Jemmie Rooney's farm, which separates the townland of Bryanstown from Beamore. These people sent their sons to the Grammar School, and afterwards got commissions in the British Army. From 1690 onwards, there was always openings in the various wars. Captain Alcock, who had taken part in the Battle of Corunna, where Sir John Moore was killed, lived in 'St.James' near the Viaduct till the lifetime of my Father (1852-1938). Col Fairclough lived in what is now Brookville.

Snippet 8 – 'The Tandy Family'

Described by Mary, as Anglo Puritans, she expounds. The Tandy Family got a grant of the land of Johnsbrook, Kells from the Cromwellian Government some time after 1656.

About a hundred years later, a younger son came to Drogheda, rented a piece of land in the Marsh, from the Landlord, Wade of Clonabreany. He built a brewery and a dwelling house on it and lived there. Afterwards the then Tandy took 12 acres of land at Donacarney from Harry Smith of Beabeg and moved from the Marsh to the new house built at Donacarney (now Connolly's).

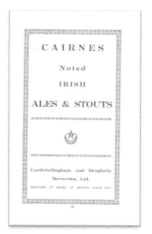

Tandy worked the brewery till about 1803 when they shut it down. Corballis was probably built before 1803 by one of the Donacarney House Family. The Brewery premises remained closed till 1827 when Thomas Cairnes, a native of Co.Tyrone, who had been a clerk in Woolsleys Brewery in Castlebellingham came to Drogheda, rented the Marsh premises from Wade, and started brewing with the use of his wife's fortune of £500.

While Mary did not live to see it, the naming of 'Father McCullen' Park in Kells would have greatly pleased her as a tribute to Fr.Dick on his retirement. His enormous contribution to the Orphanage in Kells is recalled in splendid and evocative writings in the Meath Chronicle by journalist Garret Fox, and a former orphan, Mrs Rose Clarke of Tara.

The Monsignor receiving the Freedom of Kells from the Urban District Council in 1970

One of the Tandys had gone to Dublin from Drogheda and is believed to have been an ironmonger in Thomas St. When his son was born there in 1740, he was called James Napper Tandy. This may have been after the family of Napier of Loughcrew who owned a large property in Meath and also in Cavan. James was a favourite name with them for a long time. James Lennox Napper died about 1903.

James Napper Tandy married Anne Jones in 1865. She had a profit rent of £1-1-0 an acre out of some land about Newtown Platten. I cannot say exactly where. That is shepaid rent to Metcalfe's of John St. and sublet the land to a family named Clarke and to another family named Dignam keeping a profit for herself of a guinea an acre.

The couple had at least one son, James Tandy, who become an officer in the army of the East India Co., married a woman from Castlebellingham who was related to the Woolsey family who owned the Castlebellingham Brewery.

About 1792 when James junior and his wife were home on furlough from India, they went down to Castlebellingham to visit the young Mrs. Tandy's friends. The father who had been active in Dublin public life from an early age, as an extreme radical reformer went with them. He had joined the Society of United Irishmen in 1791.

During the 18th century at different times and in different places in Ireland, the tenant farmers had formed bodies called "Defenders" to safeguard themselves from evictions.

When Tandy senior went to Co. Louth he got to meet some of the Defenders, explained the objects of the Society of United Irishmen, and went about Co. Louth swearing in recruits to that body.

He was charged with having administered unlawful oaths and returned for trial at the Dundalk spring assizes on substantial bail. However the last thing that his relatives and connections wanted was to have him tried for high treason. Consequently they allowed him to escape, paid up the two bails of £500 each and got him away to U.S.A.

The articles in the "Word" tells of the further happenings in his arrival in Hamburg, where he was taken prisoner.

The British brought him to Fort George, one of the block houses that had been put up in the Highlands of Scotland after the 1745 Rebellion.

He wanted to get money to pay for his defence in his forthcoming trial and his relatives applied to the two tenants. However they thought that as he was an outlaw, they need not pay him anything.

Then Napoleon told the British that if they executed Tandy, he would execute three British generals who were prisoners of war in France. Tandy was released, and allowed to go to Bordeaux in 1802.

The Tandy family did not lose much time in shifting Clarke and Dignam. Clarkes moved over to Lougher, where the last of them died in 1902. Paddy and Mrs. Marry own the farm now. A descendant owned   shop in Shop St. He married a Miss Gogarty from Beamore. Their only child married Thos. Owens who built Sunnyside.

Dignam lived in the house on east side of Duleek St. which is occupied now by the Misses Moore.

Tandy's wife is buried in Julianstown, probably because some of the Tandys lived in Corballis at that time.

A Col. Tandy came home from India, and settled down at the Grove, Balrath or some such place. He used to visit the Rev. John Cooper of Beamore, whose mother had been Letitia Tandy, a sister of the Tandy who built Donacarney House.

Tandy usually rode over to Beamore, about Mount Granville. Not only are these quarries on each side of the road, but the road itself is made over solid rock which could be seen quite plainly in the pre-tarred surface age. Tandy's horse slipped there, the rider's head struck the limestone and he died at once.

The horse very sensibly went back to Beamore and started making noise to attract attention. Mr. Cooper recognised what had happened. That would have been in the 1850's or 1860's. I do not know if Col. James Tandy left any family, but it is interesting to note that although all traces of the Drogheda family have gone, that the parent line from Johnsbrook is still

represented by the Bank of Ireland official in Dublin.

Major Tandy sold Johnsbrook in 1927 to the Land Commission. The herd bought the house and 25 acres of land. He sold that to P. J. Sweetman, solicitor, who is a son of Roger Sweetman who used to live at Glendalough. The house went on fire accidentally some years ago, but has been rebuilt since.

Mrs. Sweetman was born La Touche. She is a sister to Mrs. Myles Dillon.

These notes were recorded by Dr.Oliver in conversation with Mary.

CHAPTER 14

MARY'S INFLUENCE

In one of his more profound moments, William B.Yeats once said that '**History** is written at the half-door and in the marketplace', rather than in the great Assemblies of Nations. With this in mind, I set out in July 2011, to find out what effect Aunt Mary had on her nieces and nephews, over three decades after she had passed away. By the nature of things, such responses should be full of wisdom and reflection. Since this be so, there is little need for me to comment on them. All of the individuals are more than able to speak for themselves! My younger brother, **Richard**, comes first –

Auntie Mary was a frequent caller to Beamore especially in the 1950's. Sometimes she called to stay but mostly she called to visit. For weekly visits the ritual for us began when Carter pulled up on the lane outside the garden gate to allow Auntie Mary enter via the front door. Carter was referred to only by his surname and I think drove either an Austin Cambridge or Morris Oxford - as either model was in effect the same car it didn't really matter. Later I learned that he did have a Christian name - Louis. He was a small fussy taxi man who always appeared to be of the same indeterminate age i.e oldish and lived in Pearse Park or Perse Park as my father pronounced it. Sometimes if Carter was unavailable the driving duties were performed by another taxi man - Gerry Campbell but he was always got his full name and was never referred to as Campbell.

Anyway once admitted to the house over which she once ruled Auntie Mary made her way to the kitchen which was the centre of activities. She invariably took her seat in a black bent wood armchair in one corner of the room between the large kitchen press and front window. In time this chair became know as Auntie Mary's chair and it was from this throne that Auntie Mary held forth on many topics most notably the genealogy of her own family - immediate and extended and a great many other families beside.

As the kitchen was the centre of domestic activities in the house and they were performed almost exclusively by my mother it was she who invariably was the captive audience for Auntie Mary. What a lot Dolly Dolan must have learned about the family she had married into from those visits. My father seemed to have a sort of ambivalent attitude to Auntie Mary and while I don't doubt that he held her in great affection he managed to keep this well hidden for the most part. I do recall that very often the times when he seemed to be particularly busy outside maybe looking after a sick beast or sick baste as it might be called coincided with Auntie Mary's visits.

Auntie Mary's knowledge of history in general and family history in particular was prodigious. It did not even need a question to prompt her into some long ramble through the mists of time as she recalled seed breed and generation of someone either living or long departed. Coupled with that vast depth of knowledge she had an incessant way of talking and invariably went down many side roads of information without ever getting to the point. The fact that my father might interrupt in exasperation with 'Mary Mary would you ever be quiet' did little to stem the tidal wave of information that was being imparted.

The topics of conversation were wide ranging but would only have held my interest if I were an old fashioned five or six year old which of course I wasn't. I do remember that they ranged from the family tree of the Fitzharris's or Fee Harrys to the Gillicks of Oldcastle, the Derhams of Balbriggan and the pronunciation of the Halpennys from Ardee [was it Ha'penny or Halpenny ? - that seemed to be an endless question much trawled over].

It was not unusual for Auntie Mary to be hoarse from talking by the end of her visits such was the endless nature of the stream of consciousness that she delivered in her incessant and sometimes ready tones.

I'm not sure if it was the sound of her voice or the fact that she patently knew more than him that irritated my father so much, although I suspect it was the latter rather than the former. Maybe there is a lesson there for all family historians !

My mother was more polite in her dealings with Auntie Mary and knew when to make an interjection that indicated she was not only interested in what her sister in law was saying but was still listening while cleaning and cooking. I imagine both my parents were somewhat relieved when three o clock came around and Carter's reappearance signalled the end of the visit. I don't recall whether or not Auntie Mary called to our house empty handed or not and that lack of recollection would seem to suggest that she was not given to bringing sweets to her nephews. Sometimes Auntie Mary would send a postcard - possibly a black and white picture of the main street in Clonmellon which would bring the news that she intended to stay with us for several weeks. This news would necessitate a hasty check of the guest room by my mother to ensure that it was fit for purpose.

It is interesting to note that Auntie Mary never actually seemed to stay with people as she spoke of staying in Beamore or in Hartlands or the Sea [which was Laytown and its dodgy fish merchants] or of visiting Fair St. or Laurence St.

Richard mentions her prodigious knowledge of History, and being in her company this had an osmotic effect on the people in her life. Similarily the habit of reading brushed off ..... My older brother, **Pat,** writes colourfully of her presence in his life; *'Heavenly Patience! M.F's usual exclamation when anything strange or shocking was being discussed'.*

On Reading :
* *Without a word to us she sent off a subscription to the American comic 'Topix' which seemed to come fortnightly or maybe two issues a month but delivered together. This prevented us fighting over who it was really meant for. We figured out that it was American because everyone wore a baseball cap and said 'Hi!', and was called a 'Kid!'. We felt quite important that anyone in America should be sending something to us. It was of course an improving magazine with a catholic ethos.*
* *MF would really have been a reader of the 'Freemans Journal', rather than ever the 'Irish Independent' which replaced it. There was no place (other than Hell) for the 'Irish Times'. I have mentioned her subscription to the Scottish 'Weekly Sketch' or 'Weekly Graphic' to keep up with the war news. I do not think that when at Beamore she would have had access to a radio other than the rather hefty machine that was turned on for the news, Michael O'Hehir and a good German band if one could be found. All this depended on somebody (John. A) having remembered to get the set battery charged at Tiernans or McAllister's and to have bought a new dry battery (about half the size of a biscuit tin) if they were available.*
* *She also had an interest in paper back novels of the Agatha Christie type.*

On Family History:
* *Mary had a vast knowledge of families and their relationships, whether in Ireland or England (especially the titled families). This was reflected in many of the books in Beamore, whether bought in auctions or in second hand book shops.*
* *J. A McCullen shared some of her interests in families etc. but only up to point, if they were not connected with the cattle trade. Hence the outburst at dinner one day, when he, having lost the track of her conversation asked 'Mary, what are you talking about?'. The reply was swift 'D'Arcy of Platin', emphasised with a frustrated bang of her clenched fist on the table, making the cutlery hop!*

On Holidays at the seaside:
* *MF had rented three houses there at different times – first was 'The Bungalow' owned by the Lyons family. They later reserved it for themselves and she had tomove to a drafty semi-detached place called 'Overstrand' where it was said the east wind would come in through the front door without any hindrance at all. The final cottage was in the square where she stayed for a number of years.*
* *Of great interest to MF at Laytown were the Trim nuns, Kells nuns, Navan Nuns etc and probably several other convents who took holiday homes for their communities at the sea. In those days she was an avid walker on the beach and would meet with her acquaintenances from those communities.*

* *When the cars were off the road nobody seems to have gone to Mornington as the only transport was GNR or train. A great feather in her cap one day was to learn that the Manager of the Royal Marine Hotel in Dun Laoighaire had chosen Laytown for his own holidays.*
* *As children we were continuously being warned not to pick up anything that floated in onto the beach in case it should explode. (Hexagonal discharged flare casings about 12'' long were most common).*
* *During the war the Clogherhead fishermen brought their catch for sale in Drogheda (Laurence St.) using small fish carts. When the war ended they went to Balbriggan and acquired small pick up trucks and vans and were able to sell to the houses in Laytown etc. Being so the kind hearted MF could not turn them away, and so purchases were made on the double from Mr Richardston of Balbriggan and the fat Mr Rath of Clogherhead.*

On Keeping House...
* *If doing the cooking , in which she appeared to have little interest, she would always be likely to pick up and become immsersed in some book (on almost any subject).*
* *We both remember the cascade of fish bones and potato skins that emerged from the half full cornflake box when on holiday at Laytown/Bettystown. She had absent mindedly cleared the plates into the cornflakes packet the day before!*
* *When keeping house in Beamore for the menfolk during the 20's and 30's she must have used the black range (possibly made in the Drogheda Ironworks) from the heap of coal kept on the iron plate on the floor, as I think the 'Esse' cooker was with the plumbing part of the improvements necessitated by the planned arrival of Miss D.Dolan, who was still reclaiming and decorating bedrooms as late as 1944-45 and finally managed to modernise the kitchen when the house was wired for electricity '47-8 (by McAllisters, which took ages). The kitchen presses and units were made by McDonnells of John Street.*

On Open House ...
* *In the 1920-30 period Beamore seems to have been something of an Open House for neighbours and former 'maids' or serving girls. Possibly these included Mary Connor, Bridgie Clarken, Mrs Tom Crickley and others including May McCullen. I remember Auntie Jenny remarking that 'Dolly found it difficult to know where she stood with all these people when she came to Beamore at first.' Presumably all these contacts and many more from all strata of society were 'grist to the mill.' Where MF was concerned.*
* *One regular visitor in MF's time at Beamore was Miss Allen, the sister of the caretaker of the Freemason's Lodge in Drogheda (North Quay). This lady sold knitted items which MF would have bought out of sympathy. Eventually she ceased coming when our Mum declined to buy anything ' for the baby' over a period of time.*

On Politics
* *''Who did you vote for in the election, Auntie Mary?' .... 'Two sound men!'*
* *It is difficult at this remove to understand the avidness which the debates in the House of Commons on the 'Irish Question' and Home Rule were followed and analysed. As far as MF was concerned the Great Criminal in the British Establishment was Bonar Law, not apparently Lloyd George or Carson. Needless to say she had no time for a tall fellow with glasses on the Irish side either.*
* *As one who had lived through the eras of Parnell, Redmond, Cosgrave, DeValera, Lemass etc, how she would have revelled when it came to John Bruton's turn !*

On Health and Wellbeing
* *I think that the traumatic and painful experience of the broken hip, the long convalescence and the permanent handicap of the special shoes must have taken a lot out of her.*
* *Added to this would have been an erosion in the value of the stocks and shares that she had been left and which had once appeared so valuable.*
* *On my final visit to her in the Lourdes Hospital she was a tiny creature in the bed, frail and weak.*

On What might have been ?
* *MF had taken second place in Ireland (in English) the year that she had done her Intermediate Certificate (equivalent to Leaving Certificate in those days) so an academic or at least a teaching career could have beckoned but it was not to be.*
* *Was it the death of her mother that ordained that she should stay at home ? By the time I knew her she had become a self-effacing person characterised by her bun of silver hair and dressed in various shade of brown.*

Mention of the visits of Miss Allen from the Freemason Hall is a reminder of how broad Mary's sphere of interest could be. I never heard of her placing a wager on a racehorse, but like The Boss, she knew her Racing, as exemplified in this letter, probably written in 1950's.

Hartland, Clonmellon, Kells.
My Dear Eva,   *Wed 3rd May*

Many thanks for the Irish Times which was enclosed. It is interesting to note that Nano Reid's artistic outlook reminds the Irish Times critic of the spirit of Chopin.

The £1000 Red Cross Races at the Phoenix Park has been won by the single racehorse that belongs to Mr Owens of Kingscourt. On Sat it won the Irish Lincolnshire worth £500 at the Curragh. Mr Owens buys lambs, kills them and ships them to England.

Mrs E.J King, Sir Hugh Nugent's mother owns Dallington, which got second place in the Red Cross Race today. Mrs McCloughery of Clonleason beside Girley drew Pango in the Sweep. It was a non-runner in the Red Cross Race, but won a £200 hurdle. Mrs Garry, whose husband is Manager of the Kilskyre Co-op Stores was half owner of a ticket which drew £100 prizes.

Thurs

Some of the Mountnugent people went to the races yesterday to back High Spirits, owned by mystery millionaire, Mr Gray. It won at 6 to 1.

The Tramp's Ball in Kells last night offered prizes to the most realistically got up characters, male and female. A genuine tramp came accompanied by his wife and family and drew all the prizes. Give my best wishes to Jim and tell him that I hope his vegetables are doing well. They seem rather scarce around here, though Nancy has some good lettuce which have been wintered in a frame.

Best Regards,
Mary

Writing sixty years later, **Oonagh** ventures the view :

'*She had a great regard for her kith and kin, and she did not approve of my moving to Co.Kildare, as she considered it was a place, where cheating and hookery were rampant. In other words, she did not approve of the Racing Fraternity.*

I remember her coming to Salmon, and causing my mother a great deal of annoyance by her pampering of my father, which he naturally lapped up....'

Oonagh's beloved older sister, **Nancy** of Salmon, married the theatrical gentleman, **Barry** Cassin and he provides us with a view of Aunt Mary from the outsider, so to speak, in his book 'I never had a proper job', (published 2012).

Writing of the similarities between Nancy and her aunt he says-

'*Aunt Mary could enumerate the seed, breed, and generation of every Big House family and holding in Meath, North County Dublin, and places farther flung. In her declining years, Nancy and I visited her in the Lourdes Hospital in Drogheda, where she was more resident than patient.*

Visiting was a lesson in lineage. Leaving was a problem. On a day when time was short, we decided to pay our brief respects and go, but no sooner had we arrived, than Mary launched into the history of some past landlord family, and by the time we had inched backwards to the bedroom door, we were through four generations of birth, marriages and death.

Which was no more than a preamble, because Mary accompanied us to the main entrance, spreading the net wider to include inheritances, illegitimacies and squandered fortunes. If ever a natural academic was undirected, a gifted researcher lost, it was Aunt Mary.

She read avidly and kept house eccentrically. It is said that on an occasion when visitors arrived she was despatched to make tea, and when she had not returned an hour later, was found buried in a yellowed newspaper that lined a press!

The Salmon Trio, Oonagh, Nancy & Maura.

Memories from the Kilnew Twins:

Sr. Maura's strongest memory of Mary Frances is receiving bundles of The Daily Sketch from her in order to improve her mind and broaden her outlook.

Nancy always remembers John McC (Sn) saying to Mary F 'I asked you a question, I don't want a history lesson, I just want a straight answer.'

Maura and Nancy celebrating their birthday recently.

Mary's genealogical outreach was extraordinary, but not limited to Landlord or Titled families. One of her favourite complicated families to unravel was the Lenehans who had been close associates of the McCullens for several generations, with a base in South Dublin and spread through East Meath, with several marriage connections to Grimes, Taaffes, Lynch, Wall, Murray and Marry.

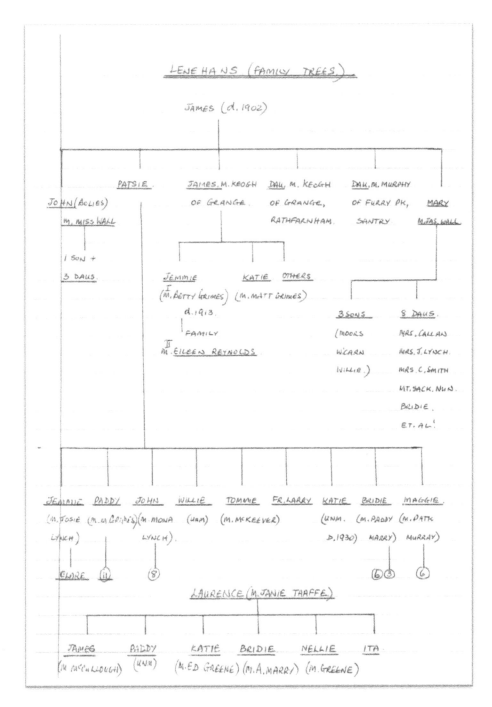

The Lenehan Family Tree as documented by Aunt Mary.

A valuable aspect of Mary's visitings is her retelling of folk memory tales, which were not recorded in the small number of local history books published before the 1960's. One such story in a letter to Jim, undated as to year, but seemingly of the 1940's, as **Jim** was starting his 'office' life.

Hartlands,Clonmellon,Kells,Co.Meath
Mon 13ᵗʰ June

Dear Jim,

This book may interest Dick, it gives an amount of information and may not be in print now. Your Uncle Joe says that just inside of Lennie Murray's gate are the remains of a mound and that he had heard always that Cromwell stood there when directing the fire of the cannon over the walls of Drogheda. This would be the mound from which the Corporation carried away to stuff to mend the roads during the lifetime of your grandfather (1852-1938). He said that the lane which runs across there to McKenny's and the railway used to be known as 'Bloody Lane'.

The town wall ran around the back of what is now the Protestant graveyard of St.Mary's and ended at the river with a tower. On the opposite side was another tower. The southern tower and part of the wall stood on the side of the present Drogheda Ironworks. Consequently my grandfather had to take down the wall and tower before he started to build the present Ironworks for St. Geo Smith in the 1840's. He said that a number of cannon balls were found in the tower.

Your Uncle Joe, Tom and myself were very interested in 'Murder in Miami'. Till I read the solution I had no idea who was the person.

Joined by the others in wishing you every success in your office life,

I remain, Yours Sincerely,

Aunt Mary

PS. I am posting the book separately.

Remnants of the wall of the Drogheda Ironworks.

Back in 2003, an archaeological dig was carried out at the Ironworks Site by Thaddeus Breen, before the building of Scotch Hall Shopping Centre. My records of James McCullen's building in 1850-51, and his workers were Pat Durnin, John Pierce, Pat Wasser, Pat Campbell and Peter Kelly. I wrote a piece in the local paper, wondering whether the cannonballs were still out there being minded by descendents. Sure enough I was stopped in the street by a lady to confirm that she was descended from Peter and still had the canonball. Aunt Mary's revelations have often led to a feedback from the local community memory bank, even after a century and a half, as in the Canonball case.

This poses the often asked, plaintive question – 'Why did we not ask Auntie Mary?', and is put into a colourful context by **John Drew**, her grand nephew and contemporary of my own....

John Drew, pictured with Nancy Long, Desmond Drew and John McCullen (l to r)

'When I was about four to five years of age both me and my cousin, P.Ball, we had a problem, so had the two Auntie Mary McCullen's, so to differentiate between them we decided to call the more senior of them Old Auntie Mary. Now Auntie Mary the younger, was soon to become Mary Collins but ever so old Auntie Mary was a very well read lady. With a mind like an encyclopaedia, you could ask her about any family in Counties Meath, Louth, Cavan, and Westmeath and she could tell you their complete history.

With all her learning there were two things she could not do, one was cook and the other was mind children. Every summer she used to rent a house in Laytown from Paddy Delany and some of the grandnephews, and grandnieces would be invited to stay on holidays. Paddy Ball and myself stayed one summer, it was a very traumatic experience for both Auntie Mary and us. For a start we lived on fried plaice and because the man with the fish cart called once a week and there was no such thing as a fridge, the fish was kept in a safe in the kitchen. The safe had a grid on the front of it and I can still get the smell of of the fish that wafted from it.

Come six o'clock both P. Ball and myself were sent off to bed. Now this was the month of July and the sun was splitting the stones outside in the Square, also the Duffners and the McQuillans and the Dolans were outside our bedroom window playing cops and robbers. We could not be off looking out at them enviously. Now as we saw them they spotted us. They came over to the window and tried to persuade us to come out.

Now our problem was Auntie Mary was outside the door and try as we might there was no way past her, so the only way out was out the window and after much huffing and puffing we got the window open enough to squeeze out. Old Auntie Mary was so engrossed in her book that she did not miss us for some time. When she did eventually miss us she marched us back into our bedroom totally humiliated in 'front of our friends' and threatening to send us home the next day. Needless to say she did not and all was forgotten soon after. Auntie Mary did not like the modern day republicans, her one and only hero was Napper Tandy. Maybe it was because he was local but she seemed to know all about hm. It was a pity that she did not write down more, as she was a very knowledgeable lady. One of her favourite rhymes that she recited to us as children was 'The House that Jack built'.

At family gatherings still Old Auntie Mary's name comes up, even years after her demise mainly in the context of conversation, some one will say 'if only Auntie Mary was here we could ask her.'

Human behaviour often repeats itself and a memory of Helen McCullen who was seven years old at Mary's death in 1970, also involved 'escape' out through an open window! Helen's older sister, Alice, spent considerable time in St.Margarets as a child, after her brother, Paddy and recalls her shock at the length of Aunt Mary's unfolded hair, her kindness and self effacing nature.

While Aunt Mary corresponded with Nuns and Priests all over the world and ladies of her own vintage, a sizeable portion of the correspondence was with what she described as 'young people of today', and her style and content would vary to suit the receivers taste, always concentrating on the human interest story. In the following letter Jim is the recipient, aged 27 years;

Hartlands,Clonmellon,Kells,Co.Meath
Mon 13th June

My dear Jim,

Many thanks for your letter and enclosures which came today. Yesterday I was in Beamore and found all in good form. They said that Mr. Charters is to live in David Cairnes's new house while the owner is in Canada. The new Rectory is to be finished before the Cairnes's come back.

On Tuesday N.Ball called here and brought Auntie Sissy and myself to Col. Bomford's auction at Oakley Park which is north of Kells. A great many British officers and their wives attended. One air commodore Chamberlain of Chamberlainstown near Girley lives with his wife and family in a yacht off Howth Hills. He succeeded to Chamberlainstown on the death of his elder brother. Now he has settled down to farming. Col Bomford's belongings included a gun (modern), a blunder bus, pistols, swords from different countries, a very large tiger skin and three leopards or tiger heads mounted with china / plaques attached, giving the place and date of their death like this 'Cholan, 1933' and 'Meiriput, 1935'.

At the auction somebody spoke of the enthusiasm with which Mrs Nicholson of Balrath has been breeding arab ponies. She has made quite a name for herself at it. She has one son and one daughter. The son does not take the slightest interest in horses and has gone into a motor business in London. The daughter has got a job in London leaving Papa and Mamma to carry on at Balrath.

Uncle John said that he was talking lately to John Hatch of Longford, Duleek. He said that both of his sons have qualified as vets and that both of them are in England now. Thanking you for your note and with best wishes,

Yours Affectionately, Auntie Mary.

Nora McCullen, who married into the McCullen family has had a lifetime to observe the family at close quarters, and knew Aunt Mary very well. She writes in 2011 –

' I had a great respect and affection for Aunt Mary. I found her to be kind and gentle, deeply caring and interested in her family and many relations. She was also a deeply religious person, and supported many good causes. When I was on holidays in June each year with my family while young, I would bring her to visit Aunt Eva in Drogheda, and the Cassins in Salmon, and other relatives. Having never driven, she was always delighted to have the chance of seeing them. I held her in high regard, and we called one of our daughters, Mary Frances, after her.

Amongst the contributions that I received in 2011 were the reflections of the two 'Senior' Mary's – and I include these in chronological order, as to age! **Mary Kingston,** daughter of Eva, who kept such a careful eye on the years of correspondence writes-

'Had Aunty Mary taken up the Exhibition she won to Camridge at the end of her school career, I have no doubt at all that she would have become a renowned scholar. So why did she not take the disciplined route, preferring instead to amass and absorb whole swathes of Irish and Britsh family history ? It might be claimed that as the only daughter in that male household of Beamore at the time, she wished to keep house; but she never acquired any skill in domestic matters, so I think the explanation lies in the word'Family'. For her, the facts and foibles of family life were paramount, and her love of and admiration for her own clan supreme.

We must all be grateful that John inherited her genealogical gift, with the added ability to interest his readers in the background from which we have sprung, so that each of us can say with the Psalmist David, ' I have a goodly heritage.'

Mary Kingston chatting with Denis Collins.

As befits the god-daughter of Aunt Mary, **Mary Collins** writes in 2011, in her 91st year, a clear and concise piece – to chronicle and to remember;

> *'My memories of Aunty Mary are happy one. She was my Godmother. When Uncle John married Dolly Dolan, Aunty Mary asked my mother if she could come and live with us in Hartlands. It must have been quite a change for her to leave Beamore and Drogheda, to come and live in our Household with all of us, Mum, Dad, three girls and Thos. She was quite happy as long as she had a book to read! Aunty Mary decided to rent a seaside cottage from Mrs.Lyons, from June to September, and keep in touch with the Drogheda connections. Over the years, we were all married, Mum and Dad moved to Laytown, and Aunty Mary joined them. She was far-sighted, and bought her own grave in Calvary Cemetary. May she rest in peace.*

Mary Collins died on Sunday 14th October 2012.

There was another **Mary McCullen**, who lived to be 102 years of age (b.1907) and knew Mary F. longer than anyone. Known as May or 'The Duchess' her cottage was adjacent to the family home of her second cousins and she lived with her brother, Jack. Her quote in the 1990's:

> *'I wouldn't have a bad word said about your Aunt Mary – she was a kind, charitable lady and she even left me and Jack a few pounds in her will.'*

'Maggie May,' with Ann McC by the hearth

Jack McCullen, in his garden

The McCullen Clan Gathering 1994

The Open Air Community Mass at 'The Castle' at Beamore
John is pictured with Fr.Denis Nulty, recently appointed Bishop.

The Loving Memory of Mary Frances McCullen

By Paddy with Eva McCullen (Clonmellon)

The Loving memory
of MF McCullen

M F
McCullen

tolerate tempers
bad good manners
all false pride
but never never repeat
or request same
focus and collect
the hornrim glasses sit By Eva
doubled even tripled.
not overbearing
but insistent with intelligence
trust a nineyearold
with time and tobacco
shanks
and listed almost daily
books –
        with nuns priests
brother Joe and cissies
friends calling
and the regular monseignor
polite precise
a virtual paragon

– after
        on co opting
your room
wandered at the high mattress
By Eva   a steely press moth balled
McCullen the buzz of your presence

Age ten
By Eva

Rosmary
Beeds